Revelation 1–3 in Christian Arabic Commentary

CHRISTIAN ARABIC TEXTS IN TRANSLATION

SERIES EDITOR
Stephen J. Davis, Yale University

ADVISORY BOARD
Jimmy Daccache, Yale University
Mark Swanson, Lutheran School of Theology
Alexander Treiger, Dalhousie University

Christian Arabic Texts in Translation (CATT) is a series dedicated to making Christian Arabic works available in English translation. Publications include works of biblical interpretation and commentary, treatises engaging with theological and ethical issues vital to Christian-Muslim encounters, as well as saints' lives, sermons, histories, and philosophical and scientific literature produced by Arabic-speaking Christians living in the medieval Islamicate world. Each accurate and accessible translation is presented with a concise, lucid, and engaging introduction to the historical context, authorship, and literary content of the work and selected critical notes providing resources for further study (biblical citations, bibliographical references, linguistic clarifications, etc.). These translations make it possible for Christian Arabic texts to be introduced to college, seminary, and graduate school curricula.

Revelation 1–3 in Christian Arabic Commentary

John's First Vision and the Letters to the Seven Churches

Stephen J. Davis, T. C. Schmidt, and Shawqi Talia

Fordham University Press
New York • 2019

Library of Congress Cataloging-in-Publication Data

Names: Davis, Stephen J., author, translator. | Schmidt, T. C. (Thomas C.), author, translator. | Talia, Shawqi N. (Shawqi Najib), author, translator. | Būlus al-Būshī, Bishop, approximately 1170– Tafsīr sifr al-Ru'yā. English. | Ibn Kātib Qayṣar, Ibrāhīm ibn Ṣafī al-Dawlah, active 13th century. Tafsir ru'yā al-Qiddīs Yūḥannā al-Lāhūtī. English.
Title: Revelation 1–3 in Christian Arabic commentary : John's first vision and the letters to the seven churches / Stephen J. Davis, T. C. Schmidt, and Shawqi Talia.
Description: First edition. | New York, NY : Fordham University Press, 2019. | Series: Christian Arabic texts in translation | Includes bibliographical references and index.
Identifiers: LCCN 2018024883| ISBN 9780823281848 (cloth : alk. paper) | ISBN 9780823281831 (pbk. : alk. paper)
Subjects: LCSH: Bible. Revelation, I-III—Commentaries. | Būlus al-Būshī, Bishop, approximately 1170– Tafsīr sifr al-Ru'yā. | Ibn Kātib Qayṣar, Ibrāhīm ibn Ṣafī al-Dawlah, active 13th century. Tafsir ru'yā al-Qiddīs Yūḥannā al-Lāhūtī.
Classification: LCC BS2825.53 .D37 2019 | DDC 228.07—dc23
LC record available at https://lccn.loc.gov/2018024883

Printed in the United States of America

21 20 19   5 4 3 2 1

First edition

CONTENTS

Preface and Acknowledgments

This book traces its roots to a session at the 2007 Society of Biblical Literature Annual Meeting in San Diego, where I presented a paper, "Angelic Vision: An Arabic Christian Commentary on Revelation," focusing on Ibn Kātib Qayṣar's thirteenth-century Christian Arabic commentary on the Apocalypse of John. After the session was over, a number of participants came up to me and asked: "When are you going to translate this work and make it available to a wider audience?" That question stuck with me ever since. Now, almost ten years later, the present volume represents an initial answer to that question, and I am exceedingly grateful to my two coauthors and cotranslators, Shawqi Talia and Thomas C. Schmidt, for their willingness to contribute their historical knowledge and linguistic expertise. It has been a delight to collaborate with them.

I also want to express my thanks to George Demacopoulos, codirector of the Orthodox Christian Studies Center at Fordham University, for his indispensable support and collegiality in helping to sponsor the Christian Arabic Texts in Translation (CATT) series; to our editors at Fordham University Press, Fredric Nachbaur and Will Cerbone, and to our copy editor, Edward W. Batchelder, for their patience and perseverance in seeing this first volume through to publication; and to the members of the CATT advisory board—Jimmy Daccache, Mark Swanson, and Alexander Treiger—for their willingness to serve in this capacity and for their wise counsel. In particular, Mark Swanson and Fordham University Press's anonymous reviewer provided invaluable critical feedback that helped us refine our analysis and translations at various points.

The Introduction and Chapter 2 each derive their principal content from the published version of my SBL conference paper, which appeared in article form under the title "Introducing an Arabic Commentary on the Apocalypse: Ibn Kātib Qayṣar on Revelation" in *Harvard Theological Review* 101, no. 1 (2008), 77–96. I once again would like to express my thanks to the following persons for their help during his preparation of that article for publication: to Adela Yarbro Collins, Mark Swanson, Samuel Moawad, and the anonymous readers for the *Harvard Theological Review* for providing valuable feedback on issues related to biblical scholarship, the history of interpretation, and the Christian Arabic literary and theological heritage; to Samir Khalil Samir and Nagi Edelby for their allowing me to acquire a photocopy of Arabic manuscript Sbath 1014 during a January 2005 visit to the Centre de documentation et de recherches arabes chrétiennes (CEDRAC) at the Université Saint-Joseph in Beirut; and finally, to the staff at the British Library for allowing access to their collection for a week of research on Arabic manuscript Or. 1329 in August 2006. Finally, I want to thank Margaret Studier and Faye Sally Bodley-Dangelo, the past and current managing editors of *Harvard Theological Review*, for their permission to reproduce and revise my work for this book.

Shawqi Talia originally translated Būlus al-Būshī's *Commentary on the Apocalypse of John* for his 1987 Ph.D. thesis at the Catholic University of America, and he kindly agreed to allow a revised version of that translation to be published for the first time here. Chapter 1 represents a distillation of his research on Būlus al-Būshī, supplemented by my own textual analysis. Chapter 4 reproduces his translation with minor revisions, along with edited selections from his critical notes (supplemented again in places by my own analysis). We would once more like to thank Father Nagi Edelby for kindly providing us with a copy of his critical edition of Būlus al-Būshī's commentary, the core component of his 2015 doctoral dissertation for the Université Saint-Joseph in Beirut.

Thomas C. Schmidt, a Ph.D. student at Yale University concentrating in the history of ancient and medieval Christianity, is currently writing his dissertation on the history of Eastern Christian commentarial practice on the book of Revelation. In the spring of 2015, he conducted an independent study on Ibn Kātib Qayṣar's *Commentary on the Apocalypse*, and Chapter 3 represents the fruit of those labors. In it, he engages in a close reading of Ibn Kātib Qayṣar's biblical interpretation, placing this Christian Arabic interpreter in the wider context of early and medieval exegesis of Revelation. In Chapter 5, Schmidt and I collaborate in translating Ibn Kātib Qayṣar's commentary on John's first vision and the letters to the seven churches. I took responsibility for translating the sections on Revelation 1–2, while Schmidt, with my editorial contributions, produced a translation of Ibn Kātib Qayṣar's commentary on Revelation 3. We both would like to thank Hany Takla of the St. Shenouda the Archimandrite Coptic Society in Los Angeles for allowing us access to his digital copy of Paris Arabic 67, which allowed us to check for errors and variant readings in the published edition of Ibn Kātib Qayṣar's text. We would also like to thank Shawqi Talia and Mark Swanson for their critical eyes in proofreading parts of our translation.

Finally, it is our collective hope that the publication of this volume will accomplish two ends: that it will help make the Christian Arabic biblical and theological heritage accessible to a wider, English-speaking readership; and that it will encourage more researchers to dedicate themselves to the close study of this literature. Such a result would indeed represent an even more satisfying and fulfilling response to the question posed to me almost a decade ago at the SBL Annual Meeting in San Diego.

Stephen J. Davis, Yale University
August 28, 2017

Editorial Notes and Abbreviations

In this volume, we sometimes cite Greek, Coptic, and Arabic terms when especially relevant to the understanding of certain passages. We only occasionally cite Greek and Coptic in the original script, but we regularly provide transliterations of words and phrases. For Greek and Coptic, we follow the transliteration standards set by the Society of Biblical Literature. For Greek, see *The SBL Handbook of Style for Ancient Near Eastern, Biblical, and Early Christian Studies*, ed. P. H. Alexander et al. (Peabody, Mass.: Hendrickson, 1999). For Coptic, see Richard Smith, *A Concise Coptic-English Lexicon*, 2nd edition, SBL Resources for Biblical Study 35 (Atlanta: Society of Biblical Literature, 1999), although for phonetic ease, we substitute *sh* for *š* in the case of the letter *shai*. For the sake of accessibility, we use transliterations for all Arabic terms. In this, we largely follow the standards set by the ALA-Library of Congress (http://www.loc.gov/catdir/cpso/romanization/arabic.pdf). Occasionally, when discussing well-known names of persons and places, we opt for recognizable Western forms, although even then we may provide Arabic transliterations for clarification.

In the notes, we make reference to relevant textual variants (the presence of differing spellings, words, or phrases) that complicate and/or illuminate certain aspects of our translation. The first time a source is cited, we provide full bibliographical information; subsequent citations usually receive an abbreviated reference. For biblical and ancient Christian primary sources, our bibliographical style (including abbreviations) again conforms to *The SBL Handbook of Style*. In all other matters, we follow the *Chicago Manual of Style*, 16th edition (Chicago: University of Chicago Press, 2010).

For the reader's convenience, we provide here a list of some of the more common abbreviations employed in this volume:

ANF	Ante-Nicene Fathers, ed. A. Roberts and J. Donaldson. Buffalo: Christian Literature, 1885–96. Repr. Grand Rapids, Mich.: Eerdmans, 1951–56.
ANRW	*Aufstieg und Niedergang der römischen Welt*. Berlin: De Gruyter, 1972–98.
CoptNT-North	*The Coptic Version of the New Testament in the Northern Dialect*, ed. G. Horner. 4 volumes. Oxford: Clarendon Press, 1898–1905. Repr. Osnabrück: Otto Zeller, 1969.
CoptNT-South	*The Coptic Version of the New Testament in the Southern Dialect*, ed. G. Horner. 7 volumes. Oxford: Clarendon Press, 1911–24. Repr. Osnabrück: Otto Zeller, 1969.
CE	*The Coptic Encyclopedia*, ed. Aziz S. Atiya. 8 volumes. New York: Macmillan, 1991.
CMR	*Christian-Muslim Relations: A Bibliographical History*, ed. David Thomas, Barbara Roggema, et al. 8 volumes. Leiden: Brill, 2009–16.
CSCO	Corpus scriptorum christianorum orientalium, ed. J-B. Chabot et al. Louvain: L. Durbecq, 1903– .
CSEL	Corpus scriptorum ecclesiasticorum latinorum. Vienna: C. Gerodi, 1866– .
*EI*²	*Encyclopaedia of Islam*, 2nd edition, ed. P. Bearman et al. BrillOnline *Reference Works*.
FC	Fathers of the Church. Washington, D.C.: The Catholic University in America Press, 1947– .
GCAL	*Geschichte der christliche arabischen Literatur*, ed. G. Graf. 5 volumes. Studi e Testi 118, 133, 146, 147, 172. Vatican City: Biblioteca Apostolica Vaticana, 1944–52.
GCS	Die griechischen christlichen Schriftsteller der ersten drei Jahrhunderte. Leipzig: J. C. Hinrichs, 1899– .

HPCC	*History of the Patriarchs of the Coptic Church*, ed. B. T. Evetts. 4 volumes. PO 1.2; 1.4; 5.1; 10.5. Paris: Firmin-Didot, 1904–15.
HPEC	*History of the Patriarchs of the Egyptian Church*, ed. A. Khater and O. H. E. KHS-Burmester. 4 volumes. Cairo: Imprimerie de l'Institut français d'archéologie orientale, 1943–74.
LCL	Loeb Classical Library. London: William Heinemann; Cambridge, Mass.: Harvard University Press, 1912– .
NPNF	Nicene and Post-Nicene Fathers, ed. P. Schaff et al. 2nd series. New York: Christian Literature, 1887–1900. Repr. Grand Rapids, Mich.: Eerdmans, 1952–56.
NRSV	The Holy Bible, New Revised Standard Version. Nashville, Tenn.: World Publishing, 1989.
PG	Patrologia Graeca, ed. J. P. Migne. Paris: Migne, 1857–66.
PL	Patrologia Latina, ed. J. P. Migne. Paris: Migne, 1844–65.
PO	Patrologia orientalis. Paris: F. Didot, 1906– .
SC	Sources chrétiennes. Paris: Cerf, 1943– .

Revelation 1–3 in Christian Arabic Commentary

INTRODUCTION

TWO ARABIC COMMENTARIES ON THE APOCALYPSE OF JOHN IN HISTORICAL AND CULTURAL CONTEXT

Stephen J. Davis

In thirteenth-century Cairo, two Arabic-speaking Egyptian Christian authors, Būlus al-Būshī and Ibn Kātib Qayṣar, wrote commentaries on the Apocalypse of John. These two long-neglected works are a veritable treasure trove for those interested in the transmission of the biblical text and its history of interpretation. Together, these two works provide a compelling witness to the currency of Revelation among Christians living in Islamic Egypt.

The Apocalypse of John had a somewhat inconsistent history of reception among early Christian churches in the eastern Mediterranean region[1]—a fact confirmed by evidence related to both canonization and formal commentary. In the third century, Dionysius of Alexandria felt it necessary to allegorize the book of Revelation in order to defend its "concealed and more wonderful meaning" over against Christian detractors who rejected the work, even as he admitted the validity of critical arguments against its apostolic authorship.[2] In compiling an official list of canonical books, the fourth-century historian Eusebius of Caesarea showed some

1. A. C. Sundberg Jr., "Canon Muratori: A Fourth-Century List," *Harvard Theological Review* 66.1 (1973), 1–41, esp. 21–26; Bruce M. Metzger, *The Canon of the New Testament: Its Origin, Development, and Significance* (Oxford: Clarendon Press, 1987), 209–28.

2. Dionysius of Alexandria, *On Promises*, preserved in Eusebius of Caesarea, *h.e.* 7.25.4 (ed. G. Bardy, SC 41 [1955], 205). On Dionysius's allegorical interpretation of Revelation as a counter to more literal, so-called "bodily" readings of the text, see Stephen J. Davis, "Biblical Interpretation and Alexandrian Episcopal Authority in the Early Christian Fayoum," in

reservation about whether to include the Apocalypse, listing it alternatively under three separate categories: genuine, dubious, and spurious.[3] Evidence from the second half of the fourth century suggests that the book of Revelation had fallen out of favor in some regions. In Asia Minor (ca. 380), Gregory of Nazianzus omits it from his list of canonical writings,[4] and Amphilochius of Iconium harbors serious reservations, reporting that "most say it is spurious."[5] In Palestine and Syria during the same period, John's Apocalypse is omitted from the canon lists compiled by Cyril of Jerusalem (ca. 350) and the *Apostolic Constitutions* (ca. 380), as well as from the Syriac *Peshitta* (ca. 400).[6]

This less-than-enthusiastic reception of the book among Eastern Christians is also reflected in a fairly sparse commentary record. In comparison, numerous commentaries on the book of Revelation were produced in the West.[7] In the third century, Hippolytus of Rome completed his major treatise *On the Apocalypse* (which unfortunately does not survive apart from selected quotations from later authors).[8] He was followed in the West by a series of Latin writers, including Victorinus of Pettau (late third century),[9]

Christianity and Monasticism in the Fayoum Oasis, ed. G. Gabra (Cairo: American University of Cairo Press, 2005), 45–61.

3. Eusebius of Caesarea, *h.e.* 3.25.1–5 (ed. G. Bardy, SC 31 [1952], 133–34).

4. Gregory of Nazianzus, *carm.* 1.1.12.39 (PG 37.474); A. C. Sundberg Jr., "Canon Muratori," 23.

5. Amphilochius of Iconium, *Seleuc.* 316–18 (ed. E. Oberg, *Amphilochii Iconiensis iambi ad Seleucum* [*Patristische Texte und Studien* 9; Berlin: De Gruyter, 1969], 39); B. Metzger, *The Canon of the New Testament*, 212–13.

6. Cyril of Jerusalem, *catech.* 4.36 (PG 33.500–501); *Const. Ap.* 7.47.85 (F. X. Funk, *Didascalia et constitutiones apostolorum*, vol. 1 [Paderborn: F. Schoeningh, 1905], 590–93). On the absence of the Apocalypse of John in the *Peshitta*, see A. C. Sundberg Jr., "Canon Muratori," 24–25. In contrast to the Syriac *Peshitta*, the Ethiopian (Ge'ez) version of the Bible includes the book of Revelation: see Josef Hofmann, *Die äthiopische Übersetzung der Johannes-Apokalypse*, 2 vols. (CSCO 281–82, Aethiopici 55–56; Louvain: Secrétariat du CorpusSCO, 1967); Josef Hofmann, *Die äthiopische Johannes-Apokalypse, kritisch untersucht* (CSCO 297, Subsidia 33; Louvain, Secrétariat du CorpusSCO, 1969).

7. For an overview, see Francis X. Gumerlock, "Patristic Commentaries on Revelation," *Kerux* 23.2 (2008), 49–67; Francis X. Gumerlock, "Patristic Commentaries on Revelation: An Update," *Kerux* 27.3 (2012), 37–43.

8. P. Prigent and R. Stehly, eds., "Les fragments du *De Apocalypsi d' Hippolyte*," *Theologische Zeitschrift* 29 (1973), 313–33.

9. M. Dulaey, ed., *Sur l'Apocalypse: suivi du fragment chronologique et de La construction du monde* (SC 423; Paris: Cerf, 1997); see also J. Hausleiter, ed., *Victorinus Petavionensis* (CSEL 49; Vienna: F. Tempsky, 1916). Jerome updated Victorinus's commentary by changing or

Tyconius (ca. 380),[10] Primasius of Hadrumetum (ca. 550),[11] Apringius of Beja (Portugal, ca. 550),[12] Bede (early eighth century),[13] and at least nine other commentators before the end of the twelfth-century.[14] By contrast, in the Greek-speaking East, Origen's *Scholia on the Apocalypse*, if authentic,[15] would represent the only commentary on Revelation produced before the sixth century, and it was only a collection of scattered glosses on selected passages, not a comprehensive treatment of the text as a whole. In

---

omitting interpretations he did not like. For a translation of this heavily edited version, see ANF 7.344–60.

10. Tyconius, *reg.*: ed. W. S. Babcock, *Tyconius: The Book of Rules* (Texts and Translations 39; Atlanta, Ga.: Scholars Press, 1989); see also Francesco Lo Bue, *Turin Fragments of Tyconius' Commentary on Revelation* (Cambridge: Cambridge University Press, 1963); and Pamela Bright, *The Book of Rules of Tyconius: Its Purpose and Inner Logic* (Notre Dame, Ind.: University of Notre Dame Press, 1988).

11. A. W. Adams, ed., *Commentarium libri quinque in Apocalypsim Joannis Evangelistae*, CSEL 92 (Turnhout: Brepols, 1985).

12. R. Gryson, ed., *Commentaria minora in Apocalypsin Johannis: Variorum auctorum*, CCSL 107 (Turnhout: Brepols, 2003), 33–97.

13. R. Gryson, ed., *Bedae presbyteri expositio apocalypseos*, CCSL 121a (Turnhout: Brepols, 2001).

14. This list of early medieval commentators includes the late eighth-century writers Beatus of Liébana, Ambrosius Autpertus, and (Ps.-) Alcuin of York; the ninth- and tenth-century writers Haimo of Auxerre, and Adso; and the twelfth-century writers Bruno of Segi, Rupert of Deutz, Richard of St. Victor, and Joachim of Fiore. On the reception and interpretation of Revelation in the early and medieval Latin West, see Georg Kretschmar, *Die Offenbarung des Johannes: Die Geschichte ihrer Auslegung im 1. Jahrtausend* (Stuttgart: Calwer, 1985), 116–60; and Francis X. Gumerlock, *The Seven Seals of the Apocalypse: Medieval Texts in Translation* (TEAMS Commentary Series; Kalamazoo, Mich.: Medieval Institute Publications; Western Michigan University, 2009). On the relation of Christian iconography to this exegetical tradition, see Yves Christe, *L'Apocalypse de Jean: Sens et développements de ses visions synthétiques* (Paris: Picard, 1996), 53–193.

15. C. I. Dyobouniotes and A. von Harnack, eds., *Der Scholien-Kommentar des Origenes zur Apokalypse Johannis* (Texte und Untersuchungen 38, no. 3; Leipzig: Hinrichs, 1911), 21–44; C. H. Turner, "The Text of the Newly Discovered Scholia of Origen on the Apocalypse," *Journal of Theological Studies* 13 (1912), 386–97; C. H. Turner., "Origen, Scholia in Apocalypsi," *Journal of Theological Studies* 25 (1923), 1–16. Dyobouniotes, one of the original editors, had doubts about the authenticity of these scholia, and these doubts have been sustained in more recent scholarship: see, e.g., Charles W. Lowry, "Did Origen Style the Son a *KTISMA*?" *Journal of Theological Studies* 39 (1938), 39–42; and Michał Wojciechowski, *Pseudo-Orygenes, Uwagi do Apokalipsy* (= *Pseudo-Origen, Scholia on the Apocalypse*) (Mała Biblioteka Ojców Kościoła 4, Wydawnictwo "M"; Kraków, 2005). Panagiōtēs Tzamalikos has recently produced a new edition of the Greek *scholia*, in which he argues that they are by a hitherto unknown author named Cassian (not John Cassian the monk): see *An Ancient Commentary on the Book of Revelation: A Critical Edition of the Scholia in Apocalypsin* (Cambridge: Cambridge University Press, 2013).

fact, only three full-length commentaries survive in Greek from late antiquity or the early medieval period. The earliest complete commentary in that language was written by a sixth-century writer named Oecumenius from Asia Minor.[16] The second and third commentaries—written in the seventh and tenth centuries by Andrew and Arethas of Caesarea in Cappadocia—are both dependent on Oecumenius's work, and the third is in many respects merely a paraphrastic expansion of the second.[17] Other Eastern Christian language groupings give the Apocalypse text even less attention. For example, no full-length Apocalypse commentaries are recorded in the Coptic language; and in Syriac we have only scattered excerpts from a twelve-century commentary by Dionysius bar Salibi (Dionysius Syrus) and one other anonymous commentary that survives in a single manuscript.[18] Thus, the presence of original Arabic commentaries on Revelation from the thirteenth century significantly expands our

16. H. C. Hoskier, ed., *The Complete Commentary of Oecumenius on the Apocalypse* (Ann Arbor: University of Michigan Press, 1928), 29–50; for an English translation, see J. N. Suggit, trans., *Oecumenius, Commentary on the Apocalypse* (Fathers of the Church 112; Washington, D.C.: The Catholic University of America Press, 2006), 19–203.

17. J. Schmid, ed., *Studien zur Geschichte des griechischen Apokalypse-Textes*, vol. 1 (Münchener theologische Studien 1; Munich: Karl Zink, 1955), 1–268 (Andrew); 207–458 (Arethas). For an English translation of Andrew of Caesarea's commentary, see Eugenia Scarvelis Constantinou, trans., *Andrew of Caesarea, Commentary on the Apocalypse* (Washington, D.C.: The Catholic University of America Press, 2011); see also Eugenia Scarvelis Constantinou, *Guiding to a Blessed End: Andrew of Caesarea and the Apocalypse* (Washington, D.C.: The Catholic University of America Press, 2013). A fourth Greek commentary was written in the twelfth or thirteenth century by the author Neophytus Inclusus: see Tzamalikos, *Ancient Commentary*, 62.

18. An unpublished Coptic homily on Revelation survives in the Pierpont Morgan collection: see Leslie S. B. MacCoull, "MS. Morgan 591: The Apocalypse Commentary of Pseudo-Cyril of Alexandria," in *Studia Patristica*, 20 (1989), 33–39; Tito Orlandi, "Cirillo Vescovo Di Alessandria," in *Omelie copte. Aegyptiorum Patrum homilias* (Corona Patrum 7; Torino: Società editrice internazionale, 1981), 121–44. For an edition of Dionysius bar Salibi's commentary, see J. Sedláček, ed., *Dionysius bar Salibi In Apocalypsim, Actus et Epistulas Catholicas*, CSCO 53, Syr. 18 (1909), 3–29 (Syriac text); CSCO 60, Syr. 20 (1910), 1–22 (Latin translation); see also www.tertullian.org/fathers/dionysiusd̦syrusd̦revelationd̦01.htm. On Dionysius's life and writings, including a discussion of his various works of biblical commentary, see Stephen Desmond Ryan, O.P., *Dionysius Bar Salibi's Factual and Spiritual Commentary on Psalms 73–82* (Cahiers de la Revue Biblique 57; Paris: J. Gabalda et Cie, 2004), chs. 1–2; reviewed by Lucas Van Rompay, in *Hugoye* 8, no. 1 (2005). On the anonymous commentary, see S. Larson, "The Earliest Syriac Commentary on the Apocalypse: Transcription, Translation and Importance of Brit. Lib. MS. ADD. 17,127" (Ph.D. dissertation, University of Birmingham, 1984), http://search.proquest.com/pqdtuk/docview/301432163/BC4985625DAE45EBPQ/1?accountid=15172.

knowledge regarding the reception of this text in the Christian East during the Middle Ages.

Having sketched out the rather sparse landscape of Eastern Christian commentary on John's Apocalypse, let me turn now specifically to the two Arabic authors who took up the task of interpreting this work. What do we know about them and their cultural context? Būlus al-Būshī and Ibn Kātib Qayṣar both participated in what has long been recognized as a Golden Age of Copto-Arabic literature—a theological renaissance that took hold of the Egyptian church during the thirteenth century.[19]

Būlus al-Būshī was a reform-minded church leader who was elected bishop of Old Cairo in 1240 and probably died around 1250 CE.[20] He was a prolific theological author. In addition to his *Commentary on the Apocalypse*, he also produced a series of eight homilies connected with major feast days,[21] as well as an apologetic work in three parts (on the Trinity, the Incarnation, and the truth of the Christian religion).[22] His *Commentary on the Apocalypse* was the first documented commentary to have been written in Arabic. Fairly spare in its wording, it becomes slightly more expansive when the author expounds upon the text's relevance for Christological doctrine—especially the Incarnation, one of his favorite themes.[23]

19. Adel Sidarus, "Le renaissance copte arabe du moyen âge," in *The Syriac Renaissance*, ed. Herman G. B. Teule et al. (Leuven: Peeters, 2010), 311–40.

20. On Būlus al-Būshī's life, see Samir Khalil Samir, *Traité de Paul de Būš sur l'Unité et la Trinité l'Incarnation, et la Vérité du Christianisme* (*Maqālah fī al-tathlīth w-al-tajassud wa-Ṣiḥḥat al-Masīḥiyyah)* (Patrimoine Arabe Chrétien 4. Zouk Mikhail: al-Turath al 'Arabi al-Masihi, 1983), v–viii, 15–27; Aziz S. Atiya, "Būlus al-Būshī," *CE* 2:423–24; and Mark N. Swanson, "Būlus al-Būshī," *CMR*, vol. 4, 280–87 (BrillOnline *Reference Works*, http://dx.doi.org/10.1163/1877-8054_cmri_COM_25673, consulted March 24, 2018).

21. An uncritical edition of Būlus al-Būshī's eight homilies was published by Manqariyūs 'Awāḍallah, in *Maqālāt al-Anbā Būlus al-Būshī* (Cairo: al-Maṭba'ah al-tujāriyah al-ḥadīthah, 1972). In the past decade, Arab scholars have produced critical editions of two of these sermons: (1) the *Homily on the Annunciation*, ed. N. Edelby, "L'Homélie de l'Annonciation de Būlus al-Būšī," *Parole de l'Orient* 22 (1997), 503–65; and (2) the *Homily on Pentecost*: ed. J. Faltas, *al-Rūḥ al-qudus: Maymar 'īd al-'anṣarah li-al-usquf Būlus al-Būshī* (Cairo: Mu'assasat al-Qiddīs Anṭūniyūs, 2006).

22. Samir, ed., *Traité de Paul de Būš*, 129–258.

23. On Būlus al-Būshī's commentary and its textual record, see Georg Graf, *Geschichte der christlichen arabischen Literatur* (= *GCAL*), volume 2 (Vatican City: Biblioteca Apostolica Vaticana, 1947), 358–59. The English translation of Būlus al-Būshī's text in Chapter 4 is primarily based on Vatican Arabic 459 (1298 CE). It is a revised version of the translation Shawqi Talia produced for his doctoral thesis: Talia, "Bulus al-Buši's Arabic Commentary on the Apocalypse of St. John: An English Translation and Commentary" (Ph.D. dissertation, The

In contrast to the figure of Būlus al-Būshī, we know relatively little about Ibn Kātib Qayṣar. Our knowledge of his biography is limited to the fact that he descended from a Copt who held a prominent position in the Islamic government under the Amīr ʿAlam al-Dīn Qayṣar—hence, the meaning of his name, "Son of the Scribe of Qayṣar (Caesar)."[24] Ibn Kātib Qayṣar applied his own writing skills in the field of theology. His literary output included biblical commentaries and translations,[25] a theological treatise on confession, and an epitome of an apologetic dialogue written by the earlier Christian Arabic writer, Yaḥyā Ibn ʿAdī.[26] He was also renowned as a grammarian and philologist. One of his influential works was a Coptic

---

Catholic University of America, 1987). The authors have also consulted other manuscripts in their analysis of the text, including Arabic manuscript Sbath 1014 (thirteenth century CE) and British Library Or. 1329 (1671 CE; formerly British Museum Arabic Supp. 16). An uncritical Arabic edition of the text was published in serial form in the Egyptian journal *Majallat Marqus* 491–503 (February 2008–April 2009): it was based on a fourteenth-century manuscript in the Monastery of St. Macarius (Commentary 22), but its editor acknowledges that he has made "some small linguistic corrections (*taṣḥīḥāt*) for the ease of reading." Because these changes are not identified or indicated in the text itself, it means that the edition must be used with some caution. In November 2015, Father Nagi Edelby completed a landmark critical edition of Būlus al-Būshī's *Commentary on the Apocalypse* as his Ph.D. thesis for the Université Saint-Joseph in Beirut: Nagi Edelby, "Le Commentaire de l'Apocalypse de Būlus al-Bušī (évêque du Caire en 1240 A.D.): Étude, edition critique, traduction et Index exhaustif," Ph.D. dissertation, Université Saint-Joseph-Beyrouth, 2015. Father Edelby kindly provided us with a copy in late May 2016, shortly before we submitted our book to press for review, and during the final stage of revisions we were able to supplement our footnotes with references to his work. Finally, Bishop Epiphanius, the head of the Monastery of St. Macarius in Wādī al-Naṭrūn, Egypt, has also published a fourteenth-century copy of Būlus al-Būshī's Revelation commentary preserved in his monastic library (Dayr Abū Maqār MS 22 Tafsīr [Commentary]), with additional consultation of manuscripts from the Church of the Holy Martyr Apa Noub in Samannud (MS 6 Lāhūt [Theology]) and from the Coptic Museum (MS 36 Ṭaqs [Liturgy]): Bishop Epiphanius (al-Anbā Ibīfānīyūs), *Tafsīr Sifr al-Ru'yā (Abūghālumsīs) li-l-Anbā Būlus al-Būshī Usquf Miṣr* (Cairo: Dār Majallat Marqus, 2017).

24. His full name was Abū Isḥāq ʿAlam al-Ri'āsah Ibrāhīm Ibn al-Shaykh Abū al-Ṭanā Ibn al-Shaykh Ṣafī al-Dawlah Abū al-Faḍā'il. On this life, see Mark N. Swanson, "Ibn Kātib Qayṣar," CMR, vol. 4, 453–56 (BrillOnline *Reference Works*, http://dx.doi.org/10.1163/1877-8054_cmri_COM_25670, consulted March 24, 2018).

25. In addition to his *Commentary on the Apocalypse*, Ibn Kātib Qayṣar also wrote commentaries on the Pauline and Catholic epistles (Graf, *GCAL* 2.384–86). According to al-Wajīh al-Qalyūbī, he also produced an Arabic translation of the Catholic epistles (Graf, *GCAL* 2.387).

26. Ibn Kātib Qayṣar's treatise on confession and his epitome of Yaḥya Ibn ʿAdī are no longer extant, but are referred to and quoted by a thirteenth-century contemporary of the author, Abū Isḥāq Ibn al-ʿAssāl (Graf, *GCAL*, 2.386–87).

grammar entitled *al-Tabṣirah* (*Enlightenment*). A polyglot, Ibn Kātib Qayṣar had some familiarity with Greek, Syriac, and Hebrew in addition to Arabic and Coptic. This linguistic training significantly shaped his approach to the Apocalypse of John.

Ibn Kātib Qayṣar's commentary on Revelation dates to 1266/7,[27] perhaps only two or three decades later than the one authored by Būlus al-Būshī. The work survives in a small handful of manuscripts, including one at the Bibliothèque nationale de France in Paris dated to the thirteenth century,[28] and another at the Coptic Patriarchal Library in Cairo dating to the year 1335 CE, but copied from an earlier manuscript dated 1305 CE.[29]

27. For a discussion of date and authorship, a brief summary of the work's contents, and an annotated bibliography listing known manuscripts, editions, and relevant studies published up to the middle of the twentieth century, see Graf, *GCAL*, 2.380–84. Ibn Kātib Qayṣar provides evidence for the date of composition himself in his comments on Revelation 17:10, when he identifies his time of writing as "year 983 of Diocletian, year 1271 of the incarnation, and year 6772 of the world" (G. Graf, "Die koptische Gelehrtenfamilie der Aulād al-'Assāl und ihr Schrifttum," *Orientalia*, n.s. 1 [1932], 51); Jirjis Fīlūthā'us 'Awaḍ, introduction (in Arabic) to *Tafsīr Sifr al-Ru'yā li-l-Qiddīs Yūḥannā al-Lahūtī li-Ibn Kātib Qayṣar*, ed. al-Qummuṣ Armāniyūs Ḥabashī Shattā al-Birmāwī (Cairo, 1939; repr. Maktabat al-Maḥabbah, 1994), 22. However, a problem is caused by the fact that these dates given by Ibn Kātib Qayṣar actually stand in conflict with one another: "year 983 of Diocletian" is equivalent to year 1266/7 after Christ, while "year 1271 of the incarnation" would be year 987 according to the Coptic martyrological calendar reckoned from the beginning of Diocletian's reign. It is Graf's judgment (one with which I concur) that the date given first (983 A.M., = 1266/7 CE) is the more reliable, since it follows the common Coptic dating system used in Ibn Kātib Qayṣar's day.

28. Par. Ar. 67 (thirteenth century CE). This Paris manuscript, the original beginning of which is unfortunately lost, served as the basis for the first modern summary of the work, published by Heinrich Ewald, in *Abhandlungen zur orientalischen und biblischen Literatur* (Göttingen: Dieterich, 1832), 1–11.

29. Cairo Arabic 666 (= Coptic Patriarchate 243): M. Simaika, *Catalogue of the Coptic and Arabic Manuscripts in the Coptic Museum, the Patriarchate, the Principal Churches of Cairo and Alexandria and the Monasteries of Egypt*, vol. 2 (Cairo: Government Press, 1942), 101 (call no. theol. 58). The first folio and some folia at the end of this manuscript were restored in 1612 CE. The Coptic Patriarchate collection also contains another manuscript of Ibn Kātib Qayṣar's work, Cairo Arabic 608 (= Coptic Patriarchate Arabic 243), which dates to the nineteenth century but is copied from the same fourteenth-century prototypes: see Simaika, *Catalogue*, 100–1 (call. no. theol. 57). A fourth copy of the commentary has been documented in Syria (Aleppo 54; Ibrāhīm Ḥarfūsh, "Die Bibliothek der Maroniten in Ḥaleb," *Mashriq* 17 [1914], 96). This Aleppo manuscript has been mistakenly transmitted under the name of Ibn al-'Assāl (Graf, "Die koptische Gelehrtenfamilie," 50). In the case of the Paris manuscript, the original title and identification of the author were lost when the first three folia went missing. At some later date, these missing pages were replaced with new leaves, which contain two separate (and spurious) authorial attributions—one gives credit to Hippolytus of Rome and

In other words, the known manuscript tradition for this commentary brings us to within thirty or forty years of its original composition.

Judging by the surviving evidence, one may safely conclude that Ibn Kātib Qayṣar never completed his commentary. His interpretation ends rather abruptly at Revelation 20:6. In one of the curiosities of the manuscript tradition, however, this lacuna has been filled by later enterprising scribes, who have supplemented Ibn Kātib Qayṣar's text with sections of commentary from Būlus al-Būshī covering the remaining chapters and verses (20:7–22:21).[30] The end result is a juxtaposition of two Arabic perspectives on the Apocalypse of John.

This publication is dedicated to making translations of these two authors accessible to an English-speaking audience. In both cases, we train our attention on the interpretation of the first three chapters of Revelation. As further introduction to the primary sources, the translators have also written chapters focusing on different aspects of these two Arabic-language commentaries, touching on matters ranging from authorship and language, to biblical interpretation, theology, and Christian-Muslim encounter. It is our hope that the end result will be a deeper appreciation for the immense cultural, intellectual, and spiritual contributions of these Christian Arabic authors.

Būlus al-Būshī (fol. 2r), the other to John Chrysostom (fol. 2v). See Graf, "Die koptische Gelehrtenfamilie," 49–50; Graf, *GCAL* 2.384; and Ewald's article in *Abhandlungen*, 2.

The first (and oldest) Cairo manuscript mentioned above (Cairo Arabic 666) was the text published by al-Qummuṣ Armāniyūs Ḥabashī Shattā al-Birmāwī: *Tafsīr Sifr al-Ru'yā li-l-Qiddīs Yūḥannā al-Lahūtī l-Ibn Kātib Qayṣar* (Cairo, 1939; repr. 1994) (henceforth, Birmāwī). Cairo Arabic 666 is not currently accessible, and therefore it has not been possible to check the reissue of his edition against the manuscript itself. In utilizing uncritical editions of Christian Arabic texts published in Egypt, one must always beware of changes (both intentional and unintentional) allowed in the process of republishing and reprinting those texts. One such example of intentional editorial "correction" occurs in Chapter 18, section 88, of Ibn Kātib Qayṣar's commentary (on Revelation 17:10: Birmāwī, 337), where a recent Egyptian editor has sought to reconcile the conflicting dates provided by the author by changing the Coptic year from 983 to 987, even while the original 1939 introduction published with the 1994 printing retains the authentic reference to 983 (Birmāwī, 22; see also my discussion of dating above in note 27). In choosing to use this edition as a basis for our studies and translation, we have therefore proceeded with caution, checking it over against Par. Ar. 67. The need remains for a critical edition that would serve as a more definitive basis for future scholarly work.

30. The end of Ibn Kātib Qayṣar's commentary is found on page 402 of Birmāwī's edition; the appended section of Būlus al-Būshī's work follows on pages 403–24.

CHAPTER

1

Būlus al-Būshī on Revelation 1–3

Christology and Christian-Muslim Encounter

Shawqi Talia and Stephen J. Davis

The book of Revelation has not been received with the same enthusiasm as the other books of Scripture. It has been the least-read canonical book in the history of the church, and yet at the same time it has captured the imagination of many who have attempted to decipher its meaning. Like much apocalyptic literature, its style is obscure, its language is difficult, and its visions are mysterious. As mentioned in the introduction, the early church produced only a small handful of ancient commentaries on the Apocalypse, and as a result this literature has not been a favored subject for scholarship.

Only two Arabic-language commentaries on the Apocalypse of John associated with specific authors have come down to us from the medieval period, both written in the thirteenth century by Christians from Egypt.[1] The author of the earlier and shorter of these two commentaries is Būlus al-Būshī, who wrote the text sometime prior to his death circa 1250 CE. The second and longer of the two commentaries was written perhaps a decade or two later by Ibn Kātib Qayṣar, who occasionally cites sections of Būlus al-Būshī's work. This chapter provides a brief introduction to Būlus al-Būshī's commentary.

1. Three Arabic manuscripts containing anonymous commentaries on Revelation also survive in the library at the Monastery of the Syrians in Egypt (MS 88, 1r–42v; MS 89, 38v–113r; MS 90, 2r–68r), perhaps three copies of the same anonymous text. The contents feature a number of quotations from patristic authors. Further study is necessary to determine whether these manuscripts preserve a single-authored work or a florilegium (i.e., a collection of excerpts from earlier writers). For further discussion of MS 88, see note 22 below.

The Life and Works of Būlus al-Būshī

Sources for the life of Būlus al-Būshī are very scant. The date of his birth is obscure but may be assumed to have taken place around 1170–75 CE. He hailed from the town of Būsh in Middle Egypt, just north of modern-day Beni Suef. He probably studied for the priesthood at one of the monasteries in al-Fayyūm, since we know that his friend Dāwūd ibn Yūḥannā al-Fayyūmī also pursued his religious studies there.[2] Unfortunately, there are no historical sources that shed any light on the date of Būlus al-Būshī's ordination or of the many works he produced. There are a number of references to him and his writings in the works of other Copto-Arabic writers, but they tell us nothing about his life.[3]

The first time we hear Būlus al-Būshī's name is in reference to the controversy surrounding the election of the new patriarch of the Coptic church following the death of Patriarch John VI (*fl.* 1189–1216 CE). The *History of the Patriarchs of the Egyptian Church* states that the death of John VI precipitated a three-way division within the ranks of the Egyptian Christian community. Būlus al-Būshī was one of three church candidates nominated to the vacant see: "Some people preferred the priest Būlus al-Būshī, some preferred Dāwūd ibn Yūḥannā al-Fayyūmī [commonly known as Dāwūd ibn Laqlaq], and some preferred the elder Abū al-Karam, archdeacon of the church al-Muʿallaqah in Cairo."[4] The matter was only resolved in Dāwūd al-Fayyūmī's favor nineteen years after John VI's death, when he and his supporters made payments to the Sultan to secure his election, which took place on June 17, 1235 CE.[5]

Dāwūd al-Fayyūmī took the patriarchal name, Cyril III, and while in office he continued to offer special favors in exchange for benefits, otherwise known as the practice of simony (Arabic, *al-sharṭūniyyah*), which caused great

2. On Dāwūd ibn Yūḥannā al-Fayyūmī (later Patriarch Cyril III), see Mark Swanson, *The Coptic Papacy in Islamic Egypt (641–1517)* (Cairo: American University in Cairo Press, 2010), ch. 6; Kurt Werthmuller, *Coptic Identity and Ayyubid Politics in Egypt, 1218–1250* (Cairo: American University in Cairo Press, 2010); and Mark N. Swanson, "Patriarch Cyril III ibn Laqlaq," CMR, vol. 4, 320–24 (BrillOnline *Reference Works*, http://dx.doi.org/10.1163/1877-8054_cmri_COM_25270, consulted March 24, 2018).

3. Samir, *Traité de Paul de Būš*, 15–17.

4. *HPEC* 4.1, 2.

5. The *History of the Patriarchs* (*HPEC* 4.1) presents a meandering and circuitous account of these events. For a concise summary, see Aziz S. Atiya, "Būlus al-Būshī," *Coptic Encyclopedia*, vol. 2 (New York: Macmillan, 1991), 423–24; see also Samir, *Traité de Paul de Būš*, 17–24.

indignation among the Egyptian clergy.[6] In response to these abuses, a synod composed of bishops met on September 8, 1240, to try to curb his behavior. At this synod, Būlus al-Būshī was commissioned as one of two wardens (or guardians) of the church designated to keep an eye on Cyril III's financial dealings and appointments.[7] At the same time, Būlus al-Būshī was also ordained bishop of Old Cairo, where he is thought to have served until his death sometime around the middle of the thirteenth century (ca. 1250 CE).[8]

In addition to his role as church leader, Būlus al-Būshī was a prolific writer. As far as can now be ascertained, over the course of his career, he wrote at least nine works. Only one of these seems to have been written prior to his elevation as bishop—a *Book on the Sacrament of Confession* (*Kitāb al-iʿtirāf*), coauthored with Dāwūd al-Fayyūmī before the latter became patriarch.[9] His other works were all composed during Būlus al-Būshī's time as bishop of Old Cairo. They include a *Book of Spiritual Sciences* (*Kitāb al-ʿulūm al-rūḥāniyyah*),[10] a *Treatise on [the Predetermination of] Lifespan and Sustenance* (*Maqālah fī al-ʿumr wa-l-rizq*),[11] a *Disputation with Ibn Laqlaq*,[12] two major theological treatises,[13] a collection of

6. These benefits included the election of forty bishops to vacant sees: see Samir, *Traité de Paul de Būš*, 24–26.

7. The Arabic term for his role was *raqīb* (pl. *ruqabāʾ*).

8. al-Ṣafī ibn al-ʿAssāl, *Kitāb al-qawānīn*: ed. M. Jirjis (Cairo: Tabaʿat al-usquf Īsūdhūrus, 1927), 31 (lines 14–16); Samir, *Traité de Paul de Būš*, 26–27.

9. Also known as *The Book of the Teacher and the Student* (*Kitāb al-muʿallim wa-l-tilmīdh*): Graf, *GCAL* 2.365–67; Samir, *Traité de Paul de Būš*, 35–36; Edelby, "Commentaire," 19.

10. Graf, *GCAL* 2.360; Samir, *Traité de Paul de Būš*, 33; Edelby, "Commentaire," 19.

11. Graf, *GCAL* 2.360; Samir, *Traité de Paul de Būš*, 32–33; Edelby, "Commentaire," 18.

12. Samir, *Traité de Paul de Būš*, 33–35; Edelby, "Commentaire," 18. The history of this disputation is confusing. According to Abū-l-Barakāt, it took place between Dāwūd al-Fayyūmī and some other scholars in the presence of al-Malik al-Kāmil ibn Ayyūb, with Būlus al-Būshī in attendance as an observer: Graf, *GCAL* 2.438–45; W. Riedel, "Der Katalog der christlichen Schriften in arabischer Sprache von Abū-l-Barakāt," *Nachrichten von der königlichen Gesellschaft der Wissenschaften zu Göttingen*, Philologisch-historische Klasse (Göttingen: Horstmann, 1902), 659. But Samir Khalil Samir (*Traité de Paul de Būš*, 33–35) has argued that Būlus al-Būshī actually played a larger role and that the disputation in fact took place primarily between him and Dāwūd al-Fayyūmī (and not between the latter and a group of Muslim scholars). According to this reading, the purpose of the debate was so that al-Kāmil could determine who should be elevated to the patriarchal see. This would make sense of the fact that it was the Coptic community who both brought the matter before al-Kāmil and supposedly participated in adjudicating the results (*HPEC* 4.41).

13. These two works consist of a freestanding treatise *On the Incarnation* (Graf, *GCAL* 2.430; Samir, *Traité de Paul de Būš*, 36–39; Edelby, "Commentaire," 22) and a three-part

eight homilies on the feast days of the Lord,[14] and biblical commentaries on Hebrews[15] and Revelation.[16]

As an author, Būlus al-Būshī participated in a renaissance of Copto-Arabic theological writing. Indeed, his near contemporaries were well familiar with his literary output and some of them utilized his works as sources for their own writings. Among them were Ibn Kātib Qayṣar, author of the other named Arabic commentary on Revelation; al-Rashīd Abū al-Khayr ibn al-Ṭayyib, best known for his *Antidote of Understanding*;[17] and the three famous 'Assāl brothers (al-Ṣafī, al-As'ad, and al-Mu'taman), whose exegetical, apologetic, philosophical, and theological works helped transform the cultural landscape of thirteenth-century Cairo.[18]

work *On the Unity of God, the Trinity, the Incarnation, and the Truth of the Christian Religion* (ed. Samir, *Traité de Paul de Būš*, 129–258; see also Edelby, "Commentaire," 20–22). Graf mistakenly attributed the latter work to a Melkite/Chalcedonian author (Graf, *GCAL* 2.92). For a more recent discussion, see Stephen J. Davis, *Coptic Christology in Practice*, 238–51. An earlier version of this study appeared in Davis, "The Copto-Arabic Tradition of *Theosis*: A Eucharistic Reading of John 3:51–57 in Būlus al-Būshī's Treatise *On the Incarnation*," in *Partakers of the Divine Nature*, ed. M. J. Christensen and J. A. Wittung (Madison, N.J.: Fairleigh Dickinson University Press, 2007), 163–74.

14. Edited by Manqariyūs 'Awāḍallah, *Maqālāt al-Anbā Būlus al-Būshī* (Cairo: al-Maṭba'ah al-tijāriyyah al-ḥadīthah, 1972); see also Graf, *GCAL* 2.357–58; Samir, *Traité de Paul de Būš*, 29–30; Edelby, "Commentaire," 16–17. Individual critical editions have been produced for two of these homilies: (1) *Homily on the Annunciation*, ed. Nagi Edelby, "L'Homélie de l'Annonciation de Būlus al-Būšī," *Parole de l'Orient* 22 (1997), 503–65 (= *Actes du I^um Symposium syro-arabicum. ii. Études arabes chrétiennes*, ed. Samir Khalil Samir [Kaslik: Université Saint-Esprit, 1997], 503–65); and (2) *Homily on Pentecost*, ed. Joseph Faltas, *al-Rūḥ al-qudus: Maymar 'īd al-'anṣarah li-l-usquf Būlus al-Būshī* (Cairo: Mu'assasat al-Qiddīs Anṭūniyūs, 2006).

15. Būlus al-Būshī's *Commentary on Hebrews* does not survive: no manuscript is extant, but Ibn al-Rāhib (Graf, *GCAL* 2.428–34) mentions it in his *Book of Healing* (*Kitāb al-shifā'*) (Graf, *GCAL* 2.430; Samir, *Traité de Paul de Būš*, 31–32; Edelby, "Commentaire," 17–18).

16. Graf, *GCAL* 2.358–59; idem, "Exegetische Schriften," 36–37; Samir, *Traité de Paul de Būš*, 30. For two editions and translations of the text, see Talia, "Bulus al-Buši's Arabic Commentary"; and Edelby, "Commentaire."

17. Graf, *GCAL* 2.344–48; Wadi Awad, "Al-Rashīd Abū l-Khayr Ibn al-Ṭayyib," CMR, vol. 4, 431–37 (BrillOnline *Reference Works*, http://dx.doi.org/10.1163/1877-8054_cmri_COM_24906, consulted March 24, 2018).

18. See Graf, "Gelehrtenfamilie," 34–56, 129–48, 193–204; idem, *GCAL* 2.388–414; and Wadi Awad, "al-Mu'taman Ibn al-'Assāl," and "al-Ṣafī Ibn al-'Assāl," in CMR, vol. 4, 530–37, 538–51 (BrillOnline *Reference Works*, http://dx.doi.org/10.1163/1877-8054_cmri_COM_24900 and 24904, consulted March 24, 2018); see also Wadi Awad's online article on "al-As'ad Ibn al-'Assāl" (http://dx.doi.org/10.1163/1877-8054_cmri_COM_25903, consulted March 24, 2018). Al-As'ad wrote a preface (*muqaddimah*) to the *Book of the Teacher and the*

Būlus al-Būshī on Revelation: Authorship and Reception, Biblical Text and Commentary

Authorship and Reception

Būlus al-Būshī's authorship of the *Commentary on the Apocalypse* is supported by three kinds of evidence: manuscript witnesses, external testimonies, and stylistic analysis. First, while most manuscripts containing the work do not identify the author by name, the two that do so exclusively attribute the work to Būlus al-Būshī.[19] There is also a paraphrase of the same commentary credited to him. Second, the later commentary written by Ibn Kātib Qayṣar provides additional confirmation of Būlus al-Būshī's authorship. It does so in two ways: by way of citation and by way of its history of transmission. On the one hand, Ibn Kātib Qayṣar actually cites sections of Būlus al-Būshī's commentary, identifying him by name. On the other hand, after the ending of Ibn Kātib Qayṣar's commentary was lost in the history of transmission, a later Arabic scribe substituted the last two chapters of Būlus al-Būshī's text to fill the gap and explicitly cites his authorship: "The remainder of the commentary is that of Būlus al-Būshī."[20]

Student, which was reportedly coauthored by Būlus al-Būshī and Dāwūd al-Fayyūmī. Al-Mu'taman himself testifies that he used some of Būlus al-Būshī's works in composing his theological *Summa Theologica*: Graf, "Das Schriftstellerverzeichnis des Abū Isḥāq ibn al-'Assāl," *Oriens Christianus* n.s. 2 (1912), 212. For a recent multivolume work including a study of Mu'taman and a critical edition (and Italian translation) of his *Summa*, see A. Wadi, OFM, ed., *Studio su al-Mu'taman Ibn al-'Assāl (Dirāsah 'an al-Mu'taman ibn al-'Assāl)* and *Summa dei principi della Religione (Majmū' uṣūl al-dīn)* (7 volumes; Studia Orientalia Christiana Monographiae 5 [intro], 6a–7a [text], 6b–7b [critical apparatus], 8–9 [Italian translation]; Cairo: The Franciscan Centre of Christian Oriental Studies and Franciscan Printing Press, 1997–99).

19. One of these manuscripts (Cairo Arabic 52, now Coptic Museum MS 185, 2) is a paraphrased or abridged version of Būlus al-Būshī's commentary: see *Catalogue, Coptic Museum*, vol. 1, 90–91; Graf, *GCAL* 2.359; Talia, "Būlus al-Būšī's Arabic Commentary," 17 and 26n10. Graf dates the text to 1484 CE, while Talia gives a date of March 20, 1688. The other manuscript (Cairo Arabic 430, now Coptic Patriarchate MS 455, 2; fourteenth to fifteenth century CE) preserves an excerpt from Būlus al-Būshī's commentary. This manuscript is identified by Samir (*Traité de Paul de Būš*, 50) as Theology (*Lāhūt*) 262, but Talia did not use it in his dissertation. While Graf raises the possibility that this authorial attribution was the product of later tradition, Samir Khalil Samir has more recently supported Būlus al-Būshī's authorship. It should be noted that Samir (*Traité de Paul de Būš*, 51–52) also identifies additional possible abridged copies of Būlus al-Būshī's commentary, including one that "contains the same text" as the second manuscript discussed above.

20. Talia, "Būlus al-Būšī's Arabic Commentary," 24; see also Graf, *GCAL* 2.358.

A comparison of those two chapters with the ending of Būlus al-Būshī's commentary in surviving manuscripts shows that the text of both the Apocalypse and the commentary are one and the same. Third and finally, a stylistic comparison of the language used in the commentary with that found in Būlus al-Būshī's treatise *On the Incarnation* provides further support for his authorship. Indeed, one passage discussing the fall of Adam, the meaning of physical and spiritual death, and the Incarnation of Christ provides an almost-verbatim match.[21]

The number of manuscripts that survive make it clear that his *Commentary on the Apocalypse* was in fact the most widely copied and, perhaps, the most widely utilized of Būlus al-Būshī's works.[22] It must have circulated soon after its composition, given the fact that Ibn Kātib Qayṣar already had access to it only a decade or two later. Furthermore, Būlus al-Būshī's commentary was also copied outside of Egypt. A copy of the commentary preserved in the Vatican library (Vat. ar. 118) also attests to the fact that Būlus al-Būshī's commentary was transcribed in Syria during the fourteenth century (May 16, 1323 CE).[23]

Biblical Text and Commentary

Before discussing the Būlus al-Būshī's interpretation of Revelation, it is important to say something about the scriptural text he was interpreting.

21. In support of this point, Talia ("Būlus al-Būšī's Arabic Commentary," 25) presents a line-by-line comparison of Būlus's *Commentary on the Apocalypse* (Vat. Ar. 459, f. 41v), and Būlus's treatise *On the Incarnation* (Samir, *Traité de Paul de Būš*, 58).

22. For a detailed discussion of the manuscript tradition, see Edelby, "Commentaire," 24–39. For a supplementary list of manuscript copies, including one from the Monastery of the Syrians (Dayr al-Suryān MS 88) in Wādī al-Naṭrūn, see Bishop Epiphanius (al-Anbā Ibīfānīyūs), *Tafsīr Sifr al-Ru'yā*, 33–34. The Monastery of the Syrians manuscript has also been documented by a team led by Stephen J. Davis as part of a project to catalogue the Coptic and Arabic manuscripts in that library: Davis, "Cataloguing the Coptic and Arabic Manuscripts in the Monastery of the Syrians: A Preliminary Report," *Studia Patristica* 90 (2018), 179–185. In a handwritten Arabic catalogue internal to the monastery, its twentieth-century monastic author associated the commentary in MS 88 with Būlus al-Būshī, but the manuscript requires further detailed study to assess its relationship with the rest of the surviving record.

23. Samir, *Traité de Paul de Būš*, 52. R. Cowley (*The Traditional Interpretation of the Apocalypse of St. John in the Ethiopian Orthodox Church* [Cambridge: Cambridge University Press, 1983], 74, 168) has suggested that Būlus al-Būshī's *Commentary on Revelation* may also have been read in the Ethiopian church.

The history of the Arabic version of the Bible, especially that of the Apocalypse, is yet to be written in full.[24] The Arabic text of Revelation has received considerably less attention than earlier Christian translations, such as the Coptic and Syriac versions, which bear a more direct relationship to the original Greek and thus have been used more extensively for text critical purposes.

In his commentary on this text, Būlus al-Būshī first copies sets of verses from the Apocalypse and then appends his own remarks after each block of biblical text. The Arabic version of Revelation he uses was translated from an earlier Bohairic Coptic version,[25] but there are many variants between his text of Revelation and extant Coptic versions. Strangely enough, there is also divergence between the primary blocks of text that serve as the basis for his commentary and the wording of shorter excerpts from the Apocalypse that he quotes within his own discourse.

These variants raise an important question. Did Būlus al-Būshī utilize for his commentary an already available Arabic translation of the Apocalypse, or was he translating Revelation from Coptic into Arabic while composing his commentary? If we imagine that he translated the biblical text directly from Coptic into Arabic, these textual idiosyncrasies would indicate that he was careless in his translation or that his facility in the language hindered him from producing a faithful translation. Given his composition of other rather sophisticated theological treatises in Arabic, however, this pair of scenarios seems unlikely. It thus makes more sense that he utilized an earlier Arabic version of the Apocalypse, but perhaps did not always check or collate it with other Coptic versions of the text.

As for Būlus al-Būshī's commentary itself, it does not cover every verse of the Apocalypse: In fact, only one-third of the total verses in Revelation are the subject of substantive interpretation. The remaining verses are either given a very cursory reading or passed over altogether. There is no evident reason for this selectivity. Perhaps Būlus al-Būshī felt it necessary to

24. But see now Sidney H. Griffith, *The Bible in Arabic: The Scriptures of the "People of the Book" in the Language of Islam* (Princeton: Princeton University Press, 2013); and Ronny Vollandt, *Arabic Versions of the Pentateuch: A Comparative Study of Jewish, Christian, and Muslim Sources* (Leiden: Brill, 2015).

25. The Arabic version of Revelation survives in four different recensions (labeled A–D). Three of these (A, B, and C) are all translated from the Bohairic Coptic version, while the fourth (D) seems to show indications of Syriac influence. For a discussion, see Graf, "Arabische Übersetzungen der Apokalypse," *Biblica* 10 (1929), 170–94, at 192–93.

comment only on those verses in which he saw some allegorical or symbolic interpretation. Or he may have focused only on those verses necessary for his discussion of the new covenant and the coming of Christ, since these are his main unifying themes.

Būlus al-Būshī's exegesis is homiletic in nature, with simple and elementary pedagogical objectives. The structure of the commentary is uneven, with many long digressions, and yet it nevertheless exhibits its own thematic unity. In particular, the text maintains a fairly consistent Christocentric emphasis. The new covenant is Christ; he is the only salvation; the church shall finally triumph; and God's kingdom is soon to be with us. These emphases are reinforced by occasional quotations from early Christian church fathers, whom he mentions individually by name or anonymously as a collective group. The most quoted patristic authors include Basil the Great, Gregory of Nazianzus (identified as "the Theologian"), and especially Cyril of Alexandria.

The language of the commentary diverges from standard Classical Arabic insofar as it reflects the influence of regional expressions characteristic of medieval Egypt. Such divergences are evident "in orthography, morphology and syntax."[26] In the past, such nonstandard forms of Arabic were sometimes labeled as "Middle Arabic" or "Christian Arabic," and attributed to a lack of education or grammatical training on the part of the writer. But such variations were in fact often stylistic choices and/or dialectical registers embraced by highly educated authors, both Christian and Muslim. Indeed, in the case of Būlus al-Būshī, the grammar of the commentary conforms specifically to what was spoken and written "by Christians [and] for Christians" in Egypt.[27] At the same time, however, like other

26. R. Y. Ebied and M. J. L. Young, *The Lamp of the Intellect of Severus ibn al-Muqaffa', Bishop of al-Ashmūnain* (CSCO 365; Louvain: Secrétariat du CorpusSCO, 1975), xii. On the history and development of "Middle Arabic," see J. Blau, *The Emergence and Linguistic Background of Judaeo-Arabic* (London: Oxford University Press, 1965), 1–18. For more recent, nuanced treatments of Arabic dialectical variations, see Jonathan Owens, *A Linguistic History of Arabic* (Oxford: Oxford University Press, 2006), 46–47; Jérôme Lentin, "Middle Arabic," in *Encyclopedia of Arabic Language and Linguistics*, Managing Editors Online Edition: Lutz Edzard, Rudolf de Jong, http://dx.doi.org/10.1163/1570-6699_eall_EALL_COM_vol3_0213, consulted March 24, 2018. The authors of this chapter want to thank Fordham University Press's anonymous reviewer for invaluable feedback and references on recent developments in the linguistic study of nonstandard Arabic.

27. On the Arabic dialect typically used by Christian authors in Egypt, see S. Kussaim, "Contribution à l'étude du moyen arabe des coptes," *Le Muséon* 80 (1967), 153–209; and 81

learned Copts of the thirteenth century, Būlus al-Būshī shows himself to be well versed in Islamic theological and technical vocabulary, including certain terms found in the Qur'ān and the *ḥadīth* literature.[28]

Būlus al-Būshī's Christological emphasis—framed by a subtle engagement with both patristic and Islamic thought—conforms to what we find elsewhere in his theological treatises and sermons. One of the key themes in his writings is the Incarnation of Christ. In addition to dedicating an independent treatise to the topic, he also made Christ's act of becoming human (*al-ta'annus*) and taking on a body (*al-tajassud*) the centerpiece of a four-part work *On the Unity of God, the Trinity, the Incarnation, and the Truth of the Christian Religion.*

In that work, the section on the Incarnation is of special interest. He structures his treatment of this theme around a series of questions. First, how did God the Word become incarnate? How did God come to dwell in the woman (Mary) whom God created? How did the Incarnation concern one person of the Trinity only? Is the one who became incarnate the eternal Creator? Second, why did God the Word become incarnate? What was it that compelled God to do so? Why did God not send an angel or a prophet to save God's people instead? Third and finally, what are the fruits of the Incarnation? How does this event relate to the conferring of eternal life and human participation in the body of Christ?[29]

(1968), 5–77. For a comprehensive investigation of Christian Arabic, see G. Graf, *Der Sprachgebrauch der ältesten christlichen-arabischen Literatur: ein Beitrag zur Geschichte des Vulgar-Arabisch* (Leipzig: Harrossowitz, 1905); and especially J. Blau, *A Grammar of Christian Arabic* (CSCO 267, 276, 279; Louvain: Secrétariat du CorpusSCO, 1966–67), quote from p. 20, no. 4.

28. For a documentation of Būlus al-Būshī's use of Islamic terminology, see Talia, "Būlus al-Būšī's Arabic Commentary," 36–41; and Edelby, "Commentaire," 44–48.

29. These themes and questions are not unique to Būlus al-Būshī or to the Arabic literature produced by Christians in Egypt. For treatments of the Incarnation by Arabic Christian authors from other regions and confessions, see, e.g., Paul Khoury, *Matériaux pour servir à l'étude de la controverse théologique islamo-chrétienne de langue arabe du VIIIe au XIIe siècle*, vol. 5 (Würburg: Oros, 2000), B.3, 177ff.; and B.4, 305ff.; Bénédicte Landron, *Chétiens et musulmans en Irak: attitudes nestoriennes vis-à-vis de l'Islam* (Paris: Cariscript, 1994), ch. 13; Martin Accad, "The Ultimate Proof-Text: The Interpretation of John 20:17 in Muslim-Christian Dialogue (Second/Eighth–Eighth/Fourteenth Centuries)," in *Christians at the Heart of Islamic Rule: Church Life and Scholarship in 'Abbasid Iraq*, ed. David Thomas (Leiden: Brill, 2003), 199–214; Mark Beaumont, *Christology in Dialogue with Muslims: A Critical Analysis of Christian Presentations of Christ for Muslims from the Ninth and Twentieth Centuries*

With respect to the first two sets of questions, on how and why God the Word became incarnate, Būlus al-Būshī engages with apologetic concerns inflected by Christian Arab encounters with Islam. This is reflected in both structure and theme. The question-and-answer format he employs follows the Islamic rhetorical and theological model of *al-Kalām*, a particular kind of rational discourse designed to frame the terms of intellectual engagement on weighty topics. The content of the questions themselves also highlight certain theological concerns he shared with his Muslim contemporaries: especially, the unity of God, the status of messengers or prophets (*rusul*, the same Arabic word used to designate Christian apostles as well), and God's divine agency in creation. With regard to this last theme, he even quotes from the Qur'ān (Surah 23:115) to underscore his point.

With respect to his third concern, on the fruits of the Incarnation, Būlus al-Būshī shifts from apologetic discourse to narrative exposition of the Bible. Here, "one begins to see more clearly his indebtedness to an Alexandrian tradition of Christology and biblical commentary in which the Incarnation and human participation in the divine nature are intimately linked."[30] His language on creation and salvation echoes that of Athanasius of Alexandria, and he shows extensive familiarity with Cyril of Alexandria's exegesis and sacramental theology. This works on two levels. On the one hand, he applies the anti-Arian soteriological arguments of Athanasius and Cyril to Christian-Muslim apologetic, as a means of underscoring a crucial difference between Christ's role and that of the prophets (including the prophet Muhammad). On the other hand, he draws on these early church fathers in order to develop his own incarnational theology regarding the life-giving eucharistic reality of Christ's flesh.[31]

These same emphases are found interspersed throughout Būlus al-Būshī's commentary on Revelation 1–3. On the text's reference to the "Son of Man" in Revelation 1:13, he notes that "he is called the *Son of Man* because he became incarnate."[32] With regard to Revelation 1:18 ("I am the living one.

(Bletchley: Paternoster, 2005). Once again, we are indebted to our anonymous reviewer for this bibliography.

30. Davis, *Coptic Christology in Practice*, 246.

31. Davis, *Coptic Christology in Practice*, 250. On the influence of Athanasius's thought on Būlus al-Būshī, see also Joseph Moris Faltas, "O megas Athanasios ōs pēgē tēs theologias tou Būlūs al-Būšī" (Ph.D. diss., University of Athens, 1994), esp. 86–191.

32. Būlus al-Būshī, *Commentary on the Apocalypse* 2 (Vat. Ar. 459, f. 2r; Edelby, "Commentaire," 5–6 [Arabic text]).

I died, but behold, I am alive forever"), he emphasizes Christ's "life-giving" and "corporeal" suffering and "the power of his divinity."[33] Commenting on the reference to "the paradise of God" in Revelation 2:7, he alludes to God's creation, underscores the fact that God "became fully incarnate with a rational soul completely like us in every way except sin," and highlights "the power of miracles" as a manifestation of the Incarnation. Then he concludes with the statement, "He is God incarnate. The one to whom divinity properly belongs is also the one to whom Incarnation properly belongs."[34]

Furthermore, in his interpretation of Revelation, Būlus al-Būshī explicitly borrows the Alexandrian language of "economy" when speaking of "the manner of the Incarnation," and quotes from "Cyril the Great, the patriarch of Alexandria who writes, 'He is the life, the living one who gives life by the power of his divinity, who does not suffer and does not die.'"[35] In this context, he subsequently interprets the "the book of life" in Revelation 3:5 as confirmation of the incarnate Word's eternality: "Although he has appeared in a body as a human, he remains eternal God, and he exists without end, along with the Father."[36] Finally, in interpreting Revelation 3:14 and 3:21, Būlus al-Būshī makes familiar Alexandrian exegetical moves when he connects "the beginning of God's creation" and the heavenly "throne" with the Incarnation.[37] Such Christological themes, backed by

33. Būlus al-Būshī, *Commentary on the Apocalypse* 3 (Vat. Ar. 459, f. 3r; Edelby, "Commentaire," 9 [Arabic text]).

34. Būlus al-Būshī, *Commentary on the Apocalypse* 4 (Vat. Ar. 459, f. 5r; Edelby, "Commentaire," 15–16 [Arabic text]).

35. Būlus al-Būshī, *Commentary on the Apocalypse* 5 (Vat. Ar. 459, f. 5v; Edelby, "Commentaire," 18 [Arabic text]).

36. Būlus al-Būshī, *Commentary on the Apocalypse* 8. (Vat. Ar. 459, f. 11v; Edelby, "Commentaire," 32 [Arabic text]).

37. Būlus al-Būshī, *Commentary on the Apocalypse* 10 (Vat. Ar. 459, f. 14r–v, 16r; Edelby, "Commentaire," 39, 44 [Arabic text]). In his *Scholia on the Incarnation* (*schol. inc.*), Cyril of Alexandria repeated links images of creation and the heavenly throne with Christ's Incarnation. On the heavenly throne, see *schol. inc.* 12 (PG 75.1384; trans. McGuckin, *St. Cyril*, 305), where Cyril writes that "[the Word of God] was humbled on account of the flesh, but even so he did not descend from the height of divine majesty for he kept his lofty throne." Three chapters later, he emphasizes that Christ sits "at the right hand of the Father in his own majesty, possessing the highest throne, even with his flesh" (*schol. inc.* 15: PG 75.1390; trans. McGuckin, *St. Cyril*, 310). On creation, see, e.g., *schol. inc.* 29 (PG 75.1402; trans. J. A. McGuckin, *St. Cyril*, 324), where Cyril (following Solomon), "is amazed by the incarnation of the Word, . . . that he dwelt with men on the earth when he himself became man," and marvels "that God did not turn away from what he had created, but rather cherished them, and sustained what was already in existence, and even created things that were not."

Alexandrian patristic rationales, continue over the course of his entire commentary.

Būlus al-Būshī's commentary also evinces a consistent apologetic with respect to Islam. His interpretation of "those who say they are apostles [*rusul*]" but are found to be "liars" in Revelation 2:2 is especially telling. His warning about the need to be "on guard" against such "false apostles and deceitful prophets" (2 Cor. 11:13, *rusul kadhabah wa-anbiyā' ghadarah*) would have been understood by his Arabic-speaking Christian audience at least in part as alluding to Muhammad's status as the Islamic prophet par excellence.[38] The connection he makes between "the throne of Satan" in Revelation 2:13 and the idolatrous "sacrifices" of Revelation 2:14, and his warnings against tolerating and associating with evil people (instantiated in the idolatrous figure of Jezebel in Revelation 2:20) may have prompted a similar apologetic posture in his readers vis-à-vis Islam.[39] Later, Būlus al-Būshī's polemical attitude in relation to Islam becomes more explicit. In commenting on Revelation 3:9 ("I have surrendered you to the synagogue of Satan"), he interprets this phrase as meaning that "they profess they are keeping the tradition [*sunnah*], but they are in opposition to it, because they have not accepted the Incarnation of the Lord."[40] The Arabic term *sunnah* was closely associated with Sunni Muslims' adherence to Islamic law and tradition. In using this language, Būlus al-Būshī is effectively demonizing Muslims for their rejection of Christian doctrine regarding the Word made flesh. Later in the commentary, this again becomes a point of emphasis when he interprets 666—the number of the beast in Revelation 13:18—as a portent of Islam's prophet: "If the letters are summed up—if each letter is counted according to its value and added together, and then all are totaled up—the name [of the beast] will be *Mametios*, i.e., Muhammad."[41]

38. Būlus al-Būshī, *Commentary on the Apocalypse* 4 (Vat. Ar. 459, f. 4r; Edelby, "Commentaire," 13 [Arabic text]).

39. Būlus al-Būshī, *Commentary on the Apocalypse* 6 and 7 (Vat. Ar. 459, ff. 7r, 9r–v; Edelby, "Commentaire," 22, 26–7 [Arabic text]).

40. Būlus al-Būshī, *Commentary on the Apocalypse* 9 (Vat. Ar. 459, f. 13r–v; Edelby, "Commentaire," 35 [Arabic text]).

41. Būlus al-Būshī, *Commentary on the Apocalypse* 24 (Vat. Ar. 459, f. 35r; Edelby, "Commentaire," 97 [Arabic text]). In Sbath 1014 (f. 77r), the scribe completes the sentence in the margin, where he writes the Coptic word ⲙⲁⲙⲉⲧⲓⲟⲥ (*Mametios*) along with its Arabic "translation"—*Muḥammad*. In the British Library manuscript, Or. 1329 (f. 41r), the entire phrase, "his name is *Mametios*" is written in Coptic as follows: ⲙⲁⲙⲉⲧⲓⲟⲥ ⲡⲉ ⲡⲉϥⲣⲁⲛ (*Mametios pe pefran*). Imme-

In sum, Būlus al-Būshī's exegesis of Revelation stands at a crucial nexus, a cultural crossroads where the inheritance of patristic Christology intersected with philosophical and theological questions motivated by Christian encounters with Islam in medieval Egypt. The result provides us with a fascinating glimpse into the way an apocalyptic biblical text and a medieval Egyptian commentator spoke simultaneously to those two sets of concerns in an Arabic-speaking ecclesiastical context.

---

diately below, the scribe has assigned each letter in the name its numerical value: 40 + 1 + 40 + 5 + 300 + 10 + 70 + 200 (= 666). For a further discussion of Būlus's interpretation of 666, in comparison to that of Ibn Kātib Qayṣar, see Chapter 2.

CHAPTER

2

Ibn Kātib Qayṣar on Visions, Angels, Prophets, and Dreams

Stephen J. Davis

Introducing Ibn Kātib Qayṣar's Commentary on the Apocalypse

Let us now turn our attention to Ibn Kātib Qayṣar, who authored the second extant Christian Arabic commentary on Revelation. Our critical introduction to his exegetical work is divided into two parts—consisting of Chapters 2 and 3 in the present volume. Chapter 2 will focus on his theory and typology of revelatory vision and his understanding of John as a privileged recipient of such a vision. Chapter 3 will present a broader, systematic analysis of his exegetical method and theology.

In this chapter, I will begin by focusing on Ibn Kātib Qayṣar's interpretation of John's initial vision, where he touches on the dual themes of angelology and visionary experience. In his interpretation of Revelation 1:1, the author presents a hierarchical classification of revelatory visions and portrays John as an angel, apostle, prophet, and priest. As I will demonstrate, these two sets of concerns reveal how Ibn Kātib Qayṣar elaborates on ancient Greek and Latin cultural assumptions—assumptions that were crucially mediated through Arabic channels—even as he engaged with subtle linguistic issues specific to his reading of a Copto-Arabic biblical text. Finally, I will also raise some questions regarding how Ibn Kātib Qayṣar's work was contextualized by, and in conversation with, early medieval Islamic theories of visionary experience.

At the outset, let me outline four distinguishing features of Ibn Kātib Qayṣar's commentary as a whole. These four features include:

1. the author's special focus on the grammar and etymology of particular words and phrases, with special reference to Coptic, Greek, and Syriac precedents;

2. his fondness for systematic classification, such as when he categorizes different meanings of the words "vision" (1:1) and "Jewish" (2:9),[1] and different classes or races of human beings according to moral and ethnic types (3:4 and 13:1);[2]

3. his healthy regard for historical context: as, for example, in the case of his discussion of John's messages to the seven churches (2:1–3:22),[3] and the reigns of kings and emperors from the Hellenistic and Roman periods, such as Antiochus Epiphanes, Tiberius, Nero, and Titus (17:10);[4]

4. his citation of earlier commentators, including Hippolytus of Rome (whose interpretations he often rejects) and a spectrum of other medieval Arabic writers ranging from the Jewish philosopher Maimonides,[5] to Christian theologians from different theological communions in the Near East, including the Nestorians Abū al-Faraj 'Abdallah ibn al-Ṭayyib and Sabrīshu' Bishr ibn al-Sirrī, as well as other anti-Chalcedonians such as 'Īsā ibn Zur'a and his near contemporaries Buṭrus al-Sadamantī and Būlus al-Būshī.[6] The ecumenical scope of his citational practice reflects the spirit of a Copto-Arabic golden age in the thirteenth century, when Egyptian theologians came into deeper, more positive engagement with the theology produced by fellow Arabic Christians in Syria and Iraq as they sought

1. Ibn Kātib Qayṣar, *Commentary on the Apocalypse* 1; 12 (Birmāwī, 30–31, 57–58).

2. Ibn Kātib Qayṣar, *Commentary on the Apocalypse* 15; 62 (Birmāwī, 75, 261–62).

3. Ibn Kātib Qayṣar, *Commentary on the Apocalypse* 11–17 (Birmāwī, 52–95).

4. Ibn Kātib Qayṣar, *Commentary on the Apocalypse* 88 (Birmāwī, 335–37).

5. While Maimonides (1138–1204 CE) was born in Spain, he spent the latter half of his life in Fusṭāṭ (a district adjacent to Old Cairo), where he wrote most of his works.

6. On Ibn Kātib Qayṣar's citations of these Arabic Christian authors, see G. Graf, *GCAL* 2, 383. On the identity of Bishr ibn al-Sirrī, see Sebastian Brock, "A Neglected Witness to the East Syriac New Testament Commentary Tradition, Sinai Arabic ms 151," in *Studies on the Christian Arabic Heritage in Honour of Prof. Dr. Samir Khalil Samir S. I. on the Occasion of His Sixty-Fifth Birthday*, ed. R. Ebied and H. Teule (Eastern Christian Studies 5; Leuven: Peeters, 2004), 205–15, esp. 213–15.

to defend their beliefs over against the intellectual challenges raised by Islam.[7]

The relevance of this apologetic context for the task of biblical interpretation—that is, the heightened sensitivities connected with Christian-Muslim encounter—becomes especially evident in the way that Ibn Kātib Qayṣar handles the number 666, the infamous mark of the beast in Revelation 13:18.[8] After citing Hippolytus, who had identified four historical personages whose names had letter values corresponding to 666, he goes on to mention the fact that his Arabic compatriot Būlus al-Būshī had more recently put forward a fifth name with this numerical value.[9] An examination of Būlus al-Būshī's own *Commentary on the Apocalypse of John* demonstrates his particular preoccupation with this detail in the biblical text. After quoting Revelation 13:11–18—eight consecutive verses of the biblical text—he reserves his only commentary for the number 666. In succinct and unsparing terms, he writes, "If the letters are summed up—if each letter is counted according to its value and added together, and then all are totaled up—the name [of the beast] will be *Mametios* [ⲙⲁⲙⲉⲧⲓⲟⲥ], i.e., Muhammad [*Muḥammad*]."[10]

This numerical association of the beast with Muhammad and the coming of the Arabs to Egypt is attested in Coptic sources as early as the seventh century. Around the year 690, the chronicler John of Nikiu wrote,

7. For studies of Arabic Christian apologetics under early Islam, especially the literature produced in Syria and Iraq that later thirteenth-century Copto-Arabic theologians utilized in developing their own apologetic discourse, see Rachid Haddad, *La Trinité divine chez les théologiens arabes (750–1050)* (Beauchesne religions 15; Paris: Beauchesne, 1985); and Samir Khalil Samir and Jørgen S. Nielsen, eds., *Christian Arabic Apologetics during the Abbasid Period, 750–1258* (Leiden: Brill, 1994). Additional essential reading: the numerous publications by Sidney H. Griffith, including those collected in *The Beginnings of Christian Theology in Arabic: Muslim-Christian Encounters in the Early Islamic Period* (Variorum Collected Studies Series; Aldershot: Ashgate, 2002); his essay, "Answering the Call of the Minaret: Christian Apologetics in the World of Islam," in *Redefining Christian Identity: Cultural Interaction in the Middle East since the Rise of Islam*, ed. J. J. van Ginkel, H. L. Murre-van der Berg, T. M. van Lint (Leuven: Peeters, 2005), 91–126; and his books, *The Church in the Shadow of the Mosque: Christians and Muslims in the World of Islam* (Princeton: Princeton University Press, 2008); and *The Bible in Arabic: The Scriptures of the "People of the Book" in the Language of Islam* (2013). Finally, see also now the multivolume CMR, especially volumes 1–4.

8. Ibn Kātib Qayṣar, *Commentary on the Apocalypse* 64 (Birmāwī, 373–75).

9. Ibn Kātib Qayṣar, *Commentary on the Apocalypse* 64 (Birmāwī, 374).

10. Būlus al-Būshī, *Commentary on the Apocalypse* 24 (Vat. Ar. 459, f. 35r; Sbath 1014, f. 77r; Edelby, "Commentaire," 97 [Arabic text]). See also note 41 in Chapter 1.

> And now many of the Egyptians who had been false Christians denied the holy orthodox faith and life-giving baptism, and embraced the religion of the Muslims, the enemies of God, and accepted the detestable doctrine of the beast, that is, Muhammad.[11]

Perhaps twenty-five years later, the author of the *Apocalypse of Ps.-Athanasius* picks up on the same theme. Written circa 715, the work presents a prophecy purportedly given by the fourth-century Athanasius of Alexandria regarding the reminting of Islamic coins under ʿAbd al-Malik (696 CE). This retrospective prophecy forecasts the coming of a "nation (that) will destroy the gold on which there is the image of the cross of the Lord our God in order to make all the countries under its rule mint their own gold with the name of the beast written on it, the number of whose name is 666."[12]

This interpretation remained current in the thirteenth century. One finds it in at least one other Arabic-Egyptian work from Būlus al-Būshī's own era. His contemporary, Ibn al-Rāhib, twice makes reference to the name *Mametios* (ⲙⲁⲙⲉⲧⲓⲟⲥ) in his *Book of Histories* (*Kitāb al-tawārīkh*).[13]

11. John of Nikiu, *Chronicle* 121.10; trans. R. H. Charles, *The Chronicle of John (c. 690 A. D.) Coptic Bishop of Nikiu* (Text and Translation Society 3; London: William & Norgate, 1916), 75–76. While it was probably originally composed in Coptic and/or Greek, John of Nikiu's *Chronicle* only survives in an Ethiopic version based directly on an Arabic *Vorlage* (ed. H. Zotenberg, "La Chronique de Jean de Nikioū," *Notices et Extraits des manuscrits de la Bibliothèque Nationale* 24.1 [1883], 125–605). This Ethiopic text serves as the basis for Charles's English translation.

12. Ps.-Athanasius, *Apocalypse* IX.9: ed. and trans. F. J. Martinez, "Eastern Christian Apocalyptic in the Early Muslim Period: Pseudo-Methodius and Pseudo-Athanasius," (Ph.D. dissertation, Catholic University of America, Washington, D.C., 1985), 247–590, esp. 529–31. Robert Hoyland argues that the name of the beast in this apocalypse also refers to Muhammad: see his book, *Seeing Islam As Others Saw It: A Survey and Evaluation of Christian, Jewish, and Zoroastrian Writings on Early Islam* (Studies in Late Antiquity and Early Islam; Princeton: Darwin Press, 1998), 283–85; pace Tito Orlandi, "Un testo copto sulla dominazione araba in Egitto," in *Acts of the Second International Congress of Coptic Studies*, ed. T. Orlandi and F. Wisse (Rome: C.I.M., 1985), 225–34. This work is preserved primarily in Arabic (Graf, *GCAL* I.277–79), but some fragments of the original Coptic also survive: see Bernd Witte, "Der koptische Text von M 602 f. 52–f. 77 der Pierpont Morgan Library—wirklich eine Schrift des Athanasius?" *Orientalia Christiana* 78 (1994), 123–30; and Harald Suermann, "Koptische arabische Apokalypsen," in *Studies on the Christian Arabic Heritage*, ed. R. Ebied and H. Teule (Eastern Christian Studies 5; Peeters: Leuven, 2004), 25–44, esp. 26–30.

13. Samuel Moawad originally called my attention to Ibn al-Rāhib's relevance for this study. For earlier editions and studies of Ibn al-Rāhib's *Kitāb al-tawārīkh*, see Louis Cheiko, ed., *Petrus ibn Rahib: Chronicon orientale* (Beirut: E Typographeo catholico, 1903; repr. Louvain: L. Durbecq, 1955); and Adel Sidarus and Samuel Moawad, "Un traité melkite sur le

First, he recalls "what John the Evangelist mentioned in the Apocalypse regarding the weeks for the coming of *Mametios* and the period of time associated with him."[14] Later, in commenting on dating systems, he notes that a particular Thursday was "the first day of the year in which *Mametioe* [*sic*], i.e., Muhammad, emigrated from Mecca to al-Medina."[15] In his commentary on Revelation, Būlus al-Būshī inherits this apocalyptic tradition regarding the significance of Muhammad's name.

In this context, just as striking as Būlus al-Būshī's embrace of this polemical reading is Ibn Kātib Qayṣar's purposeful decision to suppress it. He notably refrains from quoting the specifics of Būlus al-Būshī's interpretation and concludes by saying, "The attempt to solve the true identity [of the beast] cannot be realized apart from divine inspiration, seeing as there have already been many inventive solutions proposed. How is it possible to find a way to know that name from its sum, apart from knowing the name itself? The wisdom in hiding this name was lest one of the kings or archheretics embrace it and claim that he is that beast."[16] Far from supplying a name, Ibn Kātib Qayṣar is content here to leave the identity of the beast a mystery to his readers. His reticence to embrace Būlus al-Būshī's more controversial interpretation may be related not simply to hermeneutical

comput pascal de Yaḥyā ibn Saʿīd al-Anṭākī d'après Abū Šākir ibn al-Rāhib (auteur copte du XIIIe siècle)," *Le Muséon* 123 (2010), 455–77. But see now Part 1 of Samuel Moawad's new critical edition: Abū Shākir Ibn al-Rāhib, *Kitāb al-tawārīkh*, al-juzʾ al-awwal, al-abwāb 1–47, ed. S. Moawad (Silsilat Madrasat al-Iskandariyyah li-al-dirāsāt al-masīḥiyyah; Cairo: Madrasat al-Iskandariyyah, 2016); and Adel Sidarus, "Ibn al-Rāhib," CMR, vol. 4, 471–79.

14. London, British Library, Or. 1337, f. 2v; Berlin, Staatsbibliothek (DE-BS), Or. fol. 434, 3.

15. London, British Library, Or. 1337, f. 12v. In the London manuscript, the late eighteenth-century scribe has mistaken the final Coptic *sigma* (ϲ) in the name for an *epsilon* (ϵ). In the Berlin manuscript cited above (Or. fol. 434, 24), a different nineteenth-century scribe records the same passage but leaves an open space where he was supposed to have written the word *Mametios*. This omission is perhaps due to the difficulty he had in working with the Coptic language (this despite the fact that he successfully copied the same word earlier in his manuscript). For more information on the life and work of Ibn al-Rāhib, see Adel Sidarus, *Ibn ar-Rāhibs Leben und Werk: Ein koptisch-arabischer Enzyklopädist des 7./13. Jahrhunderts* (Islamkundliche Untersuchungen 36; Freiburg: Klaus Schwarz Verlag, 1975); Johannes den Heijer, "Coptic Historiography in the Fatimid, Ayyubid, and Early Mamluk Periods," *Medieval Encounters* 2 (1996), 67–98, esp. 83–88; and Sidarus, "Kitāb al-tawārīkh," in *Christian Muslim Relations 600–1500*, ed. D. Thomas (BrillOnline *Reference Works*, http://referenceworks.brillonline.com/entries/christian-muslim-relations-i/kitab-al-tawarikh-COM_24891, consulted March 24, 2018).

16. Ibn Kātib Qayṣar, *Commentary on the Apocalypse* 64 (Birmāwī, 274).

method, but also perhaps to the very real social and political concerns he and his family would have had as cosmopolitan Copts who interacted with Muslim colleagues on a daily basis in literary and administrative circles.

The rest of this chapter will concern itself with the opening paragraphs of Ibn Kātib Qayṣar's commentary, and especially with two textual details that highlight his understanding of divine visions and the mediatory role of "angels" in this revelatory economy. These two case studies will serve as an introduction to his unique sensibility as a commentator, an interpretive identity shaped by his inheritance of conceptual categories from late antiquity and by key issues related to the transmission and translation of the biblical text from Greek to Coptic and finally to Arabic.

Classified Vision: Revelation on the Edge of Wakefulness

The first textual detail calling for closer study relates to Ibn Kātib Qayṣar's proclivity toward semantic classification. After a brief, formulaic preface, and after quoting the first two verses of Revelation, he focuses his attention on the very first word in the text, *ru'yā*, which may be translated as "vision," "revelation," or—as I will most often render it—"revelatory vision." In his preface he had already identified the biblical book itself by the composite form derived from the Coptic and Arabic synonyms, *ru'yā al-ābūghālumsis* (lit., "revelatory vision of the Apocalypse").[17] The commentator then proceeds to classify "revelatory vision" as "one [of three] species of prophecy [*al-nubūwah*] belonging to the givers of the law."[18] He defines the broad category of prophecy as "a divine superabundance mediated through the active intellect to the rational soul, and then through it to the power of imagination."

Ibn Kātib Qayṣar draws here on the philosophical language of Ibn Sīnā (d. 1037), known in the West as Avicenna, who adapted the Aristotelian and Neoplatonic cosmology of al-Fārābī (d. 950 or 951), applying it to his understanding of the soul's faculties as the crucial point of contact or conjunction (*ittiṣāl*) with the "Active Intellect" (*al-'aql al-fā'ālah* or *al-'aql al-munfa'ilah*) that emanates from God as the first cause. According to Ibn Sīnā's schema, prophecy had three aspects or elements: intellectual (based

17. Ibn Kātib Qayṣar, *Commentary on the Apocalypse*, Preface (Birmāwī, 29).
18. Ibn Kātib Qayṣar, *Commentary on the Apocalypse* 1 (Birmāwī, 30).

on acts of intuition), imaginative (involving the experience of divinatory visions); and practical/motive (allowing the prophet to produce miraculous effects externally in the visible world). Ibn Sīnā understood prophets to be gifted with highly developed imaginative faculties especially receptive to divine inspiration—not just during sleep (*al-nawm*) in the form of dreams, but also during waking life (*al-yaqẓah*).[19]

In his *Commentary on the Apocalypse*, Ibn Kātib Qayṣar is also interested in the prophet's state of mind when divine insight is granted, but as he develops his ideas on the subject, he moves beyond a simple binary involving sleep (*al-nawm*) and wakefulness (*al-yaqẓah*) to elaborate a classificatory system involving three types or conditions of prophecy. To do so, he redefines the term *al-yaqẓah* for his own purposes, considering it in terms of either partial or full wakefulness.

The first and weakest type, which Ibn Kātib Qayṣar labels with the term "prophecy" (*al-nubūwah*), "takes place if it occurs in the condition of sleep, by means of a dream."[20] As illustrations, he points to a series of examples from the Hebrew Bible/Old Testament (dreams of Pharaoh and Nebuchadnezzar interpreted by Joseph and Daniel, the dreams of Jacob and Joseph, and Laban and Abimalech, and some of the prophecy of Daniel). The second type takes place in a condition of *al-yaqẓah*, which he understands in terms of a state of semiwakefulness characterized by light slumber

19. al-Fārābī, *Kitāb mabādi' ārā' ahl al-madīnah al-fāḍilah* 13–14: ed. R. Walzer, *Al-Fārābī on the Perfect State: Abū Naṣr al-Fārābī's* Mabādi' ārā' ahl al-madīna al-fāḍila (Oxford: Clarendon, 1985), 196–227 (with commentary on pp. 401–23); Ibn Sīnā (Avicenna), *Kitāb al-nafs* IV.2–4: ed. F. Rahman, *Avicenna's* De Anima *(Arabic Text): Being the Psychological Part of* Kitāb al-Shifā' (Oxford: Oxford University Press, 1959), 169–201. For a concise summary of al-Fārābī's and Ibn Sīnā's prophetic theories, see Marin Whittingham, "Prophecy," in *Encyclopaedia of Islamic Civilisation and Religion*, ed. Ian Richard Netton (London: Routledge, 2008), 514–15. For more in-depth treatments of Ibn Sīnā's psychology and epistemology of prophecy, see Fazlur Rahman, *Prophecy in Islam: Philosophy and Orthodoxy* (London: Allen & Unwin, 1958); Frank Griffel, "The Muslim Philosophers' Rationalist Explanation of Muḥammad's Prophecy," in *The Cambridge Companion to Muḥammad*, ed. Jonathan E. Brockopp (Cambridge: Cambridge University Press, 2010), 158–79; and Griffel, "Philosophy and Prophecy," in *The Routledge Companion to Islamic Philosophy*, ed. R. C. Taylor and L. X. López-Farjeat (London: Routledge, 2016), 385–98. On the influence of Ibn Sīnā's thought over subsequent theology, see Jean Michot, "La pandémie avicennienne au VIe/XIIe siècle: Présentation, edition princeps et traduction de l'introduction du livre de l'advenue du monde (*kitāb ḥudūth al-'ālam*) d'Ibn Ghaylān al-Balkhī," *Arabica* 40.3 (1993), 287–344 I am grateful to our anonymous reviewer for drawing attention to this Avicennian connection.

20. Ibn Kātib Qayṣar, *Commentary on the Apocalypse* 1 (Birmāwī, 30).

(*al-subāt*). Identifying this second type as "revelatory vision" (*al-ru'yā*),[21] Ibn Kātib Qayṣar notes that in Scripture it typically occurs as a kind of "sight, [a condition of] being lost in thought, and inspiration," through which God speaks and acts in a more powerful way.[22] Examples include the visions of Abraham, Isaiah, Hosea, and Obadiah, some of the visions of Daniel, as well as the one recorded by John in his Apocalypse. Finally, the third type is defined by the recipient's condition of full wakefulness not affected by any trace of sleepiness or slumber, as in the stories of Adam in the Garden of Eden, Abraham's calling, Moses at Sinai, and (again) Daniel when he was on the bank of the Euphrates. This most powerful species of prophecy he characterizes as a divine "manifestation" (*al-tajallī*) and "message" (*al-khiṭāb*).[23]

Thus, Ibn Kātib Qayṣar's classification of prophecy and vision may be graphically illustrated as follows:

Types of Prophecy (*al-nubūwah*)

1. Prophecy (*al-nubūwah*): experienced in a state of sleep.
2. Revelatory vision (*al-ru'yā*): experienced in a state of semiwakefulness or light slumber.
3. A divine manifestation (*al-tajallī*) or message (*al-khiṭāb*): experienced in a state of full wakefulness.

In addition to its connections with the philosophical thought of Ibn Sīnā, this analysis of prophetic types bears some resemblance to the threefold classification scheme found in the fifth-century Roman philosopher and grammarian Macrobius, who divides revelatory dreams into three categories: the dream (Gr. *oneiros*; Lat. *somnium*); the vision (Gr. *horama*; Lat. *visio*); and the oracular utterance (Gr. *chrēmatismos*; Lat. *oraculum*).[24] Like Ibn Kātib Qayṣar, Macrobius presents these types in terms of an ascending spectrum of revelatory insight. While the meaning of the divine message in a dream (*somnium*) remains (at least partly) concealed and therefore requires interpretation, the true meaning conveyed in an oracle (*oraculum*)

21. Ibn Kātib Qayṣar, *Commentary on the Apocalypse* 1 (Birmāwī, 30–31).

22. Ibn Kātib Qayṣar, *Commentary on the Apocalypse* 1 (Birmāwī, 31).

23. Ibn Kātib Qayṣar, *Commentary on the Apocalypse* 1 (Birmāwī, 31).

24. Macrobius, *Commentary on the Dream of Scipio* 1.3.2 and 1.3.8–10: ed. M. Armisen-Marchetti, *Macrobe: Commentaire au Songe de Scipion*, vol. 1 (Paris: Les Belles Lettres, 2001), 10, 12–13; Steven F. Kruger, *Dreaming in the Middle Ages* (Cambridge Studies in Medieval Literature 14; Cambridge: Cambridge University Press, 1992), 21–23.

is fully manifest to the recipient and does not require any interpretation. It remains an open question whether Ibn Kātib Qayṣar had access to such earlier traditions, and if so, what kind of access he had.

While it is perhaps doubtful that he had direct knowledge of Macrobius's writings, there is evidence that similar dream typologies disseminated widely during the medieval period, not only in the Latin language but also in Arabic-speaking contexts as well.[25] Ibn Kātib Qayṣar's impulse to classify these types of revelatory prophecy is also consistent with the systematic approach of other ancient theorists, the most famous of whom was Artemidorus (second century CE), who likewise ranked classes of dreamers according to their importance and level of insight.[26] By the ninth century, Artemidorus's *Oneirocriticon* had been translated (or better, adapted) into Arabic by Ḥunayn ibn Isḥāq, a Nestorian Christian physician and scholar from Iraq.[27] As a result, this standard Greek work became widely known throughout the Arabic-speaking world, and Artemidorus's penchant for classification systems and typologies became an integral component of early Islamic (and Christian Arabic) dream interpretation manuals.[28]

However, what distinguishes Ibn Kātib Qayṣar's own threefold classification scheme from that of earlier theorists is the careful attention he gives

25. Steven F. Kruger, *Dreaming in the Middle Ages*, 58–69; John C. Lamoreaux, *The Early Muslim Tradition of Dream Interpretation* (Albany: SUNY Press, 2002), 84.

26. Artemidorus, *Onir.* 1.2 (ed. R. A. Pack, *Artemidori Daldiani onirocriticon libri V* [Leipzig: Teubner, 1963], 9–10); Patricia Cox Miller, *Dreams in Late Antiquity: Studies in the Imagination of a Culture* (Princeton: Princeton University Press, 1994), 50. Gregory of Nyssa seems to have shared this perspective: according to him, "there are (only) a few who are judged worthy of divine communication" and "there are some, not all, who participate by means of their dreams in some diviner manifestation" (*De hom. op.* 13.12; PG 44.172B; trans. P. Cox Miller, 49).

27. This work has been edited by Toufic Fahd, *Artemidorus: Le livre des songes* (Damascus: Institut français de Damas, 1964); for a discussion, see J. Lamoreaux, *The Early Muslim Tradition of Dream Interpretation*, 47–49.

28. For a detailed discussion of Islamic and Islamicate oneirocritical traditions from the seventh to the eleventh century, see Lamoreaux, *The Early Muslim Tradition of Dream Interpretation*; also Nile Green, "The Religious and Cultural Roles of Dreams and Visions in Islam," *Journal of the Royal Asiatic Society*, Series 3, 13.3 (2003), 287–313. For an example of a Byzantine Greek manual that draws on both Artemidorus and Arabic dream science, see Francis Drexl, ed., *Achmetis oneirocriticon* (Leipzig: Teubner, 1925); Steven M. Oberhelman, *Oneirocriticon of Achmet: A Medieval Greek and Arabic Treatise on the Interpretation of Dreams* (Lubbock: Texas Tech University, 1991); and Maria Mavroudi, *A Byzantine Book on Dream Interpretation: The Oneirocriticon of Achmet and Its Arabic Sources* (Leiden: Brill, 2002).

to the middle category of *al-ru'yā*, which he associates with the revelation granted to John on Patmos, and to the particular cognitive state of the visionary in his semiwaking encounter with the divine. Here, one begins to get a sense of how this Arabic-speaking Christian utilized but also elaborated significantly upon the semantic categories used by ancient Greek writers. In antiquity, there were different perspectives on the relation between the condition of sleep (or wakefulness) and a person's corresponding receptivity (or resistivity) to divine influence. Thus, while Plato and Athanasius of Alexandria could describe sleep as the ideal state for "true and inspired divination,"[29] others like Gregory of Nyssa characterized the soul's higher perceptions during sleep as "weak and faint."[30] Among ancient authors there does not seem to have been a consensus regarding the definition of dreams and visions, or regarding the relationship of one to the other. Indeed, scholars have increasingly noted a blurring of these two categories, partly due to inconsistencies in the application of terminology.[31]

29. Plato, *Tim.* 71 E (trans. R. G. Bury, 187). Athanasius of Alexandria (*gent.* 31.38–44; Thomson, 87) writes: "When the body is still, at rest and sleeping, a man is in inner movement—he contemplates (*theorein*) what is outside himself, he traverses foreign lands, he meets friends, and often through them (the dreams) he divines (*manteuomenos*) and learns in advance his daily actions. What else could this be but a rational soul (*psuchē logikē*)?" For a helpful discussion of these sources, see Patricia Cox Miller, *Dreams in Late Antiquity*, 39–40 (quotation of Athanasius at p. 40).

30. Gregory of Nyssa, *De hominis opificio* 13.9 (PG 44.169A–D, quote at D); P. Cox Miller, *Dreams in Late Antiquity*, 47–48.

31. On Greek and Latin terminology related to dreams and visions, along with a brief review of scholarship, see Gregor Weber, *Kaiser, Träume und Visionen in Prinzipat und Spätantike* (Stuttgart: Franz Steiner, 2000), 32–34. John S. Hanson ("Dreams and Visions in the Graeco-Roman World and Early Christianity," in *ANRW* II.23.2 [1980], 1395–1427) also emphasizes the "fairly loose application of a variety of terms that can mean 'dream' or 'vision' or both" in the Graeco-Roman world, and the "lack of consistent discrimination between waking and sleeping in connection with any particular term" (1408). He concludes that "the rather rigid modern distinction between the terms dream (a sleeping phenomenon) and vision (a waking phenomenon) is not paralleled in antiquity" (p. 1409). K. Zibelius-Chen ("Kategorien und Rolle des Traumes in Ägypten," *Studien zur altägyptischen Kultur* 15 [1988], 277–93) has made a similar observation with respect to ancient Egyptian culture, where the etymology of the word for "dream" (*rswt*) derives from the verbal root meaning "to be awake" (*rs*): in this context, he notes that "the Egyptians do not divide conceptually, nor likewise in terms of content, between dream and vision" (282). This blurring of definitional categories in antiquity is also noted by B. Heininger, *Paulus als Visionär: Eine religionsgeschichtliche Studie* (Herdersbiblische Studien 9; Freiburg: Herder, 1996), 43.

What is clear is that Ibn Kātib Qayṣar's threefold categorization according to the states of sleeping, semiwakefulness (i.e., light slumber), and full wakefulness expands upon earlier systems of classification found in the Greek commentary tradition as well as in medieval Islamic philosophy. Andrew and Arethas of Caesarea, writing in the seventh and tenth centuries respectively, both adhere to a two-type model in their interpretation of the conditions appropriate for the visionary experience. They each describe it as "the manifestation of secret mysteries," granted to one "who is illuminated and suited for guidance, either through divine dreams [*dia theiōn oneiratōn*] or in accordance with a waking vision [*kath' hupar*], which comes from divine illumination."[32] In their tenth- and eleventh-century writings, al-Fārābī and Ibn Sīnā likewise restrict themselves, in binary terms, to a consideration of sleep (*al-nawm*) and full wakefulness (*al-yaqẓah*) as the two conditions relevant to their analysis of the prophets' reception of divine insight.[33]

While Ibn Kātib Qayṣar's concern to distinguish semiwakefulness as a receptive condition for divine vision represents a new element in Eastern Christian commentaries on Revelation, one finds at least one potential precedent in the corpus of patristic literature. In the second-century *Shepherd of Hermas*, the protagonist is said to have experienced two of his five visions after he "became sleepy" (*aphupnōsai*).[34] Modern scholars have wrestled over whether this qualified as a sleeping dream or a waking vision. However, in doing so, their oppositional discourse has had the effect of establishing a categorical distinction between two states whose boundaries

32. Andrew of Caesarea, *Commentary on the Apocalypse* 1.1 (Schmid, 11.9–11); Arethas of Caesarea, *Apoc.* (PG 106.501A); see also Elias V. Oiconomou, "Authorities and Citizens in John's Book of Revelation" (http://www.myriobiblos.gr/bible/studies/economouḍrevelation.asp).

33. Griffel, "Muslim Philosophers' Rationalist Explanation," 163–74; idem, "Philosophy and Prophecy," 388–94.

34. *Shepherd of Hermas* (*Vis.*) 1.1.3; see also 5.1.1. In other instances, he experienced visions "while (he) slept" (*Vis.* 2.4.1; 3.1.2). Over against Robin Lane Fox (*Pagans and Christians*, 382–89) and J. Reiling (*Hermas and Christian Prophecy*, 157 and note 6) who characterize the former instances as either a trance-like state or somnambulism, Patricia Cox Miller wants to argue for the status of all of these visions as full-fledged dreams: see *Dreams in Late Antiquity*, 133; and "'A Dubious Twilight': Reflections on Dreams in Patristic Literature," *Church History* 55 (1986), 153–64, esp. 158. However, her conflation of these episodes seems motivated in part by her desire to gather all instances of *horasis* (vision) under the oneirocritical category of dreams experienced in sleep.

may have been in fact quite permeable for certain ancient and medieval authors.

The permeability of vision-states in late antiquity is illustrated in early Christian saints' lives such as the *Life and Miracles of Saint Thecla* and the *Life of Saint John the Almsgiver*. Both of these hagiographical works relate accounts in which the saints appear to female supplicants at night while they are asleep, and in both cases the powerful presence of the saint causes the supplicants to wake up. However, this transition from unconsciousness to conscious awareness does not immediately disrupt the vision; instead, the divine experience is mediated across the boundary from sleeping (*onar*) to waking (*hupar*).[35] Could such accounts have raised questions in the minds of readers about the possibility of a third, liminal state of visionary receptivity? While this question cannot be answered with certainty based on late antique evidence, it was just such a middle state—a condition somewhere between sleeping and waking—that occupied a central place in the classificatory system of Ibn Kātib Qayṣar.

Conflating the Messenger: John as Angel, Apostle, Prophet, and Priest

The second textual detail I want to focus on requires a close examination of the Arabic biblical text quoted by Ibn Kātib Qayṣar in comparison with its Coptic and Greek antecedents.

Translation of the Arabic text of Revelation 1:1, as quoted by Ibn Kātib Qayṣar[36]

> The revelatory vision [*al-ru'yā*] of Jesus Christ that God gave to him who taught his servants about what must come to pass quickly and who gave a sign to them and sent it **by way of his angel, his servant John** [*min qibali malākihi 'abdihi Yūḥannā*].

35. *Life and Miracles of Saint Thecla*, Miracle 46.5 (ed. G. Dagron, *Vie et miracles de Sainte Thècle* [Bruxelles: Société des Bollandistes, 1978], 408); Leontius of Neapolis, *Life of Saint John the Almsgiver* 8 (ed. H. Gelzer, *Leontios' von Neapolis Leben des heiligen Johannes des Barmherzigen, Erzbischofs von Alexandrien* [Freiburg i. B., Leipzig: J. C. B. Mohr/P. Siebeck, 1893], 15–16). Gilbert Dagron discusses both of these works in the context of arguing for the equivocality of the conventional opposition suggested by the terms *onar* (a vision experienced in sleep) and *hupar* (a vision experienced while awake): see his article, "Rēver de Dieu et parler de soi: le rēve et son interpretation d'après les sources byzantines," in *I sogni ne medioevo*, ed. T. Gregory (Lessico Intellettuale Europeo 35; Rome: Edizioni dell' Ateneo, 1985), 42n21.

36. Ibn Kātib Qayṣar, *Commentary on the Apocalypse* 1 (Birmāwī, 29).

Translation of the Bohairic Coptic text of Revelation 1:1[37]

The revelation [ⲁⲡⲟⲅⲁⲗⲩⲙⲯⲓⲥ, *apogalumpsis*] of Jesus Christ that God gave to him [i.e., John], to show his servants those things that must happen quickly. And he signified them, having sent them **through his angel to his servant John** [ⲉⲃⲟⲗ ϩⲓⲧⲟⲧϥ ⲙⲡⲉϥⲁⲅⲅⲉⲗⲟⲥ ⲙⲡⲉϥⲃⲱⲕ ⲓⲱⲁⲛⲛⲏⲥ].

Translation of the Greek text of Revelation 1:1[38]

The revelation [*apokalupsis*] of Jesus Christ that God gave to him, to show his servants the things that must happen quickly. And he signified [them], having sent them **through his angel to his servant John** [*dia tou aggelou autou* $t\bar{o}_i$ $doul\bar{o}_i$ *autou* $I\bar{o}ann\bar{e}_i$].

The change in the Arabic text quoted by Ibn Kātib Qayṣar is attention-grabbing: The translator has conflated the roles of John and the angel in the text. John himself becomes the divine messenger through which the revelation is shared with all humanity.

The source of this variant reading of Revelation 1:1 was confusion on the part of the translator over the syntax of the Bohairic Coptic text on which he relied.[39] His error seems to have been that he mistakenly read the consecutive *m*-prefixes as marking two nouns in apposition, instead of as elements of two separate prepositional phrases.[40] It should be noted that the translator in question was probably not Ibn Kātib Qayṣar himself, but rather an earlier scribe. This hypothesis is supported by the fact that the Arabic text used by Būlus al-Būshī shares this same reading, even as it differs in other details.[41]

37. G. Horner, *The Coptic Version of the New Testament in the Northern Dialect* (= *CoptNT-North*), volume 4 (Oxford: Clarendon Press, 1905; repr. Osnabrück: Otto Zeller, 1969), 444.

38. Nestle-Aland, *Novum Testamentum Graece*, 27th rev. ed. (Stuttgart: Deutsche Bibelgesellschaft, 2001), 632.

39. For a study of issues related to the Arabic translation of the Bohairic biblical text, see G. Graf, "Arabische Übersetzungen der Apokalypse," *Biblica* 10.2 (1929), 170–94.

40. This verse is unfortunately not available for comparison in the Sahidic version, where the extant text begins with the last word of Revelation 1:3: see G. Horner, *The Coptic Version of the New Testament in the Southern Dialect* (= *CoptNT-South*), volume 7 (Oxford: Clarendon Press, 1924; repr. Osnabrück: Otto Zeller, 1969), 258.

41. Other Arabic translations of the Apocalypse do not fall prey to this syntactic confusion: See, for example, a manuscript containing the text in the Monastery of the Syrians in Wādī al-Naṭrūn, Egypt: Dayr al-Suryān MS 17, f. 106r, where Revelation 1:1 reads "He sent it

TRANSLATION OF THE ARABIC TEXT OF REVELATION 1:1, AS QUOTED BY BŪLUS AL-BŪSHĪ[42]

> The apocalypse [*apūghālimsīs*] of Jesus Christ that God gave to inform his servants about what must come to pass quickly. He taught them and sent them **by the hand of his angel John, his servant** [*'alā yad malākihi Yūḥannā 'abdihi*].

Here we have a vivid example of how idiosyncrasies in the process of early translation from Coptic to Arabic provided new contexts for creative commentary on the biblical text as it was received in medieval Egypt by Arabic-speaking writers.

In the case of Ibn Kātib Qayṣar, this textual detail becomes the focus of both etymological analysis (in relation to the language of the Hebrew Bible) and theological-ethical reflection (on Christian practice and leadership). First, he makes a point of emphasizing that "the naming of John as an angel [*malāk*] follows the custom of the Bible in the naming of all the prophets and apostles and priests as angels."[43] He makes this claim because the term *malāk* in Hebrew means "apostle" (i.e., "messenger," Ar. *rasūl*). Ibn Kātib Qayṣar then plays off this fact in drawing a correlation between the function of angels and apostles, who are both considered privileged emissaries sent by God to deliver a message.

Second, having drawn out these etymological connections, Ibn Kātib Qayṣar shifts his attention to the theological-ethical implications of John's identification as an "angel" for understanding Christian practice and leadership. In this context he identifies four additional attributes—"abstinence, the renunciation of bodily desires, contemplation of God . . . , and an abundance of knowledge"[44]—associated not only with angels and apostles, but also with prophets and priests.

The characterization of ascetic practice as angelic in character was a common trope in late antiquity: Christian monks were understood to embody the life of angels in their detachment from the world and in their teachings.[45]

by the hands of his angel to his servant John" (*wa arsalahu 'alā yaday malākihi li-'abdihi Yūḥannā*).

42. Būlus al-Būshī, *Commentary on the Apocalypse* 1 (Vat. Ar. 459, f. 1v; Sbath Arabic 1014, f. 1v. See also British Library, Or. 1329, f. 4r; and Edelby, "Commentaire," 3 [Arabic text]).

43. Ibn Kātib Qayṣar, *Commentary on the Apocalypse* 1 (Birmāwī, 32).

44. Ibn Kātib Qayṣar, *Commentary on the Apocalypse* 1 (Birmāwī, 32–33).

45. In the Alexandrian-Egyptian tradition, see for example, Origen of Alexandria, *princ.* 1.8.4 (Koetschau, GCS 22 [1913], 101–2; trans. Butterworth, 72); Athanasius of Alexandria, *C.*

It is in the context of the high cultural value placed on asceticism within the Egyptian church that Ibn Kātib Qayṣar identifies the author of Revelation not only with the apostle John but also with John the Baptist, who was understood in the early church as a biblical model or type for the monastic life.[46] Thus, he writes, "John the Baptist was called an *angel* even while he is priest, prophet, and apostle. About him it is said, 'Behold, I am sending my angel [i.e., messenger] before you'" (Mark 1:2; see also Malachi 3:1).[47] For this Arabic commentator, John the Evangelist, John the Apostle, and John the Baptist are, for all intents and purposes, one and the same.

Finally, in his commentary on Revelation 1:1, Ibn Kātib Qayṣar demonstrates a further concern to tie John's prophetic, apostolic, and ascetic legacy to the ecclesiastical role of the priest or bishop, "on account of the fact that all of them are prepared for God's service and the benefits of his servants."[48] John himself is recognized as the one who became the first

---

Ar. 3.25, 51 (*PG* 26.376B, 429C–432A); and Shenoute, *When the Word Says*, f. 2va–b* (New York, Pierpont Morgan M664A[6]), ed. L. Depuydt, *Catalogue of Coptic Manuscripts in the Pierpont Morgan Library*, Corpus of Illuminated Manuscripts, vol. 4; Oriental Series 1 (Leuven: Peeters, 1993), 145; Ann Arbor, Mich., 158, 20d: ed. and trans. D. W. Young, *Coptic Manuscripts from the White Monastery: Works of Shenute* (Österreichische Nationalbibliothek; Vienna: Verlag Brüder Hollinek, 1993), 162.41–9 and 167.228.

46. See the following examples from Alexandrian Greek and Coptic sources: Athanasius, *virg.* 191–203 (ed. R. Casey, "Der dem Athanasius zugeschriebene Traktat PERI PARTHENIAS," *Sitzungsberichte der preussischen Akademie der Wissenschaften* 33 [1935], 1033, 1044–45); see also *v. Anton.* 7 (ed. G. J. M. Bartelink, SC 400 [Paris: Cerf, 1994]), 154–56; D. Brakke, *Athanasius and the Politics of Asceticism* (Oxford: Clarendon Press, 1995), 55, 169, 188, 250–51, 259; Jerome, *v. Pauli* 1 (PL 23.17A, 26C); and the anonymously authored *Life of St. Onnophrius* 11 (in *Journeying into God: Seven Early Monastic Lives*, trans. T. Vivian [Minneapolis: Fortress Press, 1996], 177). For a study of ascetic interpretations of John the Baptist's diet in the writings of late antique and early medieval Christian authors, see James A. Kelhoffer, *The Diet of John the Baptist: "Locusts and Wild Honey" in Synoptic and Patristic Interpretation*, Wissenschaftliche Untersuchungen zum Neuen Testament 176 (Tübingen: Mohr Siebeck, 2005), 134–93 (ch. 5). J. Massyngberde Ford has put forward the hypothesis that Chapters 4–11 in Revelation actually derive from a revelation originally given to John the Baptist: see *Revelation*, The Anchor Bible 38 (Garden City, N.Y.: Doubleday, 1975), esp. 30–37, 50–53, 69–183. However, it is important to point out here that Ibn Kātib Qayṣar's identification of the visionary in Revelation with John the Baptist is manifestly not based on modern historical critical arguments, but rather on specific onomastic and thematic connections he was interested in developing within his thirteenth-century ecclesiastical context.

47. Ibn Kātib Qayṣar, *Commentary on the Apocalypse* 1 (Birmāwī, 33).

48. Ibn Kātib Qayṣar, *Commentary on the Apocalypse* 1 (Birmāwī, 33). The author also cites the witness of (Ps.-)Dionysius in support of this view, noting that "Dionysius adds a fifth virtue: namely, participation in the priesthood."

bishop in Asia Minor at the presiding city of Ephesus, where he "preached before the transfer of leadership from it to Constantinople in the days of Constantine the Great."[49] Thus, in writing to the seven churches, the divinely inspired John was directing his message to cities that "belonged to his [episcopal] seat" and to "the bishops of these churches," who are identified as his "disciples."[50]

These bishops, in their authority as heads of the churches, are understood to have inherited John's own angelic stature, and Ibn Kātib Qayṣar deciphers several more cryptic details in the first three chapters of Revelation to support this point. The seven stars in Revelation 1:16 are "the angels of the seven churches," and since priests are also identified as angels, the intended referent must be "the leaders of the seven churches."[51] This sequential interpretative logic connecting "stars" to "angels" and thence to "bishops" and "church leaders" is sustained throughout the commentary.[52] The same logic also provides the Arabic commentator with an interpretive key for understanding the peculiar form of epistolary address that appears in each of the seven messages recorded in Chapters 2 and 3 of Revelation—i.e., "to the angel of the church."[53] In this context, he repeatedly presses home the point that these "angels" were, in fact, the bishops of these historical church communities, even mentioning Polycarp (*Fīlfārīyūs*) of Smyrna by name, whose "crown of life" in Revelation 2:10 is understood to indicate his martyrdom.[54]

Dreams, Visions, and Christian-Muslim Apologetic in Ibn Kātib Qayṣar's Commentary

The two exegetical examples discussed in the previous section are meant to serve as a preliminary introduction to Ibn Kātib Qayṣar's work as a

49. Ibn Kātib Qayṣar, *Commentary on the Apocalypse* 11 (Birmāwī, 52–53).

50. Ibn Kātib Qayṣar, *Commentary on the Apocalypse* 3 (Birmāwī, 34). Since Ibn Kātib Qayṣar identifies Ephesus as the first bishopric (*ra's al-kursī*; "primary seat") prior to Constantine's establishment of Constantinople (*Commentary on the Apocalypse* 11; Birmāwī, 52–53), he accordingly views John as filling the role of archbishop and the bishops of the other cities as his followers or "disciples."

51. Ibn Kātib Qayṣar, *Commentary on the Apocalypse* 8 (Birmāwī, 48).

52. See, e.g., Ibn Kātib Qayṣar, *Commentary on the Apocalypse* 10 and 11 (on Rev 1:20 and 2:1), *et passim* (Birmāwī, 51, 52 *et passim*).

53. Ibn Kātib Qayṣar, *Commentary on the Apocalypse* 11–14; 15–17 (Birmāwī, 52–53, 56–57, 60, 65–66, 71–72, 80, 86–87).

54. Ibn Kātib Qayṣar, *Commentary on the Apocalypse* 12 (Birmāwī, 57–59).

commentator. As a pair of case studies, they provide intriguing glimpses into how this medieval author appropriated and developed categories from Greek late antiquity, and how the transmission of the biblical text into the Arabic language conditioned its interpretive reception in thirteenth-century Egypt. Much more remains to be done, however, to flesh out Ibn Kātib Qayṣar's modus operandi as an Arabic exegete reading Revelation in an Islamic intellectual and social environment. Let me suggest at least one fruitful avenue for such contextual study—an inquiry into the question of how Ibn Kātib Qayṣar's classification of revelatory vision related to early Muslim theories of prophecy and dreams.

There is abundant evidence for early medieval Islamic dream interpretation, and even a cursory glance at this large corpus reveals typologies of classification that are often quite elaborate. In one case, a Muslim oneirocritic named Sijistānī (937–1008 CE) divides dreams into six types, and then goes on to identify fourteen grades of dreamers and thirty-five different aspects of dream interpretation. Another theorist, Dīnawarī (1008 CE), introduces his work by addressing a series of fifteen topics related to dream experience, including the nature of sleep, behavior that encourages "true" dreams, the character of the angel responsible for dream revelations, as well as the definition of dreams and their relation to prophecy (to name only a few themes).[55] In the context of performing the particular task of biblical commentary, Ibn Kātib Qayṣar shares certain elements of this ethos in which systematic methodologies reigned supreme.

Indeed, in comparing his discussion of *al-ru'yā* with those of his Muslim contemporaries, one observes correspondences not only on a formal level, but also in substantive terms. In classifying *al-ru'yā* as one species of prophecy, Ibn Kātib Qayṣar follows a judgment held by most early medieval Muslim oneirocritics. One of the early witnesses to this tradition, Ibn Qutaybah (828–89 CE), describes *al-ru'yā* as a kind of "divine inspiration" (*al-waḥy*) and a mode of "prophecy" (*al-nubūwah*).[56] Later Muslim theorists

55. For a discussion of Sijistānī and Dīnawarī, see J. Lamoreaux, *The Early Muslim Tradition of Dream Interpretation*, 34–37, 59–62. My comparison of Ibn Kātib Qayṣar's understanding of "revelatory vision" with Muslim theories about dreams is indebted to Lamoreaux's important work, which has opened up the study of this previously neglected corpus of Islamic literature.

56. For a discussion of Ibn Qutaybah's dream manual, see J. Lamoreaux, *The Early Muslim Tradition of Dream Interpretation*, 27–34. The manual, entitled *'Ibārat al-ru'yā*, or *Ta'bīr al-ru'yā* in Arabic, is preserved in two manuscripts—a complete version at the Hebrew Uni-

sought to be even more precise. They frequently defined *al-ru'yā* as one of forty-six types of prophecy available to humankind, a view that was picked up by Arabic Christian authors like the tenth-century Iraqi Nestorian Bar Bahlūl.[57] In presenting his own classification of prophecy, Ibn Kātib Qayṣar may have been adapting and simplifying such models in combination with earlier threefold typologies of dream visions developed in late antiquity by writers like the aforementioned Macrobius.

Yet, while Ibn Kātib Qayṣar definitely shared similar assumptions with his Muslim contemporaries on the classification of *al-ru'yā* as a form of prophecy, he also diverged from them on one critical point. Medieval Muslim theorists primarily understood the word *ru'yā* to refer to a divinely sent dream during sleep, a form of revelation best exemplified by Muhammad's reception of the Qur'ān. In early Islam, the true dream visions (*ru'yā*, pl. *ru'ā*) experienced by the prophet Muhammad are consistently set over against the unreliable dreams (*ḥulm*, pl. *aḥlām*) that bedeviled his critics.[58] By contrast, Ibn Kātib Qayṣar interprets the words *ḥulm* and *ru'yā* in nearly synonymous terms. Both have a positive connotation, but, according to his system of classification, the former is still clearly subordinated to the latter. While the term *ḥulm* (dream) is used to describe "the weakest species of prophecy,"[59] the kind experienced in sleep, the term *ru'yā* (revelatory

---

versity of Jerusalem (Yahuda ms. ar. 196), and an incomplete copy at the Language, History, and Geography Faculty of Ankara University in Turkey (Is. Saib Sincer I, 4501.2, fols. 180r–217v). The section of text referred to above, found near the beginning of the Jerusalem manuscript (Yahuda, ms. ar. 196, f. 2r), is cited and translated by Lamoreaux (p. 28); however, my choice of English equivalents for the terms, *al-waḥy* and *al-nubūwah*, diverges from his translation.

57. al-Ḥasan ibn al-Bahlūl, *Kitāb al-dalā'il li-al-Ḥasan ibn al-Bahlūl*: ed. Yūsuf Ḥabbī (Kuwait: Manshūrāt ma'had al-makhṭūṭāt al-'arabiyyah, 1987), 384; J. Lamoreaux, *The Early Muslim Tradition of Dream Interpretation*, 83, 154–65 (esp. p. 157).

58. According to the ninth-century al-Bukhārī (= Muḥammad ibn Isma'īl al-Bukhārī, *Ṣaḥīḥ al-Bukhārī*, ed. Aḥmad Muḥammad Shākir, *al-Jāmi' al-Ṣaḥīḥ*, 9 vols. [Beirut: Dār al-Jīl, n.d.], 9.37): "The beginning of the inspired revelation (*al-waḥy al-ru'yā*) received by God's messenger took place in his sleep (*al-nawm*)." This reference corresponds to Book 91.1 in the four-volume edition edited by M. Ludolf Krehl (Leiden: Brill, 1862), 4.347; also available online at http://www.al-eman.com/hadeeth/viewchp.asp?BID=13&CID=196ṣs2. For an example of the interpretation of this text in medieval Egypt, see Ibn Ḥajar al-'Asqalānī, *Fatḥ al-Bāri'*, 13 vol. plus index (Cairo: Maktabat al-Salafiyyah, 1986), 12.368. The pejorative associations connected with the term *ḥulm* arose out of Muslim interpretations of the Qur'anic text: see esp. Suras 21.5 and 52.32. For a discussion of these *aḥādīth and tafāsīr* traditions, see J. Lamoreaux, *The Early Muslim Tradition of Dream Interpretation*, 109–17.

59. Ibn Kātib Qayṣar, *Commentary on the Apocalypse* 1 (Birmāwī, 30).

vision) refers to a higher grade of revelatory experience, one that takes place in a semiwaking, daydream state.

Ibn Kātib Qayṣar's reinterpretation of these terms would have had profound implications for interreligious dialogue and debate in medieval Egypt. If the prophet Muhammad received his messages from God while asleep, as was widely assumed by Muslim interpreters like al-Būkhāri,[60] then his experience would necessarily correspond to the first (and lowest) category of prophecy in Ibn Kātib Qayṣar's schema. It would no longer qualify as a revelatory vision (*ru'yā*), but rather as a prophetic dream (*ḥulm*). The semiwaking vision (*ru'yā*) of John is, by definition, identified with the second level of prophecy, and therefore in comparison accorded higher status. One related terminological detail should not escape our attention at this point. When Ibn Kātib Qayṣar labels John's vision as a form of divine inspiration (*waḥy*),[61] he is borrowing a term regularly used by Muslim interpreters to describe the Qur'ān, the record of the revelation conferred on Muhammad. Here, however, the Arabic Christian commentator reappropriates this language for a very different end—namely, to mark John as a divinely inspired messenger, as an apostle (*rasūl*) who rivals and surpasses his counterpart, the prophet (*rasūl*) of Islam. In this context, it is also noteworthy that this Copto-Arabic author identifies Jesus Christ as the sole source of this revelation, the one who granted this vision to John and who "taught his servants," the apostles (*al-rusul*), the "superabundance" of his truth.[62]

With these details in view, one begins to see more clearly the delicately drawn lines of Ibn Kātib Qayṣar's subtle scriptural apologetic against Islamic theology. At the beginning of his *Commentary on the Apocalypse of John*, he constructs a classification schema that utilizes Qur'ānic terminology and Islamic typological models, but that crucially reworks these elements to underscore the apostolic inspiration of John and the authority of Christ in contradistinction to rival Muslim claims regarding divine revelation. In this way, Ibn Kātib Qayṣar introduces a distinctively Arabic Apocalypse, a biblical text and commentary directed to those among his own language community who had an ear to hear "what the Spirit is saying to the churches."[63]

60. *Ṣaḥīḥ al-Bukhārī* 9.43–44.

61. Ibn Kātib Qayṣar, *Commentary on the Apocalypse* 1 (Birmāwī, 31).

62. Ibn Kātib Qayṣar, *Commentary on the Apocalypse* 1 (Birmāwī, 31).

63. Here I borrow the phrase that is repeated seven times throughout the second and third chapters of Revelation, once for each of the messages sent to the seven churches of Asia (2:7, 11, 17, 29; 3:6, 13, 22).

CHAPTER

3

IBN KĀTIB QAYṢAR ON REVELATION 1–3

THE FIRST VISION AND THE LETTERS TO THE SEVEN CHURCHES

T. C. Schmidt, with contributions by Stephen J. Davis

Introduction: The Two Visions of Revelation

Uniquely among Eastern exegetes, Ibn Kātib Qayṣar divided the text of Revelation into a "first vision," described in its first three chapters, and a "second vision" covering the remainder of the text. The present volume follows this pattern by translating all of the material designated as the "first vision." This chapter will attend to key exegetical, textual, and theological features of Ibn Kātib Qayṣar's commentary on this "first vision" of Revelation.

Ibn Kātib Qayṣar's Exegetical Methods

Ibn Kātib Qayṣar had few if any models to follow in his exegesis of Revelation. The only exegete from whom he overtly draws is Hippolytus, to whom he refers many times, but none of these occur in the first few chapters of Revelation and often our author mentions Hippolytus simply to disagree with him.[1] Pseudo-Dionysius (late fifth or early sixth century CE) is also known to Ibn Kātib Qayṣar, but that anonymous author makes very little use of Revelation. Pseudo-Dionysius quotes from the book only once, a citation of Revelation 1:8 in his treatise *On Divine Names*. Mistaken for

1. For example, see Ibn Kātib Qayṣar, *Commentary on the Apocalypse* 57 and 64 (Birmāwī, 238–39, 269).

the first-century disciple of Paul by late ancient readers, Ps.-Dionysius was also reputed to have written a letter to John during the seer's exile on the island of Patmos.[2] Other than these two sources, Ibn Kātib Qayṣar consulted the Revelation commentary of his older contemporary Būlus al-Būshī,[3] but rarely seems to draw interpretations from it. Indeed, Būlus al-Būshī's commentary is far shorter and more focused on Christology than Ibn Kātib Qayṣar's. At times our author also clearly contradicts Būlus al-Būshī's interpretation. For example, in commenting on Revelation 3:7, Būlus al-Būshī correctly interprets the etymology of *philadelphia* as meaning "brotherly love" while Ibn Kātib Qayṣar incorrectly interprets it as "the one who loves the sister." In general, it seems that, although Ibn Kātib Qayṣar was aware of Būlus al-Būshī's work, he did not follow it closely.

Despite this, Ibn Kātib Qayṣar's exegetical model will seem quite familiar to many readers, for it adheres to the familiar twofold sense of Scripture. Our author uses several different descriptive couplets when describing this model: the literal (*ḥarfiyyah*) and the figurative (*isti'ārah*);[4] the psychic (*nafsāniyyah*) and the spiritual (*rūḥāniyyah*);[5] the perceptible (*ẓāhir*) and the imperceptible (*ghayr ẓāhir*).[6] Such a model of biblical exegesis was, unbeknownst to him, made famous by Ibn Kātib Qayṣar's own Egyptian predecessors Philo, Clement, Origen, and to a lesser extent Didymus the Blind. The last three authors were familiar with the book of Revelation, and Origen and Didymus may have even written commentaries on it,[7] though Ibn Kātib Qayṣar appears to betray no direct knowledge of these authors.

2. Ps.-Dionysius Areopagite, *On Divine Names* 2.1, in *The Works of Dionysius the Areopagite*, vol. 1, trans. John Parker (London: James Parker and Co., 1897), 13; *Epistle 10 to John*, in *Works*, vol. 1, trans. Parker, 178–180. For a more recent English translation of these works, see also Colm Luibheid, trans., *Pseudo-Dionysius: The Complete Works* (New York: Paulist Press, 1987).

3. Ibn Kātib Qayṣar, *Commentary on the Apocalypse* 103 (Birmāwī, 373–75).

4. Ibn Kātib Qayṣar, *Commentary on the Apocalypse* 8 and 17 (Birmāwī, 46 and 94).

5. Ibn Kātib Qayṣar, *Commentary on the Apocalypse* 17 (Birmāwī, 93).

6. Ibn Kātib Qayṣar, *Commentary on the Apocalypse* 13 (Birmāwī, 65).

7. In his *Commentary on Matthew* (PG 13.1673–74), Origen seems to indicate that it had been his intention to write a commentary on Revelation, although in the end he may have only produced scholia and homilies on the text. See C. Diobouniotis and A. Harnack, eds., *Der Scholien-kommentar des Origenes zur Apokalypse Johannis* (Texte und Untersuchungen 38.3; Leipzig: J. C. Hinrichs, 1911); J. A. Robinson, "Origen's Comments on the Apocalypse," *Journal of Theological Studies* 13 (1912), 295–97; A. de Boysson, "Avons-nous un commentaire d'Origène sur l'Apocalypse," *Revue Biblique* 10 (1913), 555–67; C. H. Turner, "Document. Origen Scholia in Apocalypsin," *Journal of Theological Studies* 25 (1923), 1–16; E. Skard, "Zum

Like these earlier Egyptian writers, Ibn Kātib Qayṣar explains that prophets often use forms (*ashkāl*), images (*ṣuwar*), meanings (*maʿānī*), and verbal expressions (*alfāẓ*) that are not intended to be taken according to their literal (*ḥarfiyyah*) meaning, but rather "in what is called the spiritual language [*al-lughah al-rūḥāniyyah*]."[8] According to the commentator, when the prophets used these kinds of expressions the purpose was not "the visible things" themselves but rather the "enigmas [*alghāz*] and symbols [*rūmūz*]" hidden among them.[9] Once this is known "the expressions . . . become clear," but Ibn Kātib Qayṣar offers the caveat that the mysteries concealed within the images might still of course remain mysterious.[10]

Among the passages in Revelation interpreted according to this model are those relating to the senses of hearing and sight. When interpreting the sound of a trumpet that the prophet John had heard behind him in Revelation 1:10, Ibn Kātib Qayṣar observes that John did not physically hear the sound. Instead, in this instance, the sense of hearing does not refer to "the sensory perception of the ear" but to "the soul's discernment belonging to [its] rational faculties." He justifies this interpretation by explaining that the prophet John did not actually hear the sound of a trumpet but only a sound "like a trumpet," and that "something similar to a thing is not the thing itself."[11] In addition, he also argues that the meaning

Scholien-kommentar des Origenes zur Apokalypse Johannis," *Symbolae Osloenses: Norwegian Journal of Greek and Latin Studies* 15:1 (1936), 204–8; E. Junod, "À propos des soi-disant scolies sur l'Apocalypse d'Origène," *Rivista di storia e letteratura religiosa* 20 (1984), 112–21; Joseph F. T. Kelly, "Early Medieval Evidence for Twelve Homilies by Origen on the Apocalypse," *Vigiliae Christianae* 39 (1985), 273–79; J. Courreau, trans., *L'Apocalypse expliquee par Cesaire d'Arles. Scholies attribuée à Origène* (Paris: Desclée de Brower, 1989); and William C. Weinrich, *Revelation* (Ancient Christian Commentary on Scripture 12; Downers Grove, Il.: InterVarsity Press, 2005), xxi. Likewise, Didymus indicates that he had written a work on Revelation in his *Commentary on Zechariah* 8 (*comm. Zach.* III, 73 = ZaT 200.14–16; ed. Doutreleau, SC 84, 654–55; trans. R. C. Hill, FC 111 [Washington, D.C.: The Catholic University of America Press, 2006], 201). This work also does not survive, apart from a possible fragment preserved in a *catena* of patristic quotations. See Diobouniotis and Harnack, *Der Scholien-kommentar*, Scholia 1; R. Devress, "Châines exégetiques grecques," in *Dictionnaire de la Bible*, ed. F. G. Vigouroux, Supplement, vol. 1, ed. L. Pirot, *et al.* (Paris: Letouzey et Ané, 1928), 1228; and Thomas W. MacKay, "Early Christian Millenarianist Interpretation of the Two Witnesses in John's Apocalypse 11:3–13," note 42, http://publications.maxwellinstitute.byu.edu/fullscreen/?pub=1128&index=15.

8. Ibn Kātib Qayṣar, *Commentary on the Apocalypse* 8 (Birmāwī, 46).
9. Ibn Kātib Qayṣar, *Commentary on the Apocalypse* 8 (Birmāwī, 46).
10. Ibn Kātib Qayṣar, *Commentary on the Apocalypse* 8 (Birmāwī, 46).
11. Ibn Kātib Qayṣar, *Commentary on the Apocalypse* 8 (Birmāwī, 44).

of the sound was hidden, since John says that he heard it "behind me."[12] Later, the text says that John "turned and discerned the voice." This prompts our author to caution his audience that the Coptic, Greek, and Syriac words for discernment can all refer to both "the vision of the eye and the discernment of the intellect," and that therefore "some translators have erred in writing down" words that refer to physical sight instead of mental discernment.[13]

Ibn Kātib Qayṣar was a skillful exegete who brought relevant biblical verses into conversation with the text at hand, as he does, for example, with respect to the numerous references in Revelation to Old Testament figures, such as Balaam and Jezebel.[14] He does the same with prophetic imagery from the Hebrew Bible. When describing the eyes of Jesus, he compares them to other accounts of eyes found in the book of Daniel and in Zechariah.[15]

Very often Ibn Kātib Qayṣar is also concerned with proper theological understanding and hence juxtaposes relevant passages from the New Testament to help explain passages from Revelation. He works under the assumption that the John mentioned in Revelation 1:4 is John the son of Zebedee, one of the twelve apostles and author of not only Revelation, but also the Gospel of John and the three letters of the same name. This identification commonly encourages him to interpret passages in Revelation with corresponding verses from the Johannine Epistles and Gospel. When interpreting the word "seeing" in Revelation 3:18, for instance, he compares it with the text of 3 John 1:11: "And as for *seeing*, by it he means intellectual understanding as evidenced by the statement of this apostle, 'And as for the one who does evil, he will not see God.'"[16] He does the same with Revelation 3:20 and John 14:23: "As for his statement, *I will enter with him*, by that he means, 'I will pour out upon him the Spirit and will illuminate his intellect.' And for this reason this apostle says in his gospel, 'We will come and take lodging with him.'"[17]

Our author also uses verses relating to Ephesus and the island of Patmos as occasions to explain matters of church history to his audience. He

12. Ibn Kātib Qayṣar, *Commentary on the Apocalypse* 8 (Birmāwī, 44).
13. Ibn Kātib Qayṣar, *Commentary on the Apocalypse* 8 (Birmāwī, 45–46).
14. Ibn Kātib Qayṣar, *Commentary on the Apocalypse* 13–14 (Birmāwī, 60–71).
15. Ibn Kātib Qayṣar, *Commentary on the Apocalypse* 8 (Birmāwī, 47).
16. Ibn Kātib Qayṣar, *Commentary on the Apocalypse* 17 (Birmāwī, 94).
17. Ibn Kātib Qayṣar, *Commentary on the Apocalypse* 17 (Birmāwī, 95).

notes that John held the "leading [episcopal] seat" at Ephesus before this seat was transferred to Constantinople during the time of Constantine,[18] and also that John was exiled to the island of Patmos in the ninth year of the reign of Emperor Domitian.[19] He further says that the leader of Ephesus alluded to in Revelation is the "disciple" of John.[20] But far from portraying John as a detached leader, he is careful to describe him as a "brother" who participated in the communities of the seven churches.[21]

Notable among his exegetical maneuvers is his interpretation of the letter to the church in Ephesus. Here he turns to the book of Acts to help elucidate what in his mind must have been the context motivating the reference to false prophets in the letter. Accordingly, he describes how "the apostle Paul prophesied about these people" when he bid farewell to the elders of the church in Ephesus, saying, "I know that after my departure, there will enter in amongst you difficult wolves and they will not have pity on the flock."[22] He then draws on other New Testament letters from Peter, John, Paul, and James and says that they "complained about people like this a great deal in their letters."[23]

Ibn Kātib Qayṣar's training as a grammarian is abundantly evident throughout his commentary where his grammatical analysis of passages becomes a matter of course. He frequently makes technical linguistic comments such as: "Its genitive construction . . . is a genitive of possession."[24] Or: "To this [may be added] the genitive of specification, in contradistinction to the . . . second noun of" the genitive construction.[25] Or "[John] modifies the formulation of the active participle into a verbal noun for the purposes of emphasis."[26] His grammatical education was complemented by familiarity with a multitude of languages. References to Greek, Syriac, Hebrew and especially Coptic pour forth from his pen to add clarity and understanding for his readers.[27]

18. Ibn Kātib Qayṣar, *Commentary on the Apocalypse* 11 (Birmāwī, 52–53).
19. Ibn Kātib Qayṣar, *Commentary on the Apocalypse* 7 (Birmāwī, 41).
20. Ibn Kātib Qayṣar, *Commentary on the Apocalypse* 11 (Birmāwī, 53).
21. Ibn Kātib Qayṣar, *Commentary on the Apocalypse* 6 (Birmāwī, 40).
22. Acts 20:29.
23. Ibn Kātib Qayṣar, *Commentary on the Apocalypse* 11 (Birmāwī, 54).
24. Ibn Kātib Qayṣar, *Commentary on the Apocalypse* 17 (Birmāwī, 95).
25. Ibn Kātib Qayṣar, *Commentary on the Apocalypse* 17 (Birmāwī, 95).
26. Ibn Kātib Qayṣar, *Commentary on the Apocalypse* 16 (Birmāwī, 81).
27. See, e.g., Ibn Kātib Qayṣar, *Commentary on the Apocalypse* 7 (Birmāwī, 41). Such polyglossia was not unique to Ibn Kātib Qayṣar among medieval Copto-Arabic authors. Another

His philological skills also included Islamic terminology, especially from the domains of Islamic legal theory and theology, such as the term *jihād*, which he defines as a struggle due to persecution,[28] or as a struggle "against the flesh of nature" in reference to celibacy.[29] He employs the Islamic term *sunnah*,[30] which was used by Muslims to indicate the revered traditions of ancient predecessors, especially those of the prophet Muhammad.[31] The term *al-bayān* is also used by our author to refer to the book of Revelation in a way similar to how Muslims used it to refer to the their own scripture.[32] Lastly, Ibn Kātib Qayṣar appears aware of the Islamic names for God, or *al-asmāʾ al-ḥusnā* (the most beautiful names), and applies some of them to Jesus, in particular *al-quddūs* (the Most Holy),[33] *al-ḥaqq* (the Truth),[34] and perhaps also *al-ʿadl* (Justice).[35] The first two he derives from Revelation 3:7, which reads, "This is what the Most Holy, the Truth, says."

As pointed out in Chapter 2, Ibn Kātib Qayṣar delicately and only indirectly addresses the Islamic faith. He does so, for example, with his three-tiered interpretation of dreams by which he seems to subtly critique the mode of Muhammad's inspiration.[36] Another tacit reference to Islam can likely be found in his list of generic geopolitical events, "like the rise of a nation or the appearance of a religion (*diyānah*), the occurrence of economic inflation, an epidemic, a war . . . or things similar to this."[37] The

---

example is Abū al-Faraj Hibat Allāh Ibn al'Assāl's mid-thirteenth-century translation of the Bible, based on consultation of earlier Greek and Syriac versions: see Hikmat Kashouh, *The Arabic Versions of the Gospels: The Manuscripts and Their Families* (Berlin: de Gruyter, 2012), 261–63. Such philological attention to multiple languages among Syro-Arabic Christian writers was less marked during this period. We thank our anonymous reviewer for these observations and references.

28. Ibn Kātib Qayṣar, *Commentary on the Apocalypse* 13 (Birmāwī, 61).

29. Ibn Kātib Qayṣar, *Commentary on the Apocalypse* 15 and 16 (Birmāwī, 78 and 82).

30. Ibn Kātib Qayṣar, *Commentary on the Apocalypse* 16 (Birmāwī, 83).

31. G. H. A. Juynboll, and D. W. Brown, "Sunna," *EI²*, BrillOnline *Reference Works*. http://referenceworks.brillonline.com/entries/encyclopaedia-of-islam-2/sunna-COM_1123, consulted March 24, 2018.

32. Ibn Kātib Qayṣar, *Commentary on the Apocalypse* 3 (Birmāwī, 34).

33. Qu'ran 59:23; 62:1.

34. Qu'ran 6:62; 22:6.

35. Qu'ran 6:115. On the ninety-nine names of God, see L. Gardet, "al-Asmā' al-Ḥusnā," *EI²*, BrillOnline *Reference Works*, http://referenceworks.brillonline.com/entries/encyclopaedia-of-islam-2/al-asma-al-husna-COM_0070, consulted March 24, 2018.

36. Davis, "Introducing an Arabic Commentary," 94–96; see also Chapter 2.

37. Ibn Kātib Qayṣar, *Commentary on the Apocalypse* 2 (Birmāwī, 34).

"appearance of a religion" seems to be one of Ibn Kātib Qayṣar's oblique references to the rise of Islam, which he shrewdly places between global occurrences like the rise of a nation and changes in the economy, but before catastrophic events like epidemics and wars.

Textual Corruptions and Mistranslations

Ibn Kātib Qayṣar's exegesis was sometimes hampered by textual corruptions and mistranslations that, despite his own extensive philological background, sometimes proved obstacles to his explanatory efforts. For example, his text of Revelation 2:12 and 2:15 apparently omitted the proper names Antipas and Nicolaitans.[38] The latter case was simply translated generically as *mushāghib*, or "troublemakers," but the former omission led Ibn Kātib Qayṣar incorrectly to presume that the martyred "faithful witness," whom the Greek text specifies as Antipas, was actually Jesus.[39] Both of these textual omissions were also evidenced in the Revelation text presented by Būlus al-Būshī.[40]

Other infelicities include Ibn Kātib Qayṣar's inaccurate etymology of the Greek city name Philadelphia as "the one who loves the sister,"[41] his misrendering of the Greek word χαλκολιβάνον (*chalkolibanon*) as the "copper of Lebanon,"[42] and his misreading of the city Sardis as the island of Sardinia.[43] This final geographical detail must have perplexed him, because he resorted to a ninth-century work on geography—*The Book of Roads and Kingdoms* (*Kitāb al-masālik wa-l-mamālik*) by Ibn Khordadbeh, a Persian administrative official, in order to find some link between Sardinia and Asia Minor.

But the most prominent mistranslation comes in the epistle to the Laodiceans. In the Greek and Bohairic versions of Revelation 3:15–16, John accuses the Laodiceans of having "lukewarm" works instead of "hot" works and opines that it would be better for the Laodiceans to be "cold" rather

38. Ibn Kātib Qayṣar, *Commentary on the Apocalypse* 13 (Birmāwī, 60). The Nicolaitans are also omitted in Revelation 2:6 (*Commentary on the Apocalypse* 11; Birmāwī, 52).

39. Ibn Kātib Qayṣar, *Commentary on the Apocalypse* 13 (Birmāwī, 61).

40. See Būlus al-Būshī, *Commentary on the Apocalypse* 6 (Vat. Ar. 459, f. 6v–7r; Edelby, "Commentaire," 21 [Arabic text]).

41. Ibn Kātib Qayṣar, *Commentary on the Apocalypse* 14 (Birmāwī, 80).

42. Ibn Kātib Qayṣar, *Commentary on the Apocalypse* 14 (Birmāwī, 67).

43. Ibn Kātib Qayṣar, *Commentary on the Apocalypse* 15 (Birmāwī, 73).

than "lukewarm." Ibn Kātib Qayṣar's Arabic text of Revelation instead alternates confusingly between two metaphors. First, it claims that the works of the Laodiceans are "neither coarse nor refined." Second, it switches to a thermal metaphor, describing the Laodiceans as being "cold" and commanding them to "be lukewarm."[44]

Ibn Kātib Qayṣar attempts to provide a coherent interpretation of the first mistranslated verse by splitting the metaphors into two different spectrums of spiritual progression, and then relating them to one another. "Coarse" (*kathīf*) and "refined" (*laṭīf*) represent sinfulness/wickedness and righteousness/goodness—or, as he clarifies, those who are corporeal and those who are spiritual. He then situates the works of the Laodiceans in the middle of these extremes. Our author further points out that the Coptic word ϩⲟⲣϣ (*horsh*), translated by the Arabic *kathīf* (coarse), can also mean "heavy."[45] By the same token the Coptic word ϧⲏⲙ (*hēm*)[46] also has two meanings. It "indicates in its plain sense 'heat,' and [indicates] in its figurative sense 'refined,' designating what is necessarily implied by what necessarily implies it."[47] This concluding phrase is a technical marker of figurative interpretation. In other words, the plain meaning (in this case, "heat") is understood necessarily to imply its figurative correspondence (in this case, that which is "refined").[48]

Our author next tackles the second mistranslated passage, which in Greek criticizes the Laodiceans for being lukewarm, but in the Arabic text used by Ibn Kātib Qayṣar instead commands the Laodiceans to *become* lukewarm! Our author explains this passage by setting up another spectrum of spiritual progression. But instead of possessing a positive extreme and a negative extreme, this particular spectrum contains a positive center

44. Ibn Kātib Qayṣar, *Commentary on the Apocalypse* 17 (Birmāwī, 86).

45. Curiously, Ibn Kātib Qayṣar does not explicitly mention that ϩⲟⲣϣ (*horsh*) is also a homograph for the Bohairic word for "cold," but this may be implied by the context of his discussion, which takes it on assumption that cold things sink while hot things rise.

46. This word is written in the variant form ⲥϧⲉⲙ (*s-hem*) in both Birmāwī's edition (p. 88) and the Par. Ar. 67 (f. 43r, line 12).

47. Ar. *iṭlāqan lism al-malzūm ʿalā al-lāzim*. Ibn Kātib Qayṣar, *Commentary on the Apocalypse* 17 (Birmāwī, 88).

48. Ibn Kātib Qayṣar uses the same phrase in commenting on Revelation 3:3 (*Commentary on the Apocalypse* 15; Birmāwī, 76), where the phrase, "I will come like a thief," is understood not in its literal sense (i.e., that God would come in physical form as a thief), but in a figurative sense (implying that God's "command and judgment" would arrive without warning).

with two negative extremes. He describes the "hot" extreme as representing "intemperance and rash zeal beyond what is appropriate" and contrasts this with the "cold" extreme, which stands for a lack of zeal. Ibn Kātib Qayṣar's reading is further complicated because the Coptic word ϩⲑⲏ (*ḥthē*),[49] meaning "extreme," can also mean the "heart," which forces Ibn Kātib Qayṣar into yet another excursus where he explains to the reader why it means "extreme" in this instance.[50] The commentary by Būlus al-Būshī, known to Ibn Kātib Qayṣar, does a much better job at communicating the passage's meaning. This is therefore another indication that Ibn Kātib Qayṣar, for whatever reason, did not make much use of Būlus al-Būshī's commentary in his own exegesis.

Interpretive Difficulties: Recipients and Time Frames of Revelation

Recipients of John's Revelation

One of the many bewildering challenges for interpreting the text of Revelation is determining who the addressees were and which portion of the text was addressed to which individual or community. Ibn Kātib Qayṣar, well aware of this conundrum, carefully classifies the first three chapters of Revelation into three sections that we may conveniently label as the title, the blessing, and the epistolary section. He names the first two verses of Chapter 1 as "the title heading of the book" (*ʿunwān al-kitāb*),[51] and then points out that verse three contains a blessing upon those who hear and keep "the words of this prophecy," though he does not label this section as a blessing specifically.[52] The section from Revelation 1:4, beginning with "from John to the seven churches in Asia," up to and including the last verse of Chapter 3, represents the epistolary section of the text, though Ibn Kātib Qayṣar calls it "the first thing that the apostle wrote to the seven churches."[53] Chapter 4 marks the beginning of the "second vision," as Ibn Kātib Qayṣar calls it. Our author uses Revelation 1:9 to describe the

49. This word is written in the variant form ϩⲑⲏⲕ in both the printed edition and the Paris manuscript.

50. Ibn Kātib Qayṣar, *Commentary on the Apocalypse* 17 (Birmāwī, 88–91).

51. Ibn Kātib Qayṣar, *Commentary on the Apocalypse* 1 (Birmāwī, 30).

52. Ibn Kātib Qayṣar, *Commentary on the Apocalypse* 2 (Birmāwī, 33).

53. Ibn Kātib Qayṣar, *Commentary on the Apocalypse* 3 (Birmāwī, 34).

recipients as the leaders of the churches but says that the letters were meant to be followed by all Christians of that generation.[54]

Several verses later Ibn Kātib Qayṣar takes time to discuss whether or not the original addressees received the first vision of Revelation in the same format in which it exists today. He says that what the apostle wrote "has two possible senses." One of them is that John only wrote to each church "about whatever matters that specially concerned it,"[55] apparently indicating that each church only received its own letter, not the other six letters, though presumably every church received the second vision, contained in Chapters 4–22. The other possibility, he says, is that John "wrote the entire revelatory vision to each church."[56] Ibn Kātib Qayṣar at first appears unsure of which possibility is correct, but eventually settles on the second option due to his interpretation of Revelation 1:4, which seems to address the entire first vision, Chapters 1–3, to all seven cities.[57]

Our author only names one of the recipients of any of the letters: Polycarp the bishop of Smyrna, whom he calls "the disciple of the apostle."[58] Indeed, he interprets the statement, "do not fear the sufferings that you receive," as a "prophecy concerning the martyrdom of this aforementioned bishop." He then explains that Polycarp was arrested and burned to death,[59] which agrees with what little we know about his martyrdom from early Christian sources.[60]

Revelatory Time Frames

Another perplexing aspect of Revelation is the question of how John experienced the vision or visions. The three categories of revelatory vision delineated by Ibn Kātib Qayṣar have already been discussed in Chapter 2, so

54. Ibn Kātib Qayṣar, *Commentary on the Apocalypse* 6 (Birmāwī, 40).
55. Ibn Kātib Qayṣar, *Commentary on the Apocalypse* 8 (Birmāwī, 45).
56. Ibn Kātib Qayṣar, *Commentary on the Apocalypse* 8 (Birmāwī, 45).
57. Ibn Kātib Qayṣar, *Commentary on the Apocalypse* 8 (Birmāwī, 45).
58. Ibn Kātib Qayṣar, *Commentary on the Apocalypse* 12 (Birmāwī, 57).
59. Ibn Kātib Qayṣar, *Commentary on the Apocalypse* 12 (Birmāwī, 58).
60. Early Christian witnesses include Irenaeus *haer.* 3.3.4 (ANF 1.416); and Eusebius of Caesarea, *h.e.* 5.24.4, quoting from Polycrates of Ephesus, ed. G. Bardy, SC 41 (1955), 68; trans. NPNF, ser. 2, 1.242. A narrative account is preserved in the *Martyrdom of Polycarp (mart. Poly.)*, ed. and trans. H. Musurillo (Oxford: Clarendon, 1972), 2–22. For a bibliography and a discussion of dating, see Candida Moss, *The Other Christs: Imitating Jesus in Ancient Christian Ideologies of Martyrdom* (New York: Oxford University Press, 2010), 196–98.

here I would here like to restrict my attention to how the commentator understands the duration of John's vision. He describes this in his treatment of Revelation 1:19: "Write what you have seen, and it will take place after this."[61] This rendering differs from the Greek, which says, "Now write what you have seen, what is, and what is to take place after this."[62] Ibn Kātib Qayṣar is rightly confused by his own version, asking: "How did he say this but did not conclude [by telling us] anything of what the apostle saw after these things, except for his statement that *he is coming with the clouds, and the eyes will see him*?"[63] In other words, at this early point in the book of Revelation, very little has been revealed to John, so how could the remainder of the book be a written account of the little that he has hitherto seen?

Ibn Kātib Qayṣar's answer to this is that "what is revealed in this section is that the apostle saw all of the revelatory vision on one occasion, but he expressed what he saw one thing after another, because of the necessity of extending his account by [this] means of expression."[64] Such an answer posits a particular model of revelatory vision in which all of the vision is seen simultaneously and not in a linear narrative format, the format most suited to a book, which by its nature is strung out from word to word and from page to page.[65]

This bears great relevance to Ibn Kātib Qayṣar's interpretation of the concept of time in the book of Revelation. Our author seems to argue, based on the phrase "it will take place after this" (Revelation 1:19), that the visions contained in the book of Revelation are to be fulfilled in the eschatological future, and do not refer to the past (either his or John's), saying that the book "concerned what was coming later, not what happened in the past, as some interpreters have believed."[66] Who these interpreters are is unclear. His predecessors, Oecumenius and Andrew of Caesarea, did not believe that the visions in Revelation had been fulfilled at the time of John's writing. Oecumenius says, "Those things which were going to

61. Ibn Kātib Qayṣar, *Commentary on the Apocalypse* 9 (Birmāwī, 50).
62. NRSV translation.
63. Ibn Kātib Qayṣar, *Commentary on the Apocalypse* 9 (Birmāwī, 51).
64. Ibn Kātib Qayṣar, *Commentary on the Apocalypse* 9 (Birmāwī, 51).
65. Earlier, Ibn Kātib Qayṣar also mentions that after John's "hearing and vision come to an end" he was to "write about it afterward to the churches and send it to them" (Ibn Kātib Qayṣar, *Commentary on the Apocalypse* 8; Birmāwī, 45).
66. Ibn Kātib Qayṣar, *Commentary on the Apocalypse* 9 (Birmāwī, 51).

happen have not yet been fulfilled, although a very long time, more than five hundred years, has elapsed since this was said."[67] For his part, Andrew says that the things in Revelation are not yet "in sight" and that they "will happen in the future time."[68] Both Greek exegetes, however, did believe that, even though the visions in Revelation do not refer to the past, some prophecies, such as that of the seven seals in Revelation 6, had indeed been fulfilled by the time of their own writing in the sixth and seventh centuries CE. Būlus al-Būshī, by contrast, seems to have believed that certain visions referred to John's own past. For example, he interprets each of the seven seals as referring to a millennium of biblical history, meaning that the first four seals occured before the birth of Christ, well before the book of Revelation was written. It is possible that Būlus al-Būshī is among the "interpreters" with whom Ibn Kātib Qayṣar disagrees on this point.[69]

Ibn Kātib Qayṣar was also interested in the nature of time itself. Referring to Revelation 1:3, he writes, "As for the *time*, it is defined as the scope of movement with respect to what comes before and what comes later. On this subject, it is also said that the domain in which the movement [of time] is concealed has three divisions—the past, the present, and the future—and its components are fixed."[70] This threefold division of time is of course fairly standard, but it contrasts with Ibn Kātib Qayṣar's understanding of how John received his revelation, which he believed took place in a kind of instantaneous action, not in sequential, chronological order, even though what was revealed refers to chronological events.

Though the text of Revelation says that these future events are coming "quickly," our author emphasizes that this "does not mean that the events come into existence all at once, but rather it means that their beginning

67. Oecumenius, *Commentary on the Apocalypse* 1.2.6 (trans. Suggit, 22).

68. Andrew of Caesarea, prologue to *Commentary on the Apocalypse*, (trans. Constantinou, 51).

69. Another possible candidate for inclusion in this group of interpreters, with a different perspective on chronology, is a certain anonymous Syriac commentatator who believes that the seven seals mystically retell the story of salvation beginning with Adam: see Larson, "The Earliest Syriac Commentary," 133ff., http://search.proquest.com/pqdtuk/docview/301432163/BC4985625DAE45EBPQ/1?accountid=15172. There is no direct evidence, however, that Ibn Kātib Qayṣar was aware of this Syriac author or engaged with his interpretation in any other respect.

70. Ibn Kātib Qayṣar, *Commentary on the Apocalypse* 2 (Birmāwī, 33).

comes to pass quickly and that each will follow the other until the end,"[71] implying that the events in Revelation will unfold successively in a kind of linear format, similar to how they were recorded by John (as opposed to the sequence by which they were revealed to him).[72]

Lastly, in treating the "sign" of "what must come to pass" in Revelation 1:1, Ibn Kātib Qayṣar says that this is "not about a fixed time, for humankind is not informed about the times for the most part."[73] He goes on to explain that if humans were given a fixed time when the return of Christ would take place, then a false Messiah could easily sweep in and, using the revealed knowledge, claim to fulfill prophecy.

The Theology of Ibn Kātib Qayṣar's Commentary

Humans, Beasts, and Angels

Throughout our author's exegetical discussions, he frequently compares humans to animals and angels. He does so because he believes that human nature is potentially related to these two other kinds of creatures and therefore believes that humans move in a continuum, journeying either toward the nature of beasts or toward a fully human nature much like that of the angels. He writes that those who fall away from Christ have "no humanity . . . credited to them." They have become "sunken" and "tend toward that which is bestial in human nature." On the other hand, the one who resists these temptations becomes "an excellent person" and "truly a human being."[74]

One of the hallmarks of true humanity, according to Ibn Kātib Qayṣar, is virginity. He writes that "virginity is more honorable than marriage because in [the former] one associates with the pure angels and in [the latter] one associates with beasts and the rest of the animals."[75] He goes on to say that those who are described as being "worthy" in Revelation 3:4 are so because they were ready to honor abstinence, "because they struggled

71. Ibn Kātib Qayṣar, *Commentary on the Apocalypse* 1 (Birmāwī, 32).

72. Further study is necessary to determine whether Ibn Kātib Qayṣar maintains this chronological framework consistently throughout his commentary.

73. bn Kātib Qayṣar, *Commentary on the Apocalypse* 1 (Birmāwī, 32).

74. Ibn Kātib Qayṣar, *Commentary on the Apocalypse* 12 (Birmāwī, 58).

75. Ibn Kātib Qayṣar, *Commentary on the Apocalypse* 15 (Birmāwī, 77).

against the enticements of nature, and they were in their bodies upon the earth like angels in heaven."[76]

Ibn Kātib Qayṣar's comparison of married life with that of the beasts is typical of his sentiments regarding virginity, which he believed was the highest calling in the spiritual life. He says that "the purest people" are those "who fully held fast to the sum of their virtues through abstincence from touching a woman at all, whether licitly or illicitly."[77] Then he emphasizes that the disavowal of women is "generally applicable."[78] It was therefore apparently not reserved for a chosen few, but for all. He justifies this by referencing the 144,000 who stand on Mount Zion in white robes and are described as virgins who "walk with the Lamb wherever he goes."[79] He also interprets the color white as symbolizing chastity because it "is a pure color resembling light and [even] the most insignificant impurity has an effect upon it." It is then no surprise, given his penchant for classificatory systems, that Ibn Kātib Qayṣar ranks believers according to their ability and places "the category of the preeminence of abstinence" at the highest position, even above that of the martyrs.[80]

This emphasis on virginity is perhaps one of the reasons why our author seems so interested in angels, which are said not to marry.[81] In Chapter 2, we have already seen how Ibn Kātib Qayṣar identifies the author John as an "angel," but in other places the commentator goes further to develop a rudimentary angelology. In turning to Revelation 1:4, which describes the "seven spirits before the throne," he claims that such spirits "are the spirits who swim [between heaven and earth] and become manifest through their mediation of commands and prohibitions from the Most High in [carrying out] the business of nations and other entities. They come and go between [the realms of] being and corruption."[82] He then reveals that the spirits are angels, in fact the very angels that are specifically named in his Bible: Mikhā'īl, Ghubriyāl, Rūfā'īl, Sūriyāl, Sādākiyāl, Sārātiyāl, and

76. Ibn Kātib Qayṣar, *Commentary on the Apocalypse* 15 (Birmāwī, 78).

77. Ibn Kātib Qayṣar, *Commentary on the Apocalypse* 15 (Birmāwī, 77).

78. Ibn Kātib Qayṣar, *Commentary on the Apocalypse* 15 (Birmāwī, 77).

79. Ibn Kātib Qayṣar, *Commentary on the Apocalypse* 15 (Birmāwī, 77), referring to Revelation 14:4.

80. Ibn Kātib Qayṣar, *Commentary on the Apocalypse* 15 (Birmāwī, 77).

81. Matthew 22:30.

82. Ibn Kātib Qayṣar, *Commentary on the Apocalypse* 3 (Birmāwī, 37).

Amāniyāl.[83] In this our author differs from Būlus al-Būshī, who said that the seven spirits "are the seven hierarchical orders of the church."[84]

Ibn Kātib Qayṣar goes on to classify angels according to nine ranks or orders, a schema likely related to Ephesians 1:21, 6:12, and Colossians 1:16. He first names "cherubim and seraphim" and then the remaining seven ranks: "principalities, authorities, thrones, lords, powers, angels, and archangels." In this regard, he closely follows the angelic orders described by Pseudo-Dionysius in his work *The Celestial Hierarchy*.[85] Our author, however, explains that cherubim and seraphim are somehow representative of the other seven ranks and so should not be counted outside of the seven, thereby harmonizing his classificatory system with the reference to "seven spirits before the throne" in Revelation 1:4.[86] He does not elaborate, though, on the specifics of this classificatory system nor does he indicate whether the bands represent various levels of authority or whether instead they indicate types or species.

Christ and the Saints

In line with the potential for humans (and human destiny) to become either bestial or fully human and angelic, Ibn Kātib Qayṣar also describes another ontological spectrum. Into this alternative continuum Ibn Kātib Qayṣar places both sinful humans (who become more and more physical) and righteous humans (who become more and more spiritual). He describes how a sinner "sinks along with the allurements of nature and becomes rooted with them at the lowest level" and then becomes "corporeal."[87] The righteous person, on the other hand, is "elevated over the filth of nature and the allurements of lusts" and so "becomes spiritual."[88] This dichotomy between corporeality and spirituality was made famous in Christian

83. Ibn Kātib Qayṣar, *Commentary on the Apocalypse* 3 (Birmāwī, 37).

84. Būlus al-Būshī, *Commentary on the Apocalypse* 1 (Vat. Ar. 459, f. 2r; Edelby, "Commentaire," 4 [Arabic text]).

85. Ps.-Dionyius, *The Celestial Hierarchy*: ed. G. Heil and A. M. Ritter, *Corpus Dionysiacum*, II, second edition (Patristiche Texte und Studien 67; Berlin: De Gruyter, 2012); trans. J. Parker, *The Celestial and Ecclesiastical Hierarchy of Dionysius the Areopagite* (London: Skeffington & Son, 1894).

86. Ibn Kātib Qayṣar, *Commentary on the Apocalypse* 3 (Birmāwī, 38).

87. Ibn Kātib Qayṣar, *Commentary on the Apocalypse* 17 (Birmāwī, 88).

88. Ibn Kātib Qayṣar, *Commentary on the Apocalypse* 17 (Birmāwī, 88).

circles by Origen in the third century CE, and then disseminated and transmitted through many later theologians.[89] Ibn Kātib Qayṣar himself does not betray any indications of direct contact with Origen or Neoplatonic philosophy, but such ideas did pervade the Islamic world and it is possible that this framework informed his thought.[90]

Our author also situates the righteous at the summit of a hierarchy involving five levels or categories of moral behavior: the righteous, the heedful, the pure, the fallen, and the wicked. Along with each category he supplies a corresponding luminous image beginning with heavenly lights and then progressively dimming with each descending step: first, the sun; second, the moon; third, the stars; fourth, an extinguishing lamp, and fifth and finally, the outer darkness.[91]

Ibn Kātib Qayṣar connects the spiritual and luminous existence of the righteous with a theology of sanctification whereby the holiness or "perfection" of an ecclesiastical leader is mutually and symbiotically dependent upon the holiness of his flock. He writes that perfection has two degrees. The first is "the perfection of the person in himself by his faith and righteous deeds."[92] The second level, by contrast, is that of "leaders and teachers who do not benefit from their perfection in themselves; rather, their perfection abounds to someone else and it perfects [that person] through faith and deeds."[93] He explains that "the faithful wise person is the one who gives to his flock their spiritual nourishment in its proper time."[94] In other cases, Ibn Kātib Qayṣar warns slacking leaders that their "leadership will be removed" if they do not take note and observe the conditions of their repentance.[95]

Our author believed that the two spectrums mentioned above—from bestial to human, and from corporeal to spiritual—were mysteriously united in the person of Christ. When John beholds the glorified Jesus in

89. On human corporeality and spirituality in Origen, see Stephen Thomas, "Anthropology," in *The Westminster Handbook to Origen*, ed. John McGuckin (Louisville, Ky.: Westminster John Knox Press, 2004), 53–58.

90. R. Walzer, "Aflāṭūn," EI², BrillOnline *Reference Works*, http://referenceworks.brillonline.com/entries/encyclopaedia-of-islam-2/aflatun-COM_0023, consulted March 24, 2018.

91. Ibn Kātib Qayṣar, *Commentary on the Apocalypse* 15 (Birmāwī, 75).

92. Ibn Kātib Qayṣar, *Commentary on the Apocalypse* 15 (Birmāwī, 74).

93. Ibn Kātib Qayṣar, *Commentary on the Apocalypse* 15 (Birmāwī, 74).

94. Ibn Kātib Qayṣar, *Commentary on the Apocalypse* 15 (Birmāwī, 74).

95. Ibn Kātib Qayṣar, *Commentary on the Apocalypse* 11 (Birmāwī, 55).

the first chapter of Revelation, Ibn Kātib Qayṣar interprets the whiteness of Jesus's hair as symbolizing "the divinity united with the humanity of Christ our Lord."[96] This reference to the union of Christ's divinity and humanity is typical of Ibn Kātib Qayṣar, who in another passage says that Jesus is the "first and the last . . . insofar as he is God" and that he died and rose again "insofar as he is human."[97] He says much the same again when treating of the names of Jesus, "*Truth* is an attribute of our Lord insofar as he is divine. . . . *Faithful witness* is his description insofar as he is human."[98] But our author is careful to point out that the human nature described by John was Jesus's "humanity in the spiritual condition it had after the resurrection."[99] In other words, this was not the physical humanity Jesus possessed during his time on earth, but a fully spiritual, yet paradoxically still fully human, humanity. This combination of a fully human and fully spiritual existence beautifully unites the above two spectrums in which our author places all humans.

Death, Resurrection, and the End Times

Ibn Kātib Qayṣar also describes the end state of the righteous, saying, as before, that "their bodies shall become spiritual, imperishable, luminous, neither suffering pain nor being susceptible to corruptibility, which is the second death."[100] The phrase "second death" was quite productive for Ibn Kātib Qayṣar, who found it in Revelation 2:11, 20:6, and 20:14. He also labeled it the "destroying death" (*al-mawt al-ikhtirāmī*). He explains that the second death is the complete coming of Jesus in "command and judgment" and is "conditioned upon" a "failure to repent."[101] The first death is the "natural death" (*al-mawt al-ṭabīʿī*),[102] which, though not fully explained by our author in his exposition of the first three chapters of Revelation, refers either to the physical death or the death through sin that all will experience. This second interpretation seems more likely because it adequately explains Ibn Kātib Qayṣar's association of the term with the Lord's

96. Ibn Kātib Qayṣar, *Commentary on the Apocalypse* 8 (Birmāwī, 47).
97. Ibn Kātib Qayṣar, *Commentary on the Apocalypse* 9 (Birmāwī, 50).
98. Ibn Kātib Qayṣar, *Commentary on the Apocalypse* 17 (Birmāwī, 87).
99. Ibn Kātib Qayṣar, *Commentary on the Apocalypse* 8 (Birmāwī, 48).
100. Ibn Kātib Qayṣar, *Commentary on the Apocalypse* 17 (Birmāwī, 93).
101. Ibn Kātib Qayṣar, *Commentary on the Apocalypse* 15 (Birmāwī, 76).
102. Ibn Kātib Qayṣar, *Commentary on the Apocalypse* 15 (Birmāwī, 73).

criticism of the leader of the church of Sardis, when he proclaims to him, "you are dead," though he was in fact alive.[103]

Corresponding to the above-mentioned two deaths are the first and second resurrections. For Ibn Kātib Qayṣar the first resurrection is the spiritual resurrection that occurs when a person becomes a Christian. Ibn Kātib Qayṣar cites an example of this in Revelation 3:4 where the followers of Jesus are clad in white garments.[104] He argues that this imagery must be spiritual and therefore must refer to the first resurrection, because "otherwise their bodies would not have risen" at this juncture in the text of Revelation.[105] Here our author is unknowingly following the exegetical path forged by his predecessors Oecumenius and Andrew of Caesarea. The former writes that the first resurrection is that "which results from faith," and that the second is the "universal bodily resurrection."[106] Andrew says much the same: "The first resurrection is being brought to life out of 'dead works,' the second, the transformation from bodily corruption into incorruption."[107]

Curiously, certain strands of Islamic theology also speak of a "first resurrection," but this seems limited to Shiʿite beliefs, and Ibn Kātib Qayṣar shows no awareness of them. In any case the Shiʿite version of the "first resurrection" posits a literal resurrection of the righteous preceding that of the general second resurrection, a perspective somewhat in line with certain readings of the millennial reign of Christ in Revelation 20.[108]

Discussions of millennial beliefs are typically reserved for Chapter 20 of Revelation, but happily Ibn Kātib Qayṣar mentions his interpretation of the millennial reign when treating the epistle to the church of Thyatira. In Revelation 2:26–27, Jesus says to the church that those who prevail shall be given "authority over the nations, and he shall control them with an iron rod and he shall crush them like a clay vessel."[109] Ibn Kātib Qayṣar

103. Ibid. Further study is necessary to determine whether Ibn Kātib Qayṣar maintains this interpretation of the "second death" consistently throughout his commentary.

104. Ibn Kātib Qayṣar, *Commentary on the Apocalypse* 15 (Birmāwī, 77).

105. Ibn Kātib Qayṣar, *Commentary on the Apocalypse* 15 (Birmāwī, 77).

106. Oecumenius, *Commentary on the Apocalypse* 11.12 (trans. Suggit, 174).

107. Andrew of Caesarea, *Commentary on the Apocalypse* 62 (trans. Constantinou, 210).

108. Gardet, L. "Ḳiyāma." EI^2, BrillOnline *Reference Works*, http://referenceworks.brillonline.com/entries/encyclopaedia-of-islam-2/kiyama-COM_0526, consulted March 24, 2018.

109. Ibn Kātib Qayṣar, *Commentary on the Apocalypse* 14 (Birmāwī, 66).

says that the "intended referent . . . is the person who has authority over the nations in the dynasty of the thousand years that belong to the righteous." He explains that this is a "general example" for how the saints spiritually reign in the present time, reasoning that after the return of Christ there is no more opportunity to reign over the nations because, instead of being merely subjugated, unbelievers are punished according to their works.[110]

Thus, at its beginning (and in the end), this Arabic commentary articulates an apocalyptic hope: the promised realization of a dynasty of saints, sharply contrasted to the subjugation and punishment of unbelievers. Such a vision, revealed to John in the Book of Revelation and disclosed by Ibn Kātib Qayṣar, would have resonated deeply with a Christian community living in Egypt under the uncertainties and vicissitudes of Islamic rule.

110. Ibn Kātib Qayṣar, *Commentary on the Apocalypse* 14 (Birmāwī, 70).

CHAPTER

4

BŪLUS AL-BŪSHĪ, *COMMENTARY ON THE APOCALYPSE OF JOHN*, CH. 1–3

Translated by Shawqi Talia; edited by Stephen J. Davis

In the name of the Father and the Son and the Holy Spirit, one God. Glory be to him. With the help of our Lord, we begin the commentary on the Revelation of John the Evangelist: that is, the Apocalypse.[1] May the blessing of him who revealed it be with us.

Chapter One (1:1–20)

1. (1:1) The Apocalypse[2] of Jesus Christ which God gave him to show to his servants concerning what will soon come to pass. He has made it known by sending his revelation through his angel John,[3] his servant, (1:2) who bore witness to the word of God and the testimony of Jesus Christ by what he saw.[4] (1:3) Blessed is he who reads it and keeps what is written therein, for the time is near. (1:4) John writes to the seven churches in Asia: Grace be to you and peace from him who is, who is eternal, and who is to come, and from the seven spirits before the throne, (1:5) and from Jesus Christ, the faithful witness, the first born of the dead, and the ruler of the kings of the earth; he who has loved us and has saved us from our sins with his own blood, and who has made us (1:6) kings

1. From the Coptic ⲁⲡⲟⲅⲁⲗⲩⲙⲯⲓⲥ (*apagalumpsis*).

2. This time Būlus al-Būshī uses the Arabic transliteration of the Greek word ἀποκάλυψις.

3. Vatican Arabic Rosiana 924 and Vatican Arabic 466 (= MSS E and G, in Talia, "Būlus al-Būšī's Arabic Commentary") have: "He has made it known by sending his revelation through his angel to John his servant."

4. Read *ra'ā* (he saw) in place of *rā'ī* (viewer). The context presupposes a verb form.

and priests to God his Father, to whom be glory and honor forever and ever. Amen. (1:7) Behold, he comes on the clouds of heaven and every eye shall see him, even those who pierced him. All the tribes of the earth shall see him.[5] Amen. (1:8) I am the Alpha and the Omega, the first and the last, says the Lord, who is, who was, and who is to come, the Omnipotent One. (1:9) I, John, your brother and fellow sharer in the tribulation—sovereignty and power are in Jesus Christ—I was on the island called Patmos, for the sake of the word of God and the testimony of Jesus Christ. (1:10) I was taken up by the Spirit on Sunday, and I heard a voice behind me like a trumpet (1:11) saying: Write what you see in a book and send it to the seven churches in Asia, which are Ephesus, Smyrna, Pergamum, Thyatira, Sardis, Philadelphia, and Laodicea.

The seven spirits are the seven hierarchical orders[6] of the church, and *the seven churches* are the great cities and their regions, on account of

5. The Greek text reads "tribes of the earth will wail on account of him."

6. The word *rutbah* (pl. *rutab*) has two basic meanings in Christian Arabic theological terminology. The usage of this word in a religious sense is exclusively a Christian one: see Georg Graf, *Verzeichnis arabischer kirchlicher Termini* (Leuven: Imprimerie Orientaliste L. Durbecq, 1954), 51; Hans Wehr, *A Dictionary of Modern Written Arabic*, ed. J. M. Cowan (4th ed.; Wiesbaden: Harrassowitz, 1979), 375; R. Dozy, *Supplément aux dictionnaires arabes* (2 vols.; Leiden: Brill, 1881), I.508.

The first denotation is the "ecclesiastical hierarchy of the church." In this context, three different phrases are used: (1) *rutab al-kanīsah*, "ecclesiastical hierarchies of the church" (J. Périer, ed., *La Perle précieuse traitant des sciences ecclésiastiques par Jean, fils d'abou-Zakariyā, surnommé ibn Sabā'*, PO 16 [1922], 661); (2) *rutab al-khidmah*, "orders of the ministry" (Périer, *La Perle*, 660ff.); (3) *rutab al-kahanūt*, "ecclesiastical hierarchies of the priesthood" (see also J. Assfalg, *Die Ordnung des Priestertums: ein altes liturgisches Handbuch der koptischen Kirche* [Cairo: Publications du Centre d'études orientales; Coptica 1; Cairo: Centre d'études orientales, 1955], 40ff.). The number of hierarchies differs depending on the particular church rite. The Jacobite Ibn Sabā' enumerates nine—the reader, the subdeacon, the deacon, the archdeacon, the priest, the hegumen, the patriarch, the bishop, and the metropolitan—but in his eyes the last three are the same (Périer, *La Perle*, 661–66). The same number with slightly different names is given by the Melkite patriarch of Alexandria, Sa'īd ibn al-Biṭrīq (Eutychius of Alexandria, ca. 877–940 CE): "The first rank at the altars of Christ is a rank comprising three hosts, patriarchs, metropolitans, and bishops in one grade (or order). They are all high priests. The second rank beneath the first comprises three hosts, chorepiscopi, περιοδενταί, and priests in one grade. They are all priests. The third rank beneath the first and the second ranks comprises three hosts, deacons, subdeacons, and readers (*anagnostae*) in one rank. They are all serving deacons." (P. Cachia and W. M. Watt, eds., *Eutychius of Alexandria. The Book of the Demonstration [Kitāb al-burhān]*, CSCO 192–93 and 209–10 [Louvain: Secrétariat du Corpus SCO, 1960–61], I.205 [Ar.]; II.161 [Eng.]).

the congregations of the faithful who are there, for every congregation is called a church.

2. **He said: (1:12) I turned and I saw the voice that was speaking to me. I saw seven lamps of gold, (1:13) and in the midst of the lamps was one like the Son of Man, wearing a breast-plate and a golden girdle. (1:14) The hair on his head and his beard were white as snow and as pure wool. His eyes were like the flame of fire, (1:15) and his feet were like burnished brass, as if molded in a furnace.[7] His voice was like many waters. (1:16) In his right hand he held seven stars, and from his mouth there issued a two-edged sword. His face was like the sun in its strength.**

The seven lamps are the illuminating teachings of the churches. *In its midst* signifies the hidden meaning, i.e., the recognition of the glory of the Son of Man. He is called the *Son of Man* because he became incarnate. His statement, *wearing a breast-plate*, indicates his impervious power. *The golden girdle* is his kingdom, which prevails over all. The *white*ness of his *hair* signifies his eternal preexistence. Indeed, Daniel the prophet saw him in such a state.[8] *His eyes were like the flame of fire* signifies the light of his divinity, which sees and observes all nations. *His feet were like burnished brass* signifies his ordinances, which are right, without any blemishes, and which are pure and just in every way. His words, *His voice was like many waters*, indicate the spreading of his commandments without any hindrance. For just as water brings life to all the plants and trees and to everything, so too everyone who obeys his commandment shall live and be saved.

The *seven stars in his hand* signify that he holds and controls all the ordinances, and all the hierarchies, and all the ranks of created beings, the hidden and the manifest, because the stars have both a manifest appearance and a light that is not perceptible. The *two-edged sword issuing forth from his mouth* signifies his efficacious word, which will smite anyone who opposes it. Similar are the words of Paul the apostle: "The word of God is sharper than a two-edged sword,"[9] and so forth. He says: *His face is like the sun in its strength*, because in reality he is the sun of righteousness, which

The second meaning, using the word *marātib* (the verbal noun form of the same root) is with reference to the celestial hierarchies, such as the angels (Périer, *La Perle*, 660–61).

7. Read *qamīn* in place of *qāmīn*.

8. See Daniel 7:9.

9. Hebrews 4:12.

is mentioned by Isaiah the prophet.[10] He is the *day* that has come to us, just as Paul his apostle said: "The night is spent, and the day is near."[11] For this reason, John saw him in this way.

3. He said: (1:17) When I saw him, I fell before his feet, and I became as one who is dead. But he laid his right hand upon me and said: Fear not; I am the first and the last; (1:18) I am the living one. I died, but behold, I am alive forever, and with me I have the keys of the abyss and of hell. (1:19) Write all that you have seen, for it soon shall come to pass. (1:20) As for the seven stars that you saw in my hand and the seven golden lampstands, the seven stars are the seven angels of the seven churches, and the seven golden lampstands you saw are the seven churches.

This means that when he [i.e., John] witnessed his awesome glory, he fell down like a dead man. And *he put his hand upon him* means God's power and succor, for in visions of God, when a man becomes afraid, God takes away the fear from him. The same is true of the angels. When the angel appeared to Our Lady and she became afraid, he said to her: "Do not be afraid, Mary."[12] He spoke similarly to Zechariah when he was afraid.[13] As for visions of devils, they add fear to fear. For this reason, one is able to differentiate between visions of God and visions of evil spirits. He says, *I am alive*, because he is a being of eternal life. He says, *I died*, because of his life-giving suffering on our behalf. His words, *I am alive forever*, indicate that, although he suffered corporeally and died,[14] he remains alive by the power of his divinity. He exists eternally and without end. His statement, *With me I have the keys of the abyss and of hell*, does not signify literal keys. Rather, it is like what is written in the fifth book of the Torah,[15] where God says: I cause to die and I bring to life; I cast into the

10. Isaiah 51:4; see also Malachi 4:2.

11. Romans 13:12.

12. Luke 1:30.

13. Luke 1:12–13.

14. Coptic Museum MSS 32 and 61 (= MSS D and C, in Talia, "Būlus al-Būšī's Arabic Commentary") have the following: "He died, at the separation of the human soul, while he was on the cross. He brought [the soul] back to the body at the time of his resurrection."

15. Ar. *tawrāt*. In Islamic literature this term is used in a general sense for the Hebrew Bible/Old Testament. The word came into Arabic from the Hebrew term designating the Pentateuch (the first five books of the Old Testament). No doubt, Būlus al-Būshī is using it with the idea that it designates the Pentateuch only and not the whole Old Testament: see A. Jeffrey, *The Foreign Vocabulary of the Qur'ān* (Baroda: Oriental Institute, 1938), 95–96; also Hava Lazarus-Yafeh, "Tawrāt," in *EI*^{2}, BrillOnline *Reference Works*, http://referenceworks

abyss and bring out of it.[16] His statement that *the seven stars* in his hand *are the seven angels*, and that *the seven golden lampstands are the seven churches*, has the same interpretation as mentioned above: namely, that he controls all and holds everything, what is hidden and what is manifest, the seen and the unseen. Glory be to him forever. Amen.

Chapter Two (2:1–29)

4. He said, (2:1) Write to the angel of the church at Ephesus: Thus says the Almighty One, who has the seven stars in his right hand and who walks in the midst of the seven golden lampstands. (2:2) I know your works, your toils and your patient endurance, and that you are not capable of enduring evil. But you have tested those who say they are apostles and you have found them to be liars and that they are not apostles. (2:3) You have endured patiently for my name's sake, and you have not become weary. (2:4) But I have this against you: that you have abandoned your former love. (2:5) So remember how you have fallen, and repent, or I shall come to you and shall remove your lamps if you do not repent. (2:6) Yet, this thing you have: You despise the works of the foreign peoples[17] whom I myself despise. (2:7) He who has ears to hear, let him hear what the Spirit says to the churches. To him who conquers I shall give the right to eat from the tree of life which is in the midst of the paradise of God.

He means by *the angel of the church* the head of the church. The command is a general one for him and his congregation. He refers to the seven regions in which John the Evangelist preached. Therefore, the command is a general one, for these and for all believers like them. He began by mentioning the name of the bishop[18] who was in Ephesus, because it is the

.brillonline.com/entries/encyclopaedia-of-islam-2/tawrat-COM_1203, consulted March 24, 2018.

16. The verse Būlus al-Būshī quotes as being from the fifth book of the Torah is actually a conflation of different verses. The first part ("I cause to die and I bring to life") is found in Deuteronomy 32:39. The second part ("I cast into the abyss and bring out of it") is not found in Deuteronomy but in Tobit 13:2 and Wisdom 16:13.

17. Vatican Arabic 118 has "the Arab people" (*al-sha'b al-arabiyyah*).

18. Ar. *usquf* (pl. *asāqifah*), from the Greek ἐπίσκοπος (*episkopos*).

first.[19] Likewise, Paul said to them, "Take heed for yourselves and for the whole flock over which the Holy Spirit has appointed you bishops."[20] The first thing the apostle did was to admonish them; then he held them responsible for the congregation, since censuring it is incumbent upon them, just as in the apostolic command.[21]

His statement, *Thus says the one who holds the seven stars in his right hand*, means his mighty hand: that is, the power of his divinity, which controls everything. The *right hand* is power, not a literal right hand. For example, the prophet David says, "The right hand of God has upheld me. The right hand of God has acted as power."[22] It is also written in the Torah, "With the strength of your arm you have destroyed our adversaries."[23] His statement, *He who walks in the midst of the seven lampstands*, which he earlier said were seven churches, means that he is present everywhere by the power of his divinity, which is omnipresent. He encompasses everything, but nothing encompasses him. Because of this, he said, *I know your labors, your toils, and your patient endurance*, meaning that everything is known to him and that his knowledge encompasses all creatures, even our good and bad deeds. Thus, he praised his [i.e., the bishop's] patient endurance and toils. He then made known to him his human weakness when bearing[24] the trials and the tribulations, in order that he might become humble and ask for help from him. What he said about the false prophets[25] is similar to what the divine apostle Paul said, "They are false apostles and deceitful prophets, who assert that they are like the apostles of Christ,"[26] and so forth. Therefore, it is necessary to be on guard against them.

His statement that he has it *against* him [and] that he *abandoned his former* friendship[27] means the first warmth that moves within us through

19. There is some ambiguity in the use of the world *al-awwal* (the first). It may also mean "the greatest." Given the context, Būlus al-Būshī probably uses it here to indicate that Ephesus was the greatest city among the seven mentioned by John.

20. Acts 20:28.

21. Acts 20:28.

22. Psalm 18:35.

23. See Exodus 15:16; also Psalm 89:10.

24. Read *iḥtimāl* (to carry, bear) in place of *iḥtifāl* (to celebrate).

25. Revelation 2:2.

26. 2 Corinthians 11:13.

27. The text of Revelation 2:4 has "former love" (*al-maḥabbah al-qadīmah*). In his commentary, Būlus al-Būshī uses a different noun as a near synonym: "former friendship" (*al-mawaddah al-qadīmah*).

grace, but that someone has abandoned. On account of this, he said, *I have this against you*: That is, I reproach you. He humbled himself against us who are weak like a righteous lover of humankind. He did not hasten to punish us but gave us ample time to repent in order that he might show his bountiful love for us. His will was for us to be resurrected. When he said, *Remember now how you have fallen. Repent,* he let all the members of the congregation know that each one of them should be aware of his wrongdoings and that they should repent of these wrongdoings before death. But then he added, *If you do not repent, I shall come to you and remove the lamps from their places.* He showed himself to be like a merciful father. First, he showed us his mercy and his reprimand. Then, like a mighty king, he showed us the far-reaching power of his punishment[28] if we should continue in our disobedience until our death. But he was merciful and said, *Yet, this thing you have: You despise the works of the foreign peoples whom I myself despise.* By this he means: You despise sin, which I also despise. Yet, though you have neglected repentance, I did not reject you completely, for it is my wish that you may become perfect, so that your piety will be manifested before me, and your reward will be manifold.

His saying, *He who has ears to hear, let him hear*, means that this exhortation is not binding for a particular people only, but rather it is binding for everyone who is capable of hearing and comprehending. He then said, *What the Spirit says to the churches*, to signify that the Spirit of God is upon the whole community of believers. His words, *To him who conquers I shall give the right to eat from the tree of life*, do not mean a victory in a physical battle.[29] Rather, he achieves victory over depravity through the raising up of virtue. It is then that he will gain eternal life with God without end. He said, *which is in the midst of the paradise of God*, because the center of a thing is the most perfect part of it.[30] In the most inaccessible part of the eternal kingdom is the paradise that is coveted by all, one with many different noble fruits. He says, *divine*, because he became fully incarnate with a rational soul completely like us in every way except sin. And he called

28. Literally, "his revenge" (*intiqāmihi*). This word is often used in Islamic theological terminology to refer to God's punishment and judgment. The noun form, *al-muntaqim* (the avenger), is one of the 100 names of God in Islam, but it is not one of the epithets found in the Qur'ān (see Qur'ān 5:95).

29. Literally, "perceptible" or "sensory" (*maḥsūsah*) battle. Būlus al-Būshī uses the word *maḥsūsah* to signify the act of perception, hence the meaning "physical."

30. Read *aḥsan* in place of *aḥṣan*.

humankind his brothers, just as it is written, "I will proclaim your name to my brothers."[31] And the apostle also says, "Just as all the children have flesh and blood in common, so he in like manner has shared in these things."[32] Therefore, just as he manifested his divine work through the power of miracles, so too he has manifested the manner of his Incarnation by these things. He is God incarnate. The one to whom divinity properly belongs is also the one to whom Incarnation properly belongs.

5. He said, (2:8) Write to the angel of the church at Smyrna: Thus says the first and the last, the one who died and who lived. (2:9) I know your grief, your poverty and your riches, and the blasphemy of those who claim they are Jews.[33] They are not Jews, but a synagogue of Satan. (2:10) Do not fear the trials that will befall you. For Satan will cast some of you into prison to try you, and he will put you through tribulations for ten days. Therefore, be faithful until death, and I shall give you the crown of life. (2:11) He who has ears to hear, let him hear what the Spirit says to the churches. He who conquers, the second death will not defeat him.

He mentioned the head of the church at Smyrna and its environs, saying, *Thus says the first and the last.* This means that he is truly the Lord, the one who has neither a beginning nor an end. Now when you hear these revealed expressions concerning the human economy and the manner of the Incarnation, do not forget these exalted expressions that are proper to his divinity. He is the one who makes miracles and accepts suffering. His saying, *The one who died and who lived,* means that he accepted suffering and death corporeally and not as a phantasm.[34] "He is life, the living one

31. Hebrews 2:12.

32. Hebrews 2:14.

33. Vatican Arabic 459, f. 5v. The wording of this verse follows that of the Sahidic version (see Horner, *CopticNT-South* 7.272–75). When Ibn Kātib Qayṣar quotes the verse in his commentary below, however, he follows the different wording of the Bohairic text (see Horner, *CopticNT-North* 4.454–55).

34. In his defense of the resurrection of the body of Christ, Būlus al-Būshī is attacking the heresy of Docetism, which was thought to deny the reality of the material body of Christ and to view his death as only an illusion: see E. A. Livingstone, "Docetism," in *The Oxford Dictionary of the Christian Church*, ed. F. L. Cross and E. A. Livingston, 3rd ed. (Oxford: Oxford University Press, 2005), 496; M. Peel, *The Epistle to Rheginos: A Valentinian Letter on the Resurrection* (London: SCM Press, 1969); M. Slusser, "Docetism—A Historical Definition," *The Second Century* 1 (1981), 163–72. An earlier Arabic-language attack against Docetism is found in the *History of the Patriarchs of the Coptic Church.* According to this source, Patriarch James (fl. 819–30) attacked docetic beliefs found among the so-called "Phantasiasts" or "Gaianites": "Moreover Abba James was an admonition to the heretics, because they stood

who gives life by the power of his divinity, who does not suffer and does not die," as Cyril the Great, the patriarch of Alexandria, has said.[35] The Lord is neither seen nor perceived in the substance of his divinity. He has united with a human body in order to accept suffering and death on our behalf. He did not, however, unite with a body devoid of a rational soul. Rather, he became united with a rational, reasoning soul having the capacity to accept suffering and to taste death. So, he suffered corporeally. The body is his by virtue of the union.[36] Therefore, suffering is reckoned to him by virtue of the union and not by virtue of any change.[37] His saying, *I know your grief,* and so forth, means that he knows all things, as was said earlier in the commentary.[38]

He says, *I found not a single one of those who claim to be Jews. Rather, they are a synagogue of Satan,*[39] because the Jews are called pure on account of the circumcision, which they call purification. Similarly, we find that even until today there are communities that call circumcision purification. But the fact is that circumcision is the opposite of this. Rather, it is the symbol of the purification of holy baptism, just as the holy apostles have written. The Lord has given us baptism in the place of circumcision; his blood and flesh in place of the lambs' flesh. The divine apostle Paul knows its power, for he has said that not everyone who claims to be a Jew is one. The Jew is the one who is a Jew in his heart. Circumcision is circumcision

in awe of him, and because of the excellence of his faith, and his confession and his office; and they held his words in reverence. For when he was enthroned, he delivered an admonitory discourse, in which he anathematized all the banished heresies, and the impure council of Chalcedon, and the Phantasiasts, that is the Gaianites, who deny the lifegiving passion of the God the Word, which he accepted in the flesh" (*HPCC*: ed. B. T. Evetts, *History of the Patriarchs of the Coptic Church*, PO 10 [1915], 447–48).

35. See L. Wickham, *Cyril of Alexandria: Select Letters* (Oxford: Clarendon, 1982), 2–11, 21–23. The same defense is given by Cyril of Jerusalem in his thirteenth *Catechetical Lecture* (NPNF 7.82–93).

36. Read *al-ittiḥād* for *al-ījād*.

37. Ar. *istiḥālah*. While this is a classical Arabic word, it took on a technical meaning in Christian Arabic literature, where it corresponded to the Greek terms *alloiōsis* (change) and *mixis* (mixture): see Samir Khalil Samir, *Traité de Paul de Būš*, xix, 86–87.

38. See his translation and commentary on Revelation 2:2 cited above (Vatican Arabic 459, f. 4r).

39. Vatican Arabic 459, f. 6r. Būlus al-Būshī here quotes the Bohairic Coptic version of this verse (Horner, *CopticNT-North* 4.454–55) and not the Sahidic version noted above (Vatican Arabic 459, f. 5v; Horner, *CopticNT-South* 7.272–75).

of the heart by the spirit.[40] By Judaism, the apostle means cleanliness—that is, purification. It is not the name, nor even the circumcision [itself]. Rather, it is the cleanliness and the purification of the heart in the Holy Spirit by means of baptism. For this reason, the Apocalypse says, they are not like this: *Rather, they are a synagogue of Satan.* It means that they have held to the way of error[41] and have abandoned the truth. Satan triumphed over them when God abandoned his care of them because of their unbelief. Next, God encouraged the congregation not to fear the many tribulations that will befall them when they do good deeds. Then he informed them that Satan will put some of them to the test, and these will be the strong ones among them. He [Satan] will torment them for ten days, because one begins with ten in decimal counting.[42] So, it means *until death*, and he explained this by saying, *Be faithful until death, and I shall give you the crown.* Similarly, he said, *He who has persevered until the end shall be saved.*[43] Then he informed us about what the crown and salvation are. He said, *He who conquers, the second death will not defeat him.* In the same way, he testified in the Gospel that whoever believes in him and keeps his commandments will not taste death but will pass from death to life.[44]

6. He said, (2:12) Write to the angel of the church at Pergamum: Thus says the one who has the two-edged sword. (2:13) I know that you are the [dwelling] place of the throne of Satan,[45] that you have held to my name, and that you have not denied believing in me. You have stood

40. See Romans 2:28–29. Here, two different words connoting "heart" are used: *sarīrah* and *qalb*. The first is applied to the one who is "a Jew in his heart [or mind]" (*yahūdī al-sarīrah*). The second is applied to "the circumcision of the heart" (*khitān al-qalb*).

41. Read *ḍull* (error, wrong) in place of *ẓill* (shade, semblance). The latter is not correct in the context. Coptic Museum MSS 32 and 61, and British Library Or. 1329 (originally British Museum Arabic Supp. MS 16) (= MSS D, C, and H, in Talia, "Būlus al-Būšī's Arabic Commentary") have *al-bāṭil* (falsehood). Vatican Arabic 118 has *al-ẓulm* (injustice).

42. While the grammar of the commentary is often poor, the choice of vocabulary, at times, suggests an excellent knowledge of classical Arabic terminology, as in Būlus al-Būshī's use of the word *'aqd*. One of the meanings of *'aqd* is that it is the first decimal number in a system where the decimals begin with ten and end with ninety. Therefore, by analogy, since ten is the first of something (i.e., decimals) and therefore continues, so also does human suffering, which begins at birth and ends at death. For *'aqd*, see Lane, *Arabic-English Lexicon*, 2052, 2106.

43. Matthew 10:22; 24:13.

44. See John 5:24.

45. Note the variance of this verse from both the Greek and Coptic versions. The Greek reads "I know where you dwell, where Satan's throne is." The Coptic reads "I know where you

steadfast in the days when they put to death the faithful witness. (2:14) But there are a few names with you who hold the teaching of Balaam, who taught Balak to sow seeds of doubt before the children of Israel, so that they would eat the sacrifices that were presented to the idols and commit fornication. (2:15) You also have with you people[46] who hold to the practices of the nations. (2:16) If you do not repent, I shall quickly come to you and make war against you with the sword of my mouth. (2:17) He who has ears to hear, let him hear what the Spirit says to the churches. To him who conquers I shall give the hidden manna and a white garment,[47] and on it a new name will be inscribed, known only to him who receives it.

He commanded the head of the church of Pergamum, saying: *Thus says he who has the two-edged sword*, meaning that his efficacious word reaches to every place, just as the apostle Paul says.[48] His statement, *I know that you are the dwelling place of the throne of Satan*, means the remaining people among them who prefer to worship the idols. Indeed, wherever you see sacrifices presented to the idols, there no doubt you will also see the throne of Satan.

His saying, *You have held to my name*, means the faithful who hold steadfastly without fear in the midst of unbelief. He said, *You have stood steadfast in the days when they put to death the faithful witness.* By this he means the Evangelist, the head of the seven churches mentioned above. For he was a fellow sharer with them in the commandment.[49] He was the one who alone among his apostolic brethren remained steadfast with patience and love at the crucifixion of the Lord, until he saw the end. The Lord has

---

are dwelling, the place in which the throne of Satan is [located]" (Horner, *CopticNT-South* 7.276–77 [Sahidic]; Horner, *CopticNT-North* 4.454–455 [Bohairic].

46. The Bohairic text reads "Thus, you also have [one who] is laying hold to [the] teaching of the Nicolaitans" (Horner, *CopticNT-North* 4.456–457). The Greek reads "So you also have some who hold the teaching of the Nicolaitans."

47. The Greek and Sahidic versions refer to a white "stone" (Greek and Sahidic, *psēphos*: Horner, *CopticNT-South*, 7.280–81; Bohairic, *al*: Horner, *CopticNT-North*, 4.456–57). All the Arabic manuscripts of Būlus's commentary refer to a white "garment" (*libās*), but see Ibn Kātib Qayṣar, who follows the Greek and Coptic readings by referring to a white "stone" (*faṣṣ*).

48. See Hebrews 4:12. "For the word of God is living and efficient and keener than any two-edged sword."

49. See Mark 28:19. "Go, therefore, and make disciples of all nations, baptizing them in the name of the Father, and of the Son, and of the Holy Spirit."

named himself *the faithful witness.*[50] His holy and valiant apostle Paul refers to him in the same way when he says that before Pilate he gave a "good witness,"[51] which came at the crucial moment. For he said to Pilate that his kingdom was not of this world[52]—[a world] that is passing away, but [his kingdom] will last forever—and that he was born and had come into the world. This means that he is eternal for this reason: "that I might witness to the truth. He who is of the truth will hear my voice."[53] He also said to the high priest and to the Jewish congregation, "You shall see the Son of Man sitting at the right hand of the Power and coming on the clouds of heaven."[54] Right up to the moment of surrendering his spirit, he proclaimed that he was the Son of God, when he cried out with a loud voice, "O Father, into your hand I commend my spirit."[55] In this, he taught us that we must die for the truth, that we should have no fear, and that we should not be swayed by falsehood. The holy martyr Stephen, the first deacon and the first of the martyrs,[56] followed in his footsteps when they brought him forward in the synagogue and bore false witness against him that he was blaspheming against the Law. But the holy one would not countenance being put to death on account of such false testimony. He started with Abraham, the chief patriarch, giving a summary account, one by one, up to the time of Moses the lawgiver, and even up to this own time. Then, at the end, he informed them that they were the ones who had not kept the Law, but had been in opposition to the prophets; that they had not accepted the coming of the Blessed Holy One to whom the prophets had given testimony; that they had been constantly and in every time and circumstance in opposition to the Holy Spirit; and that they had received the commandment but had not kept it. And so, he died witnessing to the truth, and he became the first of the martyrs.[57] So it is with all the good and courageous witnesses.[58]

50. Revelation 1:5; 3:14.
51. 1 Timothy 6:13.
52. John 18:36.
53. John 18:37.
54. Mark 14:62.
55. Luke 23:46.
56. Acts 6:5.
57. Acts 6:1–8:2.
58. Ar. *shuhadā'* (witnesses, martyrs).

His saying, there are with you some who have held fast to *the practices of the nations*, means the remaining idolators whom we have mentioned above.[59] Should they not repent, he will bring upon them a quick death and he will destroy them with his word, which is sharper than the sword. Then he gave the proclamation to each church: *He who has ears to hear, let him hear*, to let us know that the command will reach all the believers. His statement, *To him who conquers I shall give the hidden manna*, does not mean the physical manna, which was eaten by the corporeal children of Israel. They died because there was no ultimate purpose connected with it.[60] He said, His *garment* is *white, and upon it a new name will be inscribed.* He did not mean a physical garment but the radiance of the souls and bodies of the righteous at the general resurrection, just as he testified when he said, "The righteous will shine forth like the sun in the kingdom of their father."[61] His saying, it is *known only to him who receives it*, is like what is written, "that no eye has seen nor ear heard what the Lord has prepared for his beloved ones."[62] Indeed, it is beyond description. Therefore, no one can recognize this munificence exactly, except the one who receives it.

7. He said, **(2:18) Write to the angel of the church at Thyatira: Thus says the Son of God whose eyes are like the flame of fire and whose feet are like the burnished brass. (2:19) I know all your works, your faith, your love,[63] your service, and your patience, and that your more recent works are better than the first ones. (2:20) But I am angry with you because of your toleration of Jezebel, who says that she is a prophetess and a teacher and leads astray my servants so that they fornicate and eat sacrifices to idols. (2:21) I have now given her time to repent from her fornication, but she did not repent. (2:22) Therefore, if she does not repent for her deeds, I shall cast her and those who joined with her onto the bed of great sorrow.[64] (2:23) I shall cause her children to perish by death, and all the**

59. Vatican Arabic 459, f. 7r.

60. See John 6:58.

61. Matthew 13:43.

62. See 1 Corinthians 2:9.

63. Note the reversed order of "faith" and "love" in the Arabic text. Both the Greek and the Coptic have "your love and your faith."

64. The Bohairic Coptic version (Horner, *CoptNT-South* 4.458–59) reads: "Lo, I will put (lit., give) her into (the) bed, and them who commit adultery with her into a great tribulation." Compare to the Sahidic Coptic version (Horner, *CoptNT-North* 7.284–85: "Behold, I shall cast her into a sickness and those who commit adultery with her into a great tribula-

churches will know that I examine hearts and minds.[65] I will give to each of you in accordance with his deeds. (2:24) I say to you who have remained in Thyatira, [you] who have not held to this teaching and who do not know what they call the profundity[66] of Satan, I shall not lay a heavy burden on you, save the one you already have. (2:25) Hold fast to it until I come. (2:26) To him who conquers and who keeps my works to the end I shall give dominion over the nations, (2:27)[67] so that he may shepherd them with an iron rod and shatter them like earthenware vessels, even as I also received from the father. (2:28) And I shall give him the star that rises in the morning. (2:29) He who has ears to hear, let him hear what the Spirit says to the churches.

He commanded the head of the church of Thyatira, saying: *Thus says the Son of God.* He means the preexistence and eternity that belong to him, along with the Father. He said, *whose eyes are like the flame of fire and whose feet are like burnished brass.* He means that he examines all creation,[68] that he knows about everything, and that his ways are without blemish. Thus, he examines [the church leader's] works of faith, love, service, and patience. He then praised [that leader] in that his more recent deeds were better than his previous ones,[69] because they are virtuous and because they turned from the path of their errors. Then he mentioned that he was angry with him, not on account of evil deeds he had done, but on account of his toleration[70] for evil people without any chastisement. These [evil people] he compared to the wicked Jezebel. If he were to forego chastising them and

tion"); and to Greek text (NRSV: "Beware, I am throwing her on a bed, and those who commit adultery with her I am throwing into great distress").

65. Lit., "hearts and kidneys" (*al-qulūb wa-l-kulā*). In antiquity, the kidneys were considered the seat of the emotions, desires, and moral reflection, while the heart was understood as the seat of wisdom: see G. Maio, "The Metaphorical and Mythical Use of the Kidney in Antiquity," *American Journal of Nephrology* 19.2 (1999), 101–6; see also E. Dvorjetski, "The History of Nephrology in the Talmudic Corpus," *American Journal of Nephrology*, 22.2–3 (2002), 119–29.

66. Ar. *'umq* (depth).

67. Note the variance with the Greek and Coptic texts, which read: "And he will rule over and shatter them with an iron scepter, as the potter's earthenware is broken into pieces."

68. The word *barāyā* means "beings or things that are created," or simply "creation," but here Būlus al-Būshī seems to be referring to humankind in particular.

69. Revelation 2:19.

70. Read *tarkihi* in place of *tarkihim*. This is a good example of Būlus al-Būshī's proclivity for using a pronoun in the singular (*a'mālihi*) and then following up with a plural in a complementary sentence (*tarkihim*). Vatican Arabic 118, Coptic Museum MSS 32 and 61, and British

allowed Christ's people, the servants of God, to associate with them, they would lead [Christ's people] astray and incline them to their kind of deeds. Therefore, it is incumbent upon all the leaders to preach to their people, to show them the right way, and to warn them against associating with those who follow the evil path, just as the apostle admonishes when he says, "Withdraw from every brother whose life is irregular and who does not live according to the instructions that you have received from us."[71]

His statement, *I have given her time to repent*, shows the abundance of his mercy and his forbearance to make repentance more accommodating to us. His statement [about the fact that] *if she does not repent* he will punish her and those who follow her, means the wicked nation and those believers who agree with her. He mentions *all the churches*, meaning the whole inhabited world. They know that he *examines hearts*. Nothing is hidden from him. He alone is the judge of justice.[72] Then he mentioned the simple among them, those who do not know the profundity of the Tempter and who do not participate in the teaching of the unbelieving nations. He said that he will not impose a burden on them,[73] but that they must keep the teaching of the apostles until his coming. This means that they shall meet him with faith. To the one he finds keeping it to the end he will give dominion and the iron rod,[74] as it is written in the Psalms.[75] By this, he means his indomitable power to smash those who oppose him, as if they were earthenware vessels. For the iron rod smashes earthenware vessels without any difficulty. So too, the power of God crushes all thoughts and every enemy power similar to them. For he is the master of his servants and those who keep the commandments until the end, just as he said, "Without me, you are not capable of doing anything."[76]

His saying, *even as I received from the Father*, signifies that by becoming incarnate he became the firstborn and the source of all the blessings. This

Library Or. 1329 (= MSS B, D, C, and H, in Talia, "Būlus al-Būšī's Arabic Commentary") all share the reading, *bal li-tarkihi*.

71. 2 Thessalonians 3:6.

72. Ar. *dayyān al-ʿadl*. That is, one who does not neglect to requite for any deed, whether good or bad. The noun *dayyān* with the definitive article *al-* is used as a divine epithet (Lane, *Arabic-English Lexicon*, 944).

73. See Revelation 2:25.

74. See Revelation 2:27.

75. Psalm 2:9. "You shall rule them with an iron rod; you shall shatter them like earthenware."

76. John 15:5.

is similar to what the apostle says.[77] His statement, *I shall give him the star that rises in the morning*, means the knowledge that removes from us the darkness of error, a knowledge that precedes the rising of holiness in our hearts. Glory be to him forever. Amen.

Chapter Three (3:1–22)

8. He said, (3:1) Write to the angel of the church of Sardis: Thus says the one who has the seven spirits of God and the seven stars. I know your works and that you have a reputation for being well.[78] You are alive, but you are dead. (3:2) Be awake and strengthen what remains lest you die.[79] For I have not found your works to be perfect in the sight of God.[80] (3:3) Remember how you received,[81] but you went astray. Repent! If you do not repent and watch, I shall come like a thief, and you will not know at what hour I shall come to you. (3:4) But I have the names of a few in Sardis who have not defiled their garments with a woman.[82] These will walk with me in white garments, for they are worthy. (3:5) Anyone who so conquers will wear white garments, and their name will not be erased from the book of life. I will present their name before my Father and before his angels. (3:6) He who has ears to hear, let him hear what the Spirit says to the churches.[83]

The Lord commanded the bishop of Sardis, saying: *Thus says the one who has the seven spirits of God and the seven stars.* The *seven spirits* mean the orders of the church, and the *seven stars* mean that he holds all things as

77. See Colossians 1:17ff.

78. The Arabic phrase translated here as "a reputation for being well" is *ism khalāṣ*, which could also mean (more literally) "a name of salvation."

79. This verse is at variance with the Sahidic version, which reads: "Arouse and strengthen what remains and is on the point of death."

80. Coptic Museum MSS 32 and 61, Vatican Arabic Rosiana MS 924, Vatican Arabic 466, and British Library Or. 1329 (= MSS D, C, E, G, and H, in Talia, "Būlus al-Būšī's Arabic Commentary"), along with the Greek text, all have "before my God."

81. Coptic Museum MS 32, Vatican Arabic Rosiana 924, Vatican Arabic 466, and British Library Or. 1329 (= MSS D, E, G, and H, in Talia, "Būlus al-Būšī's Arabic Commentary"), along with the Greek and Coptic texts, all have "You received and heard."

82. Neither the Greek nor the Sahidic has the phrase "with a woman."

83. The following commentary on the letter to Sardis is completely absent in Vatican Arabic 118 and 466, Vatican Arabic Rosiana MS 924, and British Library Or. 1329 (= MSS B, G, E, and H, in Talia, "Būlus al-Būšī's Arabic Commentary").

was stated above.[84] He said that he knows your works:[85] that is, that he examines everything. It was for this reason that he said, *You have a reputation for being alive but you are dead.*[86] He means, as a lesson for all, that [your] deed is not in accordance[87] with [your] reputation but is in fact opposed to it.[88]

He then awakened him, and us too, by saying, *Be awake and strengthen your works,*[89] and the rest also, meaning the whole congregation. He said, *lest you die,* meaning that if he were remiss with himself or with his congregation, he would be condemned on both counts. Just as God said to Ezekiel the prophet, "If you do not warn them, they will die in their sins, but I shall require the blood of everyone at your hand."[90] On account of this, the Lord said, *I have not found your works to be perfect,* meaning: You have been slack in reforming the congregation.

His saying, *before my God,*[91] means the body that he acquired from our nature. He called us his brothers, and he became like us in every way except sin, as was stated above.[92] He then reminded him about his responsibility for the congregation and about obedience to the commandment, in order that he and everyone who assists him might continue to keep [it],[93] providing leadership with cautious attention. For he said, *Remember now how you have accepted and heard;*[94] *continue this and repent.*

And then he put fear into our hearts, all of us who are remiss, because the end of things has come upon us, when he said, *If you do not awaken, I shall come like a thief, and you will not know at what hour I shall come to you.*[95] He means our departure from this life[96] through death. As it says in

84. See his commentary on Revelation 2:1 above (Vatican Arabic 459, f. 4r.).

85. See Revelation 3:1.

86. See Revelation 3:2.

87. Read *mulā'imah* (suitable, in accordance) for *malūmah* (censured).

88. That is, his "bad deed" is not consistent with his reputation for being "alive," because a person becomes dead when he or she sins.

89. See Revelation 3:2. Note here the addition of "your works" (*a'mālaka*).

90. See Ezekiel 33:8.

91. See Revelation 3:2. Note the variation with the text of Revelation cited above, where Būlus al-Būshī uses *al-ilāh* (God) (Vatican Arabic 459, f. 10r). Here, he uses *ilāhī* (my God).

92. See his commentary on Revelation 2:7 above (Vatican Arabic 459, f. 5r).

93. Read *taḥaffuẓ* (keeping).

94. Note here the addition of the word "hear." Compare this with the primary text of Revelation cited above (Vatican Arabic 459, f. 10r).

95. See Revelation 3:3. Note again the variance between this reading and the reading in the text of Revelation quoted above (Vatican Arabic 459, f. 10r).

96. Literally, "from this existence [*wujūd*]".

the holy Gospel, "Awaken, therefore, for the Son of Man will come at an hour you do not know."[97] When he rebuked the insolent people with this, he did not remain silent about the holy ones, so that we would come to know that he observes the good and the bad, that everything is revealed before him, and that he rewards us in accordance with our deeds, be they good or bad.

He said, *But there remain with you in Sardis some people who have not defiled their garments. They shall walk with me in white garments for they are worthy.*[98] With this, he has justified the virtuous and pure people who have kept pure the baptismal garment and who have not defiled their bodies or their souls with the muddiness of sin. He distinguished them from the wicked ones who defiled their souls with despicable offenses, saying, *They shall walk with me, for they are worthy.* He means that they are deserving of the grace of sonship, and that they have become fellow-sharers with all the pure ones in the inheritance of the eternal kingdom, as it is written: "Here am I, along with the children whom God has given me."[99] For this reason, they and those who follow their example walk with him in truth, following in his footsteps without turning aside, with good hope in the age to come. And so, he accepted them by reason of worthiness, because he did not discount their righteous effort, nor did he forget their struggle, until they defeated vice by good action and overcame their despicable offenses[100] by good intentions. Consequently, he emphasized this by saying, *To the one who conquers I shall give a white garment.*[101] He means the light of the souls of his chosen ones in the world to come. To this he testified by saying: "The righteous will shine forth like the sun in the kingdom of their Father."[102]

Then he said, *I shall not remove his name from the book of life.* With this, he made clear his equality with the Father in pre-existence and eternity.

97. Luke 12:40.

98. Note the variance of this verse with the reading of the text of Revelation quoted above (Vatican Arabic 459, f. 10r).

99. Hebrews 2:13.

100. Read *al-āthām* (offenses) in place of *al-ālām* (sufferings). Considering the context of the paragraph itself and the modifying adjective (*al-mardūlah*), the latter makes less sense (see Vatican Arabic 459, f. 11r).

101. This verse is at variance with the text of Revelation quoted above (Vatican Arabic 459, f. 10r.)

102. Matthew 13:43.

Although he has appeared in a body as a man, he remains eternal God, and he exists without end, along with the Father. He is without change and without divisibility in common action, just as he said one time to Moses, "Whoever sins before me, I shall erase his name from my book."[103] He now makes it increasingly clear, that whoever does righteousness before him, he will not erase his name from his book. Furthermore, he made it even clearer by saying, "I shall confess his name before my Father and before his angels."[104] What an exceeding generosity, what a noble glory, and what an exalted splendor, that they will be with him in a splendid white garment! Their names will be forever inscribed in the book of eternal life. He will announce them before his Father, who is equal to him in substance, and before his holy angels, for they are his chosen ones and the inheritors of his kingdom.

By [the statement], *they walked with him* while still in corporeal bodies on account of the splendor of their garments,[105] he means the purity of their souls. *These will walk with me* means that he is God, present in every place, abiding in everyone who invokes his name and who endeavors to keep his commandment. To this he testified when he said, "He who keeps my commandments, the Father and I will come to him and make him our abode."[106] At the end, he will deliver them from death to life, as he promised,[107] and their souls will shine like the angels of God. On the day of the general resurrection, he will resurrect their bodies, which will shine like the splendor of their souls. Everyone will be given glory and honor in body and soul, each according to his virtuous endeavor. As the apostle says, "We must all stand before the tribunal of Christ, where he will reward each one of us according to the deeds his hands have wrought in the body, be they good or evil."[108] For when the righteous ones believe that the body will rise up and will remain forever, they keep it pure and holy, so that the

103. Exodus 32:33.

104. Note the variance in the wording of this verse in comparison with the text of Revelation cited above (Vatican Arabic 459, f. 10r).

105. Note the variance in the wording of this verse in comparison with the text of Revelation cited above (Vatican Arabic 459, f. 10r).

106. See John 14:23.

107. See John 5:24. "Truly, truly, I say to you, the one who hears my word and believes the one who sent me has eternal life; that one does not come into judgment but has passed from death to life."

108. 2 Corinthians 5:10.

glorious resurrection may be theirs. It is in this hope that they exercise their endeavor, just as the righteous Job said in his worst trials and tribulations, "I believe that this skin of mine, in which I endure tribulations, will rise in the resurrection to come."[109] And just as he will acknowledge his chosen ones, he will also disown those who have disobeyed his commandments. So he has testified when he said, "Truly I say to you, I know you not,"[110] and so forth.

He said, *He who has ears to hear, let him hear what the Spirit says to the churches.* He means that this statement extends to all the congregations of believers in all nations, generation after generation. Whoever has hearing, let him hear; and whoever has intelligence, let him understand what the Spirit of God speaks to the holy churches concerning the promise of the kingdom and the threat of the punishment.[111] Therefore, if a man takes heed of the fear of God and acts piously, his reward will be doubled since he has forsaken evil and has not committed it. Instead, he has hastened to the good and has done it. Because of the love of God, he has brought it to completion and has kept his commandments. Glory be to him forever. Amen.

9. He said, (3:7) Write to the angel of the church of Philadelphia: Thus says the holy one, the righteous one, the one who has with him the keys of the house of David. When he opens, no one can shut; and when he shuts, no one can open. (3:8) I know your works and your faith. Behold, I have set before you an open door that no one can shut. Your power is small, yet you have kept my word and you have not denied my name. (3:9) Behold, I have surrendered to you the synagogue of Satan, those who assert they are Jews, but are liars. I will summon them to come, to bow down before you, and to prostrate themselves before your feet. Then all of them will know that I love you, (3:10) because you have kept my

109. Job 19:26 (LXX). The verse quoted here is based on the Septuagint, which is quite different from the Hebrew at this point. The concluding phrase, "in the resurrection to come," is not from the Septuagint, however. It may be Būlus al-Būshī's own insertion.

110. Matthew 25:12.

111. Ar. *al-waʿd wa-l-waʿīd* (the promise and the threat). This expression is one of the five pillars of the Muʿtazili school of Islam: see W. M. Watt, *Islamic Philosophy and Theology* (Edinburgh: Edinburgh University Press, 1962), 68; see also Ibn al-Ṭayyib, *Commentary on Genesis* (*al-waʿīd wa-l-waʿd*): ed. J. C. J. Sanders, *Ibn aṭ-Ṭaiyib, Commentaire sur la Genèse*, 2 vols. (CSCO 274–75; Louvain: Secrétariat du CorpusSCO, 1967), I.25 (Arabic text), II.24 (French translation).

word of patient endurance. Therefore, I too shall protect you from the trials that will befall everyone and will try everyone on earth. (3:11) I will come soon. Hold fast to what you have so that no one removes your crown. (3:12) The one who conquers I shall present as a pillar in the temple of my God. He shall not be cast out. Upon him I shall write the name of my God and the name of the city of my God—the new Jerusalem, the city that comes down from God from heaven, and my new name. (3:13) He who has ears to hear, let him hear what the Spirit says to the churches.

He sent a message to the city of Philadelphia, which means "brotherly love," saying: *Thus says the holy one, the righteous one.* He means that he is the *holy one* and that in him all will become holy. *The righteous one* means that he is without any blemish and that he has the power to absolve and to condemn. His saying, *the one who has with him the keys of the house of David*, means that he has settled leadership and dominion on the house of David and the house of Jacob, as it is written.[112] On account of this, *When he opens no one can shut* refers to the power of the dominion of his divinity; when he justifies, no one can condemn, and when he passes judgment, no one can escape his hands. Furthermore, he knows what has come about previously and what has come to pass later.

His saying, *Before you I have set an open door, which no one can shut*, means the door of repentance that he has opened before us, which no creature can invalidate. His saying, *Your power is small*, means the weakness of humankind. He then praised him for keeping his word and for undergoing struggle for his name. For this reason, he said: *Behold, I have surrendered to you the synagogue of Satan, those who assert they are Jews but are liars.* He means that they profess they are keeping the tradition,[113] but they are in opposition to it, because they have not accepted the incarnation of the Lord.

As for his saying that he summons them to bow down before him,[114] it shows that the splendor of Christianity was increasing in those districts and that [the Christians'] power was becoming greater, so that the enemies

112. See Luke 1:32–33: "And the Lord will give to him the throne of his father David, and he will reign over the house of Jacob forever."

113. Ar. *sunnah* (way, path, mode of living). This term, however, took on a technical sense in Islam, meaning "the practices of the orthodox Islamic community," including the word and deeds of the prophet Muhammad as illustrated by the essential precepts of the Qur'ān: see I. Goldziher, *Muhammedanische Studien*, 2 vols. (Halle: Niemeyer, 1888–90), II.1–27.

114. See Revelation 3:9.

of the truth were becoming subject to their teachings, as they were keeping the commandments of his apostles. In addition, he praised him [i.e., the leader of the church], saying: *Because you have kept my word of patient endurance, I too shall protect you from the trial that shall befall everyone on earth.*[115] By this he made clear the magnitude of the hope, that he will protect those who keep God's commandment from trials and that he will give them a share in his kingdom.

His saying, *I will come soon*, means that we have but a short time left on this earth and that he will seek us out in death, both the good and the wicked.[116] Therefore, whoever keeps the talent he has and trades with it will gain and will be saved. But he who neglects this will lose the eternal gift forever.[117] His saying that he *will present the one who conquers as a pillar*, does not mean a pillar of stone. Rather, it is glory standing firm forever in the city of Jerusalem, which is prepared to be the kingdom to come. His statement, *my Lord*, is on account of the Incarnation, as has already been explained.[118] The *new* means that the old things[119] have passed away, and that everything has been made new through Christ. Glory be to him forever. Amen.

10. He said, (3:14) Write to the angel of the church of Laodicea: Thus says the Amen [or "the faithful one"],[120] the true witness, the beginning of God's creation.[121] (3:15) I know your works and that you are neither cold nor hot; (3:16) but you are lukewarm, neither hot nor cold.[122] (3:17) For you say, I am rich and I do not need anything. But you do not know that you are weak, wretched, poor, naked, and blind. (3:18) I counsel you to buy from me refined gold so that you may get rich with it, and to put on white garments so that the shame of your nakedness is not manifested, and to anoint your eyes with ointment so that you may see. (3:19) For I

115. See Revelation 3:10.

116. The phrase "the good and the wicked" (*al-ṣāliḥ wa-l-ṭāliḥ*) involves a rhyming play on words.

117. Matthew 25:14 (i.e., the Parable of the Talents).

118. See above (Vatican Arabic 459, f. 5r).

119. That is, the things of the old covenant.

120. The Greek and Coptic texts have: "the Amen." The Arabic has *al-amīn*, which could mean "the faithful." This would be a possible, although unusual, interpretation of the Greek *ho amen*.

121. Read *ra's* (beginning, head) for *ra'īs* (president, leader).

122. This verse is not given in full. The ending of the full verse is supplied in the Greek and Coptic versions: "I will spew you out of my mouth."

reprove and chastise those whom I love. So be zealous now and repent. (3:20) Behold, I am standing at the door and I am knocking. Whoever hears and opens the door for me, I shall enter with him into the banquet, and he with me. (3:21) Whoever conquers, I shall grant to him to sit with me on my throne, just as I conquered and sat with the Father on his throne. (3:22) He who has ears to hear, let him hear what the Spirit says to the churches.

He commanded the head of the church of Laodicea, saying: *Thus says the faithful, true witness.* This expression belongs exclusively to the Holy Trinity, because the Father is called the *true* one, as it is written: "That they might know you, the only true God."[123] And concerning himself, he says, "I am the truth, the resurrection, and the life."[124] And concerning the Holy Spirit, he says, "The Spirit of truth who proceeds from the Father."[125] Because of this, he has affirmed this meaning here as well.

His words, *the beginning*[126] *of God's creation*, concern the Incarnation, just as the apostle Paul says "that the Son might be the firstborn among many brothers."[127] For [the fact that he is] the only one[128] indicates there is no one like him. The *firstborn* indicates that there are other brothers after him. Therefore, in reality, he is "the only one" and he is equal to the Father in substance. He has become the firstborn, the head, and the giver of all good things. Even though he is the firstborn, he remains "the only one" of the Father, since he has the glory of God's eternal divinity.[129] Therefore, he said, *I know your works*, to signify that he knows all the works of humankind. His saying, *neither cold nor hot*, means that in [the head of the church] there is not "the chill of the nations"[130] due to loss of faith, but he also does not have the power of fervent faith by reason of good works. He let [this head] know that if there had been no hope left in him, he would have erased his name from the book of life.

123. John 17:3.
124. This quoted verse conflates John 11:25 and John 14:6.
125. John 15:26.
126. Read *ra's* (beginning, head) for *ra'īs* (president, leader).
127. Romans 8:29.
128. Ar. *al-waḥīd*.
129. Read *al-lāhūtiyyah* for *alāhūtiyyah*.
130. The meaning of this phrase is obscure. It may refer to communities (or to individuals) who have accepted Christ but remain nominal Christians. Perhaps Būlus al-Būshī uses this phrase as figure for "the Jews who claim they are Jews, but they are liars" (see Revelation 3:9).

When he says, *You say, I am rich and do not need anything*, it means that that [head] has forsaken the teaching and the search[131] for what is necessary for the salvation of souls. And *lukewarm of intention* concerns what is necessary and obligatory, so that the conduct of life is virtuous and suitable[132] to the name of Christianity. Then he informed him that he [i.e., the head] is in opposition to this, because he is satisfied with himself—that is, [he is satisfied] with neglect, thinking that it is perfection. Therefore, he said to him, *You are wretched, poor, blind, and naked.* These defects characterize the soul,[133] along with its various kinds of impoverishment in relation to God.[134] Thus he said, *I counsel you.* How merciful this is! See how this mercy is mingled with forgiveness and compassion. Indeed, his saying, *I counsel you*, is like a friend counseling his best friend concerning whatever would be for his own good. And what is this counsel? He said, [a counsel] that you *buy from me*, and from no one other than me.[135] But how does one *buy* except by having humility and by prayer? And what does he *buy*? He said, *refined gold.* Now, among the characteristics of refined gold is that it contains no impurity and that it is not dull, but it is a gold that is refined and made pure. By it he means virtuous works, works that are free from every hypocrisy, vainglory, and desire for worldly rewards. Instead, all his acts are virtuous for God's sake, so that he might inherit the richness of the kingdom of heaven, a kingdom that cannot be impoverished.

Then he said, *to put on white garments so that the shame of your nakedness is not manifested.* By this he means the purity of the soul and body in chastity, which is [to be] like God. As Paul, the chosen apostle, says: "You who have been baptized into Christ have put on Christ."[136] He said, *to anoint your eyes with ointment,*[137] *so that you may see.* He means the inner sight that the soul attains when it receives the ointment. This ointment is

131. Read *al-baḥth* (search) for *al-taḥt* (what is below).

132. Read *mulā'imah* in place of *mulāwamah.*

133. That is, only the spirit is subject to these infirmities, since it is the spirit, not the body, that has failed to accept God's word.

134. Ar. *anwā' faqrihā min Allāh*: see the printed edition of Būlus al-Būshī's *Commentary on the Apocalypse*, in *Majallat Marqus* 494 (May 2008), 11. In his critical edition, Edelby ("Le Commentaire," 40) reconstructs the text as *anwā' faqrihā min dhawāt illāh.*

135. This phrase does not appear in the text of Revelation quoted above (Vatican Arabic 459, f. 14r).

136. Galatians 3:27.

137. Read *dharūr* in place of *darūr.*

the word of God, which removes from the eye all the veils that result in the darkness of disobedience,[138] causing the soul to move along a crooked path, [and] to stumble and fall. Therefore, whoever receives this ointment will shine brightly in works of virtue and will sharpen his "mind's eye." His heart will be purified, and there will be fulfilled in him that which is written, "Blessed are the pure in heart, for they shall see God."[139]

Then he drew our mind to accept his work with joy and to receive his chastisement with a cheerful countenance because of the benefit. For he said, *I reprove and chastise those whom I love.* He means that a father reproves only his favorite son, so that he will be upright and will inherit whatever belongs to his father, so that he will not become estranged from him. He said, *Be zealous now, and repent.* He means: Be solicitous about [the fact of your] favored sonship, so that you may become God's son and a sharer in the inheritance.

He then informed us about the great effort he expends on our behalf and that he actually wants salvation for us more than we want it for ourselves. Thus he said, *Behold, I am standing at the door, and I am knocking. Whoever hears me and opens the door for me, I shall enter with him into the banquet, and he with me.* O lover of rightness, you see how he loves our race. His saying, *I am standing*, means that he is not neglecting us,[140] for he has handed himself over for everyone's sake. His *knocking* at the door means that he is always beating on our ears with instruction. This is his true word and what he spoke by the power of the Holy Spirit through his prophets and apostles. Therefore, whoever hears the life-giving words and opens his heart, Christ the Lord will abide in him, just as he said: "Whoever keeps my commandment, the Father and I will come and take him to our abode."[141] On this same subject, he also said in the Gospel, "Blessed are those who, when their master comes and knocks, open the door for him straightaway,"[142] and so forth.

By *banquet*, he means the kingdom that the Lord has prepared for those who keep his commandments. His saying, *to whoever conquers*, means the

138. Ar. *illātī tusabbib lahā ẓulmat al-maʿṣiyyah.* See the printed edition of Būlus al-Būshī's *Commentary on the Apocalypse*, in *Majallat Marqus* 494 (May 2008), 12; and Edelby, "Le Commentaire," 42.

139. Matthew 5:8.

140. Read *amrinā* in place of *amrikum.*

141. John 14:23.

142. This is a conflation of two verses: Luke 12:36 and 12:37.

conquering of sin by virtuous action. He said, *I shall grant to him to sit with me on my throne,* just as the apostle says, "If we endure, we shall reign with him."[143] He also said, "We shall enter when we pass beyond the curtain of the door, a place where Jesus previously entered in our stead[144] and became a high priest forever."[145] By this he means the Incarnation. Furthermore, the Lord (glory be to him) said, *As I conquered and sat with my Father on his throne.* This expression is spoken of the Incarnation with which he conquered Satan, crushed death, vanquished hell, opened paradise, prepared for us a path to the kingdom, and granted to us that, through his help, we too may conquer. Then he lifted the body that was falling into the abyss up to the highest heaven, "the heaven of heavens,"[146] above the angels and above the principalities and powers, and he put everything under his feet. Glory and homage be to him forever. Amen.

143. 2 Timothy 2:12.
144. Read *badalanā* in place of *badhalnā*.
145. See Hebrews 6:19–20.
146. See Deuteronomy 10:14; 1 Kings 8:27; and Psalm 148:4.

CHAPTER

5

IBN KĀTIB QAYṢAR, *COMMENTARY ON THE APOCALYPSE OF JOHN*, CH. 1–3

Translated by Stephen J. Davis and T. C. Schmidt

In the name of the Father and the Son and the Holy Spirit, one God, to whom be the glory. Amen.[1]

With the help and mercy of God (may he be exalted) we begin writing the commentary on this book that contains the vision of the apocalypse—unveiling its mysteries, deciphering its symbols, disclosing its cryptic

1. The text on which this translation is based was edited by Qummuṣ Armāniyūs Ḥabashī Shattā al-Birmāwī [= Birmāwī] (Cairo, 1939; repr. 1994), from Cairo Arabic 666 [= Coptic Patriarchate 243], dated 1335 CE, but transcribed from an earlier copy dated 1306; see also Georg Graf, *Geschichte der christlichen arabischen Literatur*, volume 2 (Vatican City: Biblioteca Apostolica Vaticana, 1947), 380–84. In our footnotes, we selectively make reference to variant readings in Par. Ar. 67 (thirteenth century CE), a manuscript containing the same work. According to Graf (vol. 2, 384), in this Paris manuscript, the beginning of the commentary by Ibn Kātib Qayṣar is missing and has been replaced by sections of commentary attributed to John Chrysostom, Hippolytus, and Būlus al-Būshī. Būlus al-Būshī's near contemporaneous *Commentary on the Apocalypse* survives independently and we will occasionally draw on it for comparison. In quoting from Būlus al-Būshī's text, we cite, where possible, Shawqi Talia's translation in this volume (which is based principally on Par. Ar. 459), but we will also make reference to a thirteenth-century manuscript in the Sbath collection (Sbath 1014) and to another copy of the work now preserved in London at the British Library (Or. 1329, dated 1671 CE; originally British Museum Arabic Supp. MS 16), as well as to the recent critical edition by Nagi Edelby ("Commentaire"). Stephen Davis would like to thank Father Samir Khalil Samir and Nagi Edelby for allowing him to acquire a photocopy of the Sbath text during a January 2005 visit to the Centre de documentation et de recherches arabes chrétiennes (CEDRAC) at the Université Saint-Joseph in Beirut. He would also like to thank the staff at the British Library for allowing him access to their collection for a week of research in August 2006. Finally, the translators would like to thank Shawqi Talia and Mark Swanson for their helpful feedback during the penultimate stage of revisions to this translation.

aspects, and reporting the interpretation of its meanings—from what the honored pilgrim,[2] the most excellent leader, the teacher known as Ibn Kātib Qayṣar (may God rest his soul), was concerned to report and what he disclosed to his students.[3]

Chapter One (1:1–20)

1. (1:1) The revelatory vision[4] of Jesus Christ that God gave to him who taught his servants about what must come to pass quickly and who gave a sign to them and sent it by way of his angel, his servant John,[5] (1:2) the one who testified regarding the word of God and the witness of Jesus Christ that he beheld.

This section is the title heading of the book and is translated from it. A *revelatory vision* is one species of prophecy belonging to the givers of the law. Even if the word is synonymous with [the word] "dream" in literal terms, from the classification of prophecy the difference between revelatory vision and dream becomes clear. Let us mention the definition of prophecy first. We say: Prophecy is a divine superabundance[6] mediated

2. In an Islamic context, the honorific noun *al-ḥājj* designates one who has performed the pilgrimage to Mecca. In Christian circles, it sometimes could be used to refer to those who had visited Jerusalem and the Holy Land.

3. The incipit and opening section of Par. Ar. 67 attribute the work not to Ibn Kātib Qayṣar but to John Chrysostom (f. 2v, lines 5 and 8). At the first of these attributions (f. 2v, line 5), however, the name of John Chrysostom is crossed out and "Hippolytus, the Pope of Rome" (*Inqūlīdus/Bābā Rūmiyah*) is written in the margin. The second attribution to John Chrysostom is preserved without alteration.

4. The Arabic word translated as "revelatory vision" is *ru'yā*. Occasionally, we will also simply translate it as either "revelation" or "vision."

5. While the original Greek text of Revelation 1:1 identifies the angel as the divine messenger who mediates the divine vision to its recipient John, the Arabic text that Ibn Kātib Qayṣar quotes conflates these two figures, identifying the term "angel" as referring to John himself. The reason for this divergence relates to a point of confusion in the Arabic translation from the Bohairic Coptic version on which the translator relied. The end of the verse in Bohairic reads ⲉⲁϥⲧⲁⲟⲩⲱⲟⲩ ⲉⲃⲟⲗ ϩⲓⲧⲟⲧϥ ⲙ̄ⲡⲉϥⲁⲅⲅⲉⲗⲟⲥ ⲙ̄ⲡⲉϥⲃⲱⲕ ⲓⲱⲁⲛⲛⲏⲥ; "having sent them through his angel to his servant John." However, instead of distinguishing between the respective functions of the two ⲙ-prefixes (i.e., "through his angel" and "to his servant John"), the Arabic translator has read the prefixes in parallel as markers of two nouns in apposition (i.e., "by way of his angel, his servant John"). For the Bohairic text, see G. Horner, *CoptNT-North*, IV.444. This verse is not present in the Sahidic version edited by Horner (*CoptNT-South*, VII.258), where the extant text begins with the last word of Revelation 1:3.

6. The word *fayḍ* (superabundance) can also mean "flood" or "inundation." This term would have resonated strongly with Ibn Kātib Qayṣar's Egyptian readership, who would have

through the active intellect to the rational soul, and then through it to the power of imagination.[7]

Prophecy takes place if it occurs in the condition of sleep, by means of a dream. This is the first and weakest species of prophecy, like the dream of Pharaoh that Joseph interpreted for him,[8] and the dream of Nebuchadnezzar that Daniel interpreted for him in Babylon,[9] or like the dream of Jacob and Joseph,[10] and like the dream of Laban and Abimalech,[11] and some of the prophecy of Daniel. Indeed, [the category of] dream unites all of these [examples], even if there are differences between them with respect to other considerations.

But as for that which takes place in the condition of wakefulness, even if it occurs in [a state of] dozing,[12] it is said to be a *revelatory vision*. The vision[13] of prophecy is described as sight, (a condition of) being lost in thought, and inspiration, as well as God's speaking, God's hand, and other things as well. This species is more powerful than the first, like the vision of our father Abraham at the time of the division and settlement of the animals, because the text said, "[A state of] dozing, fear, and the darkness of his fainting fell upon Abraham at the setting of the sun."[14] It is also like the vision of Isaiah, Hosea, Obadiah, and others, and like some of the prophecy of Daniel.

As for that which it is not accompanied by [a state of] dozing, it is a [divine] manifestation and a message,[15] and it is the utmost extent of the levels attained by humankind, like the message of God to Adam,[16] to

---

been intimately familiar with the seasonal flooding of the Nile and its life-giving effect on the agricultural cycles of planting and harvest.

7. This conception of prophecy as "a divine superabundance mediated through the active intellect to the rational soul" draws on the philosophy of Ibn Sīnā. For a brief discussion and bibliography, see Chapter 2, note 19.

8. Genesis 14:25–32.

9. Daniel 2:31–45.

10. Genesis 28:10–22 and 37:5–11.

11. Genesis 20:3–7.

12. The word used here, *subāt*, refers to a condition of lethargy or light rest, which the author differentiates from deep sleep (*nawm*).

13. Here, the cognate form *mar'ā* is used as a synonym for *ru'yā*.

14. Genesis 15:12.

15. Arabic, *al-tajallī wa-l-khiṭāb*. The first term, *al-tajallī*, functions as a close synonym for *al-ru'yā* (apocalypse, revelation).

16. Genesis 9:2.

Abraham at his calling,[17] to Moses in Sinai,[18] and some of the prophecy of Daniel when he was on the bank of the Euphrates.

With regard to *revelatory vision*, there are other distinctions, for which this is not the place [to elaborate]; but the distinction between dream, *vision*, and manifestation has already been made clear to you. The use of this term in a genitive construction with Jesus Christ [i.e., "the revelatory vision *of* Jesus Christ"] is a genitive of specification—that is to say, as for this *superabundance* that was given to Jesus Christ (to him be the glory), he himself *taught his servants* by means of it. His statement, *gave*, is only correct with regard to his being a human, and it describes the connection of the vision to Jesus Christ. Finally, by *his servants* here it means his apostles.

As for his statement, *what must come to pass*—that is, in the future time—by means of it we refute whoever thinks that this revelatory vision is a report of past events that already took place and passed by. The word *must*—in other words, it is necessary—connotes a necessity on account of what divine knowledge has disclosed. The word *quickly* does not mean that the events come into existence all at once, but rather it means that their beginning comes to pass quickly and that each will follow the other until the end. The phrase, *he gave a sign*, means that he warned by means of signs. [This was] not about a fixed time, for humankind is not informed about the times for the most part since [humankind] is subject to the influence of whoever becomes preoccupied with the times even to the extent of [teaching] lying pretenses and heresies, as if it were said: "The prophet so-and-so comes on such-and-such a day or such-and-such a month." If this becomes known, some person could come and claim that he is that prophet in question, in any region that tallies [with the prophecy]. And if it were said, "Such-and-such a king dies on the first day of a certain year," claimants get excited on all sides, and other people claim that this happened by means of their machinations.

On the whole, most aims have come to naught and most strategems have gone astray. All matters related to acts of building, planting, and [other] activities pass away. And you find our Lord saying, "But as for knowledge of the day and the hour, the Father has brought it under his own authority. The angels of heaven are not acquainted with it."[19] And the apostle

17. Genesis 12:1.
18. Exodus 19 and 20.
19. Matthew 24:36.

Paul says, "But as for the times and the seasons, my brothers, I have no need to write to you about them."[20]

As for its statement, he *sent it by way of his angel, his servant John*, the *it* in the phrase *he sent it* refers back to the things that had to *come to pass quickly*. This is made clear from the order of the Coptic language.

The naming of John as an *angel* follows the custom of the Bible in naming all the prophets and apostles and priests as angels, for various reasons, including the fact that the term *malāk* in Hebrew means apostle [i.e., messenger, *rasūl*]. This is also on account of the fact that abstinence, the renunciation of bodily desires, contemplation of God (may he be exalted), and an abundance of knowledge—these four attributes—are common to the angel, the apostle, the prophet, and the priest. Dionysius adds a fifth virtue: namely, participation in the priesthood. This is [also] on account of the fact that all of them are prepared for God's service and the benefits of his servants. John the Baptist was called an *angel* even while he is priest, prophet, and apostle. About him it is said, "Behold, I am sending my angel [i.e., messenger] before you."[21]

Now as for his statement, *and the witness of Jesus Christ that he beheld*, it means that he testified to the word of God and testified to [Jesus Christ's] *witness that he beheld*.[22] The implied direct object of the verb *beheld* refers back to the witness of Jesus Christ, and the pronoun subject of the verb pertains to John, because he was with our Lord when he gave his good witness before Pilate.

2. (1:3) Blessed are those who read and those who hear the words of this prophecy and keep what is written in it because the time has come near.

The word *blessed* [*ṭūbā*] comes from a Syriac term that means "happiness," and to *keep* this prophecy means to be warned by it and to act in accordance with it. *What is written in it* means its meanings. As for the *time*, it is defined as the scope of movement with respect to what comes before and what comes later. On this subject, it is also said that the domain in which the movement [of time] is concealed has three divisions—the past, the present, and the future—and its components are fixed. Either [they are] the movements of heaven, which are four in number—the hour,

20. 1 Thessalonians 5:1.

21. Mark 1:2; see also Malachi 3:1.

22. The words for "testified" and "witness" come from the same root in Arabic (*shahida*).

the day, the month, and the year (the hour is part of the subdivision of the day into twenty-four parts; the day is from the rise of the sun until its setting; the month is one complete cycle of the moon; the solar year is one complete revolution of the sun)—or [they are] the annual conditions, which are the seasons, like the times of heat and the times of cold and the times of dryness and the times of wetness.

Among them are components that are not fixed, such as great events that occur in them, like the rise of a nation or the appearance of a religion, the occurrence of economic inflation, an epidemic, a war, or a heavenly sign, such as a flood, a great bolt of lightning, a widespread earthquake, a fire, or things similar to that. Here the text means a *time* during which the occurence of this prophecy begins, as well as its fulfillment—that this time will be fixed in advance. This will become clear [later] in its proper place.

3. **(1:4) From John to the seven churches in Asia, grace to you and peace from the one who is and who was and who is to come and from the seven spirits who are before the throne, (1:5) and from Jesus Christ, the faithful witness, the firstborn of the dead, and the ruler of all the kings of the earth, the one who loved us and purified us from our sins through his blood, (1:6) and who made us a kingdom and a priesthood to God his Father, to whom be the glory and the power, for ever and ever. Amen.**

This section is the first thing that the apostle wrote to the seven churches, which were from the regions of Asia Minor. These places belonged to his [episcopal] seat, in which he proclaimed the gospel along with his disciples, the bishops of these churches, for he was commanded in [the spirit of] inspiration to write to them concerning what his report[23] presents in detail. He prefaced what he wrote with this statement, just as he wrote in his letters and just like the custom of the rest of the apostles.

His statement, *the one who is and who was and who is to come*, has divided these three conditions according to the division of time—the past, the present, and the future. The meaning is that God (may he be exalted) is established eternally. He does not undergo alteration or change in all the conditions of time, because he (may he be greatly magnified) is beyond "when" and "where" and all other contingent states [i.e., "accidents"]. As

23. Ibn Kātib Qayṣar uses the Arabic term *bayān* here to refer to John's revelatory message, a usage probably conditioned by his Islamic cultural context, where Qur'ānic scripture was often referred to by Muslims as *al-bayān*.

for *the seven spirits before the throne*, they are the spirits who swim [between heaven and earth] and become manifest through their mediation of commands and prohibitions from the Most High in [carrying out] the business of nations and other entities. They come and go between [the realms of] being and corruption, just as was mentioned in the book of Daniel the prophet. Some of their names were designated in the books of the prophets in the Old Testament, but also in the New Testament: They are Michael [*Mikhā'īl*], Gabriel [*Ghubriyāl*], Raphael [*Rūfā'īl*], Suriel [*Sūriyāl*], Sedakiel [*Sādākiyāl*], Sarathiel [*Sārātiyāl*], and Ananiel [*Amāniyāl*].

Another point: namely, that the ranks are nine in number. Among them are the two ranks of the cherubim and the seraphim. Seven ranks remain, and they are the principalities, authorities, thrones, lords, powers, angels, and archangels. The heads of these seven ranks may signal the rest. As for his mentioning these seven spirits before mentioning Jesus Christ, this does not indicate a ranking. Rather, the mention of Jesus Christ is followed by much speech concerning him. If the mention of the spirits had followed it, then its signification would have been at a remove [from the rest] and its unity [of expression] would have been broken up.[24]

Now, as for the word *witness* [*shahīd*], its form is that of an active participle. On this subject, you say: He witnessed, he witnesses, [an act of] witnessing, and he is a *witness*. The word *witness* is said to have two meanings. The first of them is related to the act of witnessing purely by speech. The second is a more special case: It is the act of witnessing with the shedding of the witness's [i.e., martyr's] blood on account of that witness.[25] What is intended here is the more special connotation.

The word *amen* has three meanings in the Coptic language. The first is from the word "trustworthiness" [*al-amānah*]. The second is from the world "faith" [*al-īmān*]. The third is "the eunuch" [*al-khaṣī*]. This is the case in the Coptic language on the basis of what the most excellent Bashīr Ibn Sirrī mentioned in his commentary on the prophecy of Daniel.

As for his statement, *firstborn of the dead*, it is made because he was the first who rose from the dead in a resurrection that was not followed by death. On account of this priority, he became a *firstborn*, just like the

24. In contrast to Ibn Kātib Qayṣar's more elaborate angelological interpretation of the *seven spirits*, Būlus al-Būshī (Sbath 1014, f. 2v) simply interprets them as signifying the seven rites (or sacraments) of the church.

25. In Arabic, the word *shahīd* can mean either "witness" (in a general sense) or "martyr" (when used in special contexts).

priority of the physical birth that belongs to the firstborn child. His *rulership over all the kings of the earth*, is the rulership of a master over his servant, whether the servant wills it or rejects it.

As for the phrase, *the one who loved us and purified us from our sins through his blood*, he made clear the proof of his love by means of what he says in the Gospel: "What love is greater than this, that a person gives himself up for his loved ones?"[26] As for his purification of us from our sins, it has three aspects. The first is the one that is mentioned—his purification of us through his blood—and this is more excellent than the blood of animals, which used to purify sins through the shedding of their blood. The second is through baptism. The third is through his act of elucidating a way, the observance of which preserves us from error.

After that comes his statement that he *made us a kingdom and a priesthood*, like the word of the Torah in the second chapter of the second book belonging to the children of Israel: "You are for me a kingdom, a priesthood, and a people."[27] The kingdom is for the execution of his command with regard to things that benefit and things that cause harm, as when Peter passed judgment on Ananias and his wife,[28] and when he healed the crippled man with a word,[29] or when Paul healed the other blind man with a word,[30] and when he raised a dead man who had fallen from the roof with a word.[31] As for his *priesthood*, that is clear, and likewise the rest of the section.

4. (1:7) Behold, he is coming with the clouds, and all eyes will see him, and those who pierced him, and all the tribes of the earth will truly see him.[32]

26. John 15:13.
27. Exodus 19:6.
28. Acts 5:1–10.
29. Acts 9:32–35.
30. This is probably a reference to the apostle Paul's healing of Hermippus in Myra in one episode of the noncanonical *Acts of Paul*: "But they and Paul [prayed] to God. And when Hermippus recoverd [*sic*] his sight, he turned to his mother Nympha, saying to her: 'Paul came and laid his hand upon me while I wept. And in that hour I saw all things clearly'" (ed. Carl Schmidt, *Acta Pauli aus der Heidelberger koptischen Papyrushandschrift Nr. 1*, rev. ed. [Leipzig: J. C. Hinrichs, 1905; repr. 1965], 34; trans. W. Schneemelcher, in *New Testament Apocrypha*, rev. ed., vol. 2 [Cambridge: James Clarke & Co.; Louisville: Westminster/John Knox Press, 1992], 249).
31. Acts 20:9–12.
32. Here, the repetition of the verb "see" follows the Bohairic Coptic version (Horner, *CoptNT-North*, 4.446–47). In Greek and Sahidic Coptic (Horner, *CoptNT-North*, 7.258–59), the tribes of the earth are said to "wail" or "lament."

Thus he said in his holy gospel, "Then you will see the Son of Man coming at that time on the clouds of heaven along with powers and great glory. Then all the tribes of the earth will mourn."[33] And the prophet says, "Those who pierced him will see him."[34]

5. (1:8) I am the Alpha and I am the Omega, the beginning and the end, says the Lord God, the one who is and who was and who is to come, the Pantocrator [i.e., "Ruler of All"].

In this section, with respect to what precedes, what comes after, and his decree, the Lord God says, *I am the Alpha and I am the Omega*. He is the first and the last, by way of analogy, for the purpose of making this understood. Just as the alpha is the first Greek letter and the omega is the last, so too God (may he be praised and exalted) is the first and last of all existing things. As for the title, *ruler of all*, he is the one who upholds the existence of every reality, even though he is [also] the original cause of its being. The link between this section and what comes before is at the point when [John] says, *all the tribes of the earth will see him*. It declares that he is the beginning and the end.

6. (1:9) I am John, your brother and close relation[35] in hardships. Indeed, sovereignty and patient endurance come through Jesus.[36]

The message of the apostle here is directed toward the leaders of the seven churches who will be specially mentioned, even if this also applied to the people belonging to this generation of believers generally. The participation of the apostle along with them made it like the kinship relationship of a community to its *brother*. The comparison is just as it is said, "This one is the brother of that one," or "This one is the *comrade*[37] of that one," if the two have agreed on one thing. As for his intention with respect to *sovereignty*, he has assumed leadership, just as he himself explained. As for *patience*, [it is] endurance in the midst of hardships on account of faith. It

33. Matthew 24:30.

34. Zechariah 12:10.

35. Arabic, *qarīb*.

36. I read *bi Yasū'* ([come] through Jesus) here instead of simply *Yasū'* ([are] Jesus), since the former is repeated elsewhere in the commentary. In the printed edition, the preposition *bi-* has been mistakenly omitted.

37. The Arabic term used here, *qarīn* (companion, comrade), differs from the word used in the biblical text above, *qarīb* (close relation). This divergence is probably due to the fact that, sometime in the manuscript tradition, the letter *nūn* has been mistakenly substituted for the letter *bā'*, or vice versa.

is known that these two would not have been complete except through divine providence, and for this reason it says that these two things *come through Jesus.*

7. (1:9 cont.) I was on the island called Patmos [*Batmū*] on account of the word of God and the witness of Jesus Christ.

He apocopated the term *Patmos* [*Batmus*], except in the case of direct address,[38] for the purpose of abbreviation. He said *Patmos* [*Batmū*], and that form is used in the Greek and Coptic languages. He indicated the place where he saw the revelatory vision—namely, the above-mentioned island. He also indicated the reason he was exiled to the island when he says, *on account of the word of God*—that is, because after nine years of the kingdom of the emperor Domitian, on account of his preaching of the gospel, [the emperor] exiled him to this island where he recorded this vision in writing. By that means he made clear to his addressees that he had fallen into hardships just like them and had shared their lot.

His statement, *the witness of Jesus Christ,* means *on account of the word of God* (which is the good news) and *on account of* my [i.e., John's] *witness* to *Jesus Christ,* the expected one. He put *witness* in a genitive relation to *Jesus* because the verbal noun is sometimes placed in a genitive relation to its subject, as we say, "This is the work of so-and-so," but at other times it is put in a genitive relation to its object, as we say, "The wound of so-and-so was healed." This latter sense is what is intended here.

8. (1:10) I was in the spirit on that Sunday, and behind me I heard a loud voice like a trumpet (1:11) saying to me, "Whatever things you see, write them down in a book and send them to the seven churches that are in Asia—Ephesus, Smyrna, Pergamum, Thyatira, Sardis, Philadelphia, and Laodicea." (1:12) I turned and discerned the voice that I had heard speaking with me, and when I turned I saw seven lampstands made of gold, (1:13) and in the midst of the lampstands there was someone resembling the Son of Man, and upon him was armor, and tied around his loins was a golden belt. (1:14) His head and his hair were white like wool and snow, and his eyes were like a blaze of fire. (1:15) His legs were like the copper of Lebanon,[39] smelted in fire, and his voice was like many

38. Literally, "in the place of the vocative case."

39. The wording of this verse in the Arabic version quoted by Ibn Kātib Qayṣar differs from that of both the Greek and Coptic texts due to a misreading of the Greek word χαλκολιβάνον ("fine or glowing brass"). This word was also used in the Bohairic Coptic text upon which the Arabic translation was based: see Horner, *CoptNT-North*, 4.449. The Sahidic

waters. (1:16) He had seven stars in his right hand, and a sword that strikes on two faces[40] came out of his mouth, and his face shone like the sun in its power.

This is the beginning of the first revelatory vision, and it is the vision of the Son. His statement, *in the spirit*, means [that he was] in a condition of freedom from the body, such that his spirit united with the Holy Spirit, becoming wholly immersed [in the Spirit] so as to receive inspiration. This was his condition for the revelatory vision.

As for his statement, *on that Sunday*, what is the benefit of his specifying the day and not mentioning which month or year it belonged to? I think that his statement, *that Sunday*, refers to a Sunday known to the addressees at that time. [This was] on account of the proximity of the time of his writing to them. He announced the *Sunday* on which the revelatory vision took place, but he took their knowledge for granted, and neglected to specify [the time frame] for us. Thus, in this matter, we derive no great benefit.

A single term in the Coptic language is used both for the "day," meaning the sum of the day[time] and the night[time], and for the "day[time]" particularly. For this reason, there was no differentiation in [that term] as to whether this revelatory vision applied to one or the other. The Greek account indicates that it occurred during the day[time]. As for his hearing *behind* him *a loud voice like a trumpet*, the voices in the revelatory vision came from a number of directions, so let us mention them according to the method of classification for the purpose of clarification. Let us say then: [the word] *voice* has three [mental] images.[41]

---

text translates the Greek as ⲟⲩϩⲟⲙⲛⲧ ⲛⲃⲁⲣⲱⲧ ("bronze copper"): see Horner, *CoptNT-South*, 7.264. In his commentary on Revelation 1:15, Ibn Kātib Qayṣar mistakenly takes the noun as two words (according to its two component parts), χαλκο (~ Gr. χαλκός; "bronze") and λιβανον (read by the author as an adjective meaning "Lebanese"). Compare to Būlus al-Būshī's quotation of the biblical text in Sbath 1014, f. 3r: "His legs were like flashing copper, as if smelted in a furnace."

40. Lit., "a sword that strikes with two mouths." The Arabic text of Revelation 1:16 quoted by Ibn Kātib Qayṣar follows the Bohairic, which reads ⲟⲩⲥⲏϥⲓ ⲉⲥϩⲓⲟⲩⲓ ⲛ̄ⲣⲟ ⲃ̄ ("a sword striking with two mouths" [Horner, *CoptNT-North* IV.450]). By contrast, the Sahidic text reads ⲉⲣⲉ ⲟⲩⲥⲏϥⲉ ⲛⲏⲩ ⲉⲃⲟⲗ ϩⲛ̄ ⲣⲱϥ ⲉⲥⲧⲏⲙ ⲙ̄ⲡϩⲟ ⲥⲛⲁⲩ ("with a sword that was sharp on its two faces coming out of his mouth"; Horner, *CoptNT-South*, 7.264–66). My intention in using the word "face" in my translation is not to bring the Arabic text into conformity with the Sahidic (on which the Arabic does not directly depend); rather, it represents an attempt to render the phrase more fluidly in English, while still retaining enough of the original dynamic of Ibn Kātib Qayṣar's Arabic phrasing so as to make his comments on word choice intelligible.

41. Ar. *ṣūrah* (pl. *ṣuwar*).

[In the case of the first image,] either it is a voice of speech from which there is understood to be a certain intended meaning, as [John] says in the twenty-third section: "I saw a powerful angel repeating in a loud voice, saying, 'Who is worthy to open the book.'"[42] Or it is a plain voice, as he says in the nineteenth section: "Bursting forth from the throne were bolts of lighting and voices."[43] From these voices, nothing is understood apart from their extent.

The second image is in accordance with the voice that is voiced. On the one hand, the one producing the voice is known, and thus it is not out of the question then that [the vocalizer] is an angel, as [John] says in the twenty-third section, "I saw a powerful angel repeating in a loud voice,"[44] and as he says in the twenty-fourth section, "I heard the voice of many angels."[45] Or, if the voice is not that of an angel, then it is that of a human, as he says in the twenty-ninth section on the souls of the martyrs, "They cried out with a loud voice, saying . . . etc.,"[46] or that of an animal, as he says in the forty-third section, "I heard an eagle in the midst of heaven crying out and saying in a loud voice,"[47] or that of an inanimate being, as he says in the fifty-first section, "seven peals of thunder screamed,"[48] and in the one hundredth section, "like the voice of many waters and like the voice of powerful thunderclaps."[49] On the other hand, perhaps the one producing the voice may not be known, as he says in the forty-eighth section, "I heard a voice from the horns of the golden altar,"[50] and as he says in the fifty-first section, "I heard a voice from heaven saying to me, 'Seal it.'"[51]

The third image is in accordance with the source of the voice. For either the source of the voice is known, as when he says in the fifty-second section, "The voice that I heard from heaven,"[52] or it is not known, as when he says

42. Revelation 5:2. The section references indicated by Ibn Kātib Qayṣar here and elsewhere are consistent with the textual divisions found in Birmāwī's edition, unless otherwise noted.
43. Revelation 4:5.
44. Revelation 5:2.
45. Revelation 5:11.
46. Revelation 6:9–10.
47. Revelation 8:13.
48. Revelation 10:3.
49. Revelation 14:2.
50. Revelation 9:13.
51. Revelation 10:4.
52. Revelation 10:8.

in this section, *I heard behind me a loud voice like a trumpet, saying to me, Whatever things you hear, write them down.*[53]

These are the classifications of voices. The intended referent for all of them in the revelatory vision is [a person's] discernment of the things heard, and the relation of what is heard to the intellect is like the relation of spoken voices to [the sense of] hearing. If you have come to know this foundational principle, then [you will understand that] hearing therefore is not enabled by the sensory perception of the ear (for its senses are idle and its operations are static); rather, it is [enabled by] the soul's discernment belonging to [its] rational faculties. The voice is not the sound of a trumpet,[54] but rather it says, *like a trumpet.* Something similar to a thing is not the thing itself; but rather a terrifying voice is like the terrifying sound of the great trumpet of war. In the same way, it is reported with regard to the episode at Sinai that when Moses came down from the mountain to the people, "on the morning of the third day, thunder, lightning, and thick clouds came over the mountain, and there was the sound of a very loud trumpet."[55]

When he says, *I heard behind me*, it gives notice that the matter was hidden from him, since it is customary that what is behind a person is hidden from him. Now, when he says, *whatever things you see, write them down*, the pronouns that are used in this [sentence]—along with whatever is similar in what follows—are plural pronouns referring to things that are not endowed with reason. They are not feminine pronouns. In the Arabic language, they have a single form, which is used in common for both,[56] but in Coptic there is a difference between the two [usages]. It is as if the implicit meaning of the statement in Arabic is: *The things that you see, write them down.*[57]

As for the statement, *write them down in a book and send them to the seven churches that are in Asia*, it is known that the apostle in this situation did not have command over [his] sensory perception or [his] movement, apart from

53. Revelation 1:11.

54. In Arabic, the meanings of "voice" and "sound" are conveyed by the same word (*al-ṣawt*).

55. Exodus 19:16.

56. In Arabic, the feminine singular form is used for adjectives and pronouns modifying or referring to impersonal plural nouns (e.g., "inanimate objects"). Here, the pronominal suffix *-hā* is used in reference to both feminine singular nouns and impersonal plural nouns.

57. Here the author adds a definite noun (*al-ashyā'*; "the things") to the relative pronoun (*illatī*; "that") to emphasize his point that what is being referred to is a group of things (an impersonal plural).

the act of writing. Rather a languor took command of him. The implicit meaning of the statement is: "When your hearing and vision come to an end, write about it afterward to the churches and send it to them."

The thing that the apostle wrote has two possible senses. One of them is that he was writing to each church about whatever matters that specially concerned it. The other is that he wrote the entire revelatory vision to each church, so that its leader and people would pay attention to what specially concerned them in it and would observe everything that the revelation made clear to them. This is the more appropriate understanding, unless it was incumbent upon him not to write the greater part of the revelation to each of the seven churches originally because that which specially concerned each church might have led [them] astray from the revelatory vision [as a whole]. By specifying the names of the seven cities where the seven churches were found (even though they were well-known cities), he invalidated the opinion of anyone who believed that his intended audience was a single church.

As for his statement, *I turned and discerned the voice*, the term ⲛⲁⲩ [Copt. *nau*, "to see"] in the Coptic language holds in common the vision of the eye and the discernment of the intellect.[58] In the same way, the term also holds in common these two senses in the Greek and Syriac languages. For this reason, some translators have erred in writing down one meaning in place of the other, with the result that one sense has been translated apart from the other. [In this case, we are to understand,] "I had the voice in view," and thus *I discerned the voice*, but the voice is not seen [in a literal sense]. Now then, it was necessary after he said, *I discerned the voice*, for him to say, *the one whom I heard speaking with me*. This was so that no one might imagine that it was the voice of someone other than him. For along with the clarifications and confirmations found in the divine books, there occur a great many analogies, especially for whoever does not have penetrating insight into such things.

As for his saying, *when I turned I saw seven lampstands made of gold*, and what follows up to the end of the section, it may be explained as follows:

58. Here, the author refers to the Bohairic Coptic text of Revelation 1:12, which reads ⲁⲓⲫⲟⲛϩⲧ ⲁⲓⲛⲁⲩ ⲉϯⲥⲙⲏ (lit., "I turned myself and saw that voice"; Horner, *CopticNT-North*, 4.448–49), commenting on the peculiar use of the verb "to see" in relation to the discernment of a voice. In contrast, the Arabic text uses the verb, *adraka*, which means "to perceive or discern." He reconciles the Coptic usage by explaining that the verb ⲛⲁⲩ conveys both the literal or tangible act of seeing and the intellectual act of discerning with the mind.

The prophets, just as they used to utter terms and not intend literal meanings but rather other things in what is called the spiritual language, likewise saw and spoke about forms and images, whose purpose was not the visible things but rather something else in their midst. Between them [i.e., the literal and the spiritual] there is a certain correspondence. These things are called enigmas and symbols concerning what you will come to know. They [i.e., the prophets] use images and meanings figuratively, just as they use [verbal] expressions figuratively. If you have knowledge of this, then the expressions in this section become clear, except that the images and meanings that are concealed[59] in them, and thus are enigmas, just as we have said.

The seven lampstands symbolize the seven aforementioned churches, just as our Lord interprets them later on [in Revelation]. The fact that they are made of gold symbolizes five meanings.[60] The first of them is justice; the second, honor; the third, purity; the fourth, eternal life; and the fifth, endurance in times of testing and trial. For gold is the most uniform substance to the touch: the noblest, the purest, the most lasting, the most durable. By the lampstand he symbolized that Zechariah the son of Berechiah saw in his prophecy that it, along with whatever accompanied it, was the word of God in Zerubbabel.[61] But this is not what is intended here.

As for *the Son of Man*, the allusion is to Christ our Lord (to him be the glory), with respect to his humanity. And *the armor*[62] and *the golden belt* symbolize his rule, because they are its emblems. Our Lord (to him be the glory) has said, "I have been given every authority in heaven and on earth."[63] The fact that *his head and his hair were white like wool and snow* symbolizes the divinity united with the humanity of Christ our Lord, even though in the revelatory vision of Daniel, he had symbolized by it [the Lord's] eternity and infinite pre-existence, since white hair is proof of age.

The fact that *his eyes were like a blaze of fire* symbolizes two meanings. The first of them is the power of his penetrating knowledge, because knowledge acquired by the sense of sight is more powerful than knowledge acquired by the other senses. The two eyes on the horn in the vision of

59. Reading *kāminah* for *al-kāminah* (Birmāwī, 46).

60. Birmāwī (p. 46) mistakenly has "seven meanings" here, but Par. Ar. 67 (f. 13r) has the correct reading enumerating five.

61. Zechariah 4:1–7.

62. Read *dirʿ* in place of *dūʿ* (Birmāwī, 47).

63. Matthew 28:18.

Daniel have been interpreted like this,[64] and so too the many eyes on the four creatures,[65] as well as the seven eyes on the stone in the prophecy of Zechariah.[66] That angel [in Zechariah] explained that it was the stone of distinction. The second concept is the fact that he inspires fear, as evidenced by what happened to the apostle and to others among the prophets upon seeing such sights out of fear and terror.

The fact that *his legs were like copper smelted in a furnace*[67] symbolizes that it is something difficult to comprehend, because the rays of flashing *copper* make it impossible for it to be looked at. Its placement [i.e., the placement of the word *bronze*] in a genitive construction with *Lebanon* is on account of the excellence of the metals belonging to that place and the purity of their substance above anything else from [other] places. The fact that it is *smelted* is on account of the high degree of its purity from polluting elements—that is, from defects—and its remaining unsullied by rust and corrosion that would corrupt its material substance. The fact that the *belt* was in the middle, between the higher part and the lower part [of his body], symbolizes two insights, one higher than the other. His *armor* did not cover his *legs* because, since had it covered them, it would not have become clear that they were *like bronze*. This is another insight.

Thus, we have arrived at four insights, if we consider them [one at a time], beginning with one insight and proceeding to the one highter than it. The first of them is the following: namely, the reference to his legs, which were like *bronze*. That symbolizes his humanity in the spiritual condition it had after the resurrection—refined, able to pass through things, unimpeded by dense bodies of matter, just as when he entered the room of the apostles with the doors locked, and anything else included among the divine lights[68] that prevents full understanding.

The second insight, which is higher than that one, is the thing we observed about what is connected to the *belt*: It symbolizes the human

64. Daniel 8:5.

65. Revelation 4:6–11.

66. Zechariah 3:9.

67. The wording of Revelation 1:15 as cited here differs from the verse quoted above: *al-Lubnān* ("of Lebanon" in the genitive construction) is omitted, and the word *qamīn* (a furnace) is substituted for *al-nār* (fire). Because of these differences, the Arabic text quoted here in fact conforms more closely to the Greek and Coptic versions on which it is based.

68. This usage of the Arabic term *nūr* (pl. *anwār*) to refer to revelatory acts that manifest divine guidance corresponds to its usage in the Qur'ān (Lane, *Lexicon*, vol. 8, 2865).

intellect. For this reason, it signaled two insights, and they are the second and the third. Both [insights] are concealed in the *armor*, on account of the fact that they are higher than the first. The fourth insight is the highest of all. It is what we observed about his head and his hair. It symbolizes his great divinity united with his humanity, as we have said. Just as the head is higher than the body and is united to it, so too in this case. It is precisely the following insight: the face that is like the sun in its power.

Now as for his statement, *his voice was like many waters*, this also symbolizes that he is terrifying, because the sound of the sea inspires fear. For this reason, the Gospel says in its concluding chapter, "Many souls came out due to the sound of the sea."[69] As for his statement, *seven stars in his right hand*, he means by *stars* the angels of the seven churches,[70] as he elucidated in the [quoted] section. You have learned about his calling a priest an angel: His intended referent is the leaders of the churches. The fact that the *stars* are *in his hand* symbolizes that they are in obedience to him and are under his command, just like something in his grasp.

As for his statement, *a sword that strikes on two faces*[71] *came out of his mouth*, the *sword* symbolizes his destructive power, and the act of *striking* symbolizes his piercing sharpness. Regarding the fact that it has *two faces*, the *face* of the sword is its edge, and it symbolizes the doubling of its sharpness and strength. The fact that [the sword] comes *out of his mouth* symbolizes that it [i.e., his power] pierces merely by [his] word or will, with the piercing sharpness of a sword that has two edges, according to an act of imaginative association[72] belonging to whoever[73] can imagine it [i.e., the sword] in terms of the condition of [his power], despite the fact that no

69. Luke 21:25–26. The Bohairic Coptic text, on which the Arabic version is based, reads "the people's souls came out of them on account of fear" (ϩⲁⲛⲣⲱⲙⲓ ⲉⲣⲉ ⲧⲟⲩⲯⲩⲭⲏ ⲓ ⲉⲃⲟⲗ ⲛ̄ϧⲏⲧⲟⲩ ⲉⲃⲟⲗ ϧⲁ ⲧϩⲟϯ; Horner, *CoptNT-North*, 2.278). The Greek text reads "There will be signs in the sun, the moon, and the stars, and on the earth distress among nations confused by the roaring of the sea and the waves (ἤχους θαλάσσης καὶ σάλου). People will faint from fear (ἀποψυχόντων ἀνθρώπων ἀπὸ φόβου)." Ibn Kātib Qayṣar's divergent translation therefore is due to an overly literalistic reception of the Greek verb ἀποψύχειν, which he (following the Bohairic) takes to mean "to have one's soul (ⲯⲩⲭⲏ) come out (ⲉⲃⲟⲗ ⲛ̄ϧⲏⲧⲟⲩ)."

70. Arabic, *malā'ikat al-kanā'is al-sab'ah*, which can also mean either "the angels of the seven churches" or "the seven angels of the churches."

71. See note 40 above regarding the wording of Revelation 1:16 in the Arabic and Bohairic texts.

72. Arabic, *al-taqrīb al-mutaṣawwar* (the conceptual approximation).

73. Reading *li-man* for *man* in Arabic (Birmāwī, 49).

sword has any relation to [his power], [or] to that will, at which the fig tree dried up at its appointed time,[74] and which Paul the apostle describes in the third chapter of Hebrews, "For the word of God is alive and its work is sharper than any sword with two faces [i.e., having two edges]. It penetrates until it divides the soul and the spirit, the joints and the marrow."[75]

As for his statement, *his face shone like the sun in its power*, this is from the clause of the fourth insight mentioned earlier, for the power of the light of the sun prevents anyone from [truly] perceiving it. For example, God said to Moses the prophet when he stood on Sinai, "You are not able to look at my face because no human being can see it and live."[76] There are likenesses and correspondences to this revelatory vision: Thus, Daniel said, "I saw thrones being set up, and the Ancient of Days was seated with clothing like white snow and the hair on his head was like pure wool."[77] Then he said after that, "I saw on the clouds of heaven someone like the Son of Man. He approached and came [to stand] before the Ancient of Days, and to him was given authority, dominion, and honor, that all of the peoples, nations, and languages might worship him. His authority—the authority of eternity—will not end, and his kingdom will not be destroyed."[78] As for Stephen, he said, "Behold, I see the heavens opened and the Son of Man standing at the right [hand] of God."[79] But as for the Law, it said: On Mount Sinai, "the sound of the trumpet was loud."[80]

9. (1:17) When I saw him, I fell down under his feet and became like one dead, but he put his right hand on me, saying to me, "Do not be afraid. I am the first and the last, (1:18) and the one who lives. I died, and behold I am alive forever and ever. I have the keys to the abyss and to hell. (1:19) Write what you have seen, and it will take place after this."

74. Matthew 21:18–22.

75. Hebrews 4:12 (note that Ibn Kātib Qayṣar is utilizing here a different chapter numbering system). The commentator's dependence upon the Bohairic Coptic text of Hebrews is evident here, as elsewhere: see Horner, *CoptNT-North*, 3.488 (ⲟⲩⲟϩ ϥϣⲱⲧ ⲉϩⲟⲧⲉ ⲥⲏϥⲓ ⲛⲓⲃⲉⲛ ⲛ̄ⲣⲟ ⲃ̄; lit., "it is sharper than every sword of two mouths"). As in the case of Revelation 1:16, the Sahidic text of Hebrews 4:12 uses ⲛ̄ϩⲟ ⲥⲛⲁⲩ ("two faces") where ⲛ̄ⲣⲟ ⲃ̄ ("two mouths") is found in the Bohairic: see Horner, *CoptNT-South*, 5.30.

76. Exodus 33:20.

77. Daniel 7:9.

78. Daniel 7:13–14.

79. Acts 7:56.

80. Exodus 19:16.

Indeed, as for these terrifying sights—the fiery rays and the dazzling, overpowering, and miraculous events—the powers of humankind are truly incapable of withstanding them. For this reason, the apostle *fell down* to the ground like someone dead, even if that happened in the vision and not according to outward appearances.[81] As for the excessive fear, it fulfilled his statement: *He put his right hand on me, saying to me, "Do not be afraid."* This touch restored his power, which had [previously] disappeared; and this statement revived it after it had dissipated.[82]

His statement, *I am the first and the last*, is true insofar as he is God, and this interpretation has already taken place.[83] His statement, *I died, and behold I am alive forever and ever*, is true insofar as he is human.[84]

As for his statement, *I have the keys to the abyss and to hell*, by *the keys* he means the judgment that is to be obeyed, and by *the abyss* he means the nether regions of the earth—that is to say, the most remote [regions]. *Hell* is the lowest depth of the earth, like pits, trenches, graves, and sarcophagi. The sixth Psalm says, "I have no one among the dead who will remember you, nor anyone in hell who will recognize you,"[85] and by hell, it means the grave. In the same way, David said to Solomon, "As for that man who has mocked his father's gray hairs, let him go down to hell, unless he is stained by his blood,"[86] and by that [i.e., hell] he intends the grave. By *hell* is also meant the fire by which the evil ones will be punished at the promised time.

As for his statement, *Write what you have seen, and it will take place after this*, there are three problems in this section. The first is, how did he say this but did not conclude [by telling us] anything of what the apostle saw after these things, except for his statement that *he is coming with the clouds,*

81. Lit., "on the outside."

82. Būlus al-Būshī uses the angel's words, "Do not be afraid," as a springboard for a brief reflection on how one is able to distinguish between the presence of God and angels on the one hand, and Satan on the other. While God's awe-inspiring aspects ultimately take away fear, "the aspects of Satan multiply fear upon fear" (Sbath 1014, f. 5r).

83. The edited text mistakenly prints *raqada* (he slept) in place of *wa qad* (and already).

84. Būlus al-Būshī comments on 1:17–18 as follows: "Now as for his statement, *I am living*, it is because he possesses eternal life. His statement, *I died*, is on account of his life-giving sufferings on our behalf. And when he says, *I am alive forever and ever*, he means that he suffered in the body and died, but he remained alive through the power of his divinity. He remained eternal, without end" (Sbath 1014, f. 5v).

85. Psalm 6:5.

86. This is perhaps a corrupted quotation of 1 Kings 2:9.

and the eyes will see him?[87] This [small] amount [of information] is not enough [to cover] what he was going to write about. The response [to this problem] is as follows: What is revealed in this section is that the apostle saw all of the revelatory vision on one occasion, but he expressed what he saw one thing after another, because of the necessity of extending his account by [this] means of expression. Here, his statement, *Write what you have seen*, indicates the revelatory vision as a whole. The second problem is his statement, *it will take place after this*. This is a second proof that the revelatory vision concerned what was coming later, not what happened in the past,[88] as some interpreters have believed. The third problem: It appears from his statement that the phrase, *it will take place after this*, means that these events absolutely must occur.

10. (1:20) "As for the mystery of the seven stars you saw in my right hand and the seven golden lampstands, the seven stars are the seven angels who belong to the seven churches, and the seven lampstands you saw are the seven churches."

In this section, the Lord of All has interpreted the words *stars* and *churches*. Indeed, he has used [each] term in a way different from its established meaning, and he has introduced that to us in its [proper] place, just as he has interpreted it here.

Chapter Two (2:1–29)

11. (2:1) "To the angel of the church that is in Ephesus, write: 'This is what the one who holds the seven stars in his right hand, the one who walks amidst the seven golden lampstands, says. (2:2) "I know your works, your labor, and your endurance, since you cannot stand evil and you have tested those who are called prophets (but are in fact nothing) and have found them to be false prophets. (2:3) You have endurance. You withstood these things on account of my name and you have not grown weary. (2:4) But I have against you the fact that you have left your first love behind. (2:5) Remember then how you have fallen, and repent, lest I come to you and shake your lampstand from its place, unless you

87. Revelation 1:7.

88. Birmāwī (p. 51) mistakenly repeats the phrase *ya'tī ba'd* (was coming later) in the second clause. Par. Ar. 67 (f. 15r) supplies the correct verbal reading: *maḍā* (happened in the past).

repent. (2:6) But this is what you have in your favor: You hate the works of the troublemakers, whom I also hate. (2:7) Whoever has ears to hear, let him hear what the Spirit is saying to the churches. Whoever achieves victory, to him I will give permission to eat from the tree of life, which is in the midst of a divine paradise."'"

The city of *Ephesus* where the church is located was the leading [episcopal] seat in which the apostle John preached before the transfer of leadership from it to Constantinople in the days[89] of Constantine the Great. By *stars*, he means the leaders of the churches, and the *lampstands* are the churches. As if conferring the honor of his speech on the leader of the church of Ephesus—his disciple—this is what the one who holds the leaders in his grasp and who rules in judgment over the churches says. As for his statement, *I know your works, your labor, and your endurance*, he means by *works* his diligence in worship, asceticism, and self-renunciation. By *labor* he means [his] exertion in learning, and [his] labor in teaching and in imparting [that teaching] to the minds of his people. By *endurance* he means that he endured those archheretics—these are people from among the Jews who rebelled in the days of the apostles, pretending [to preach] the message in every place, propagating wicked opinions and [inviting people] to hold to outdated ordinances like circumcision, the observance of the Sabbath, the celebration of feasts on the first day of the month,[90] and the defilement of food and marriages, etc. The apostle Paul prophesied about these people in the Acts of the Apostles in the final days of the reign of Nero the Great. His prophecy came to fulfillment after some thirty years, during the final days of Domitian's reign. Namely, he sent [a message] from Miletus to Ephesus petitioning the elders of the church and then said to them, "[Watch] over yourselves and over all the flock, whom the Holy Spirit left you [in your role] as bishops [charged with] examining them."[91] He said, "I know that after my departure, there will enter in amongst you difficult wolves and they will not have pity on the flock. People who accept subversive speech will arise from among you in order to entice the disciples [to follow] after them."[92]

89. The edited text leaves the final *mīm* off the word *'ayām* (days), but the correct spelling of the word appears in Par. Ar. 67, f. 16r.

90. Lit., "the first days of the months."

91. Acts 20:28a.

92. Acts 20:29–30.

The community of the apostles—such as Peter, John, Paul, and the others—complained about people like this a great deal in their letters. Indeed, [the former] were following in the footsteps of the apostles in every respect, while [the latter] were corrupting the consciences of the faithful by their many designs. Among [these designs] were the following: their opposition to the [apostles'] teaching and their enticement of people to obey them; the fact that they made that [opposition] take the form of indolence, gluttony, and immorality; their fanatical enthusiasm for Judaism such that they compelled [people] to act in accordance with its commandments; the corruption of whatever the apostles had established; as well as other worldly opinions and wicked heresies. For this reason, [divine] inspiration[93] spoke truly about the one who presided at Ephesus, (saying), "Even if you have *endured* these people and have *withstood* them with gentleness and humility *on account of my name*,"[94] you have used that [name] outside its proper place, and you fell away when you corrupted the condition of the faithful and enabled the wolves [to attack] the flock.[95] Truly, the love that is in God, along with the [righteous] jealousy that belongs to God, requires [you] to have compassion for [the flock] and to defend it. But you preferred rest, and you did not see agreement, but rather resistance. Thus his statement: *You cannot stand evil.* If bearing this evil were in fact a good thing, and you had suffered their disregard humbly, just as I thought, indeed you would have remained at rest. This is his statement: *You withstood these things on account of my name and you did not grow weary.* But in this trust, you forfeited and failed to carry out the conditions of love, as it was written.[96] Thus his statement: *But I have against you the fact that you have left your first love behind. Remember then how you have fallen, and repent.* That is, take note of this fall, observe it closely, and turn away from it. Otherwise,

93. Par. Ar. 67 (f. 17r) provides the correct reading, *waḥy* (inspiration), instead of *wa'y* (consciousness; Birmāwī, 54). The difference is a single (middle) letter: Birmāwī has an *'ayn* where he should have had a *ḥā'*.

94. See Revelation 2:3.

95. This statement of direct address begins a sequence of interpretations that tries to align the leadership of the church at Ephesus in Ibn Kātib Qayṣar's time with the admonitions directed to the bishop of Ephesus in the book of Revelation. That is to say, the author's commentary here seems to take up a (less than explicit) polemic against the pro-Chalcedonian "corruption" of the Greek church in Asia Minor.

96. Birmāwī (p. 55) mistakenly records the phrase, *kamā kunta* (as you were); but Par. Ar. 67 (f. 17v) retains the correct reading, *kamā kutiba* (as it was written). In this passage, the commentator employs language associated with financial contracts and transactions.

your leadership will be removed [from you] if you do not observe its conditions.[97] Thus his statement: *lest I come and shake your lampstand from its place, unless you repent.* As for the *lampstand*, even if an interpretation of this same section has already been put forward regarding it—namely, that it is the church—what he intends by this is the leadership of the church, for he applied the genitive [i.e., possessive] construction to the noun, and the proof of this is the syntactical context.[98]

His statement, *But this is in your favor: You hate the works of the troublemakers, whom I also hate*, is an expression of esteem, but that which is *against you* is an expression of censure—I have already reported to you on account of it—and it means, "If you could not reason with them and you reject them, then you should feel disgust toward them." The *troublemakers* are the ones who hold disgraceful and stupid conversations in an unseemly manner, utilizing whatever methods are undesirable. This is the *trouble*: Its intended meaning is strife and disturbance—[in this case,] what is proper and true is not desired. Saint James the apostle pointed this out in his letter when he said, "Do not boast or tell lies about the truth, for this knowledge does not come from above but from below, [from what is] earthly, psychic, and devilish."[99] This is the disease that bishop disregarded with respect to those archheretics, for he was compelled to resemble [those troublemakers] in their way of life, and he came to be hated, just as was stated earlier. However, more hateful than this was the deepening influence of the wolves over the flock. Regarding something like this it was said, "Obedience is better than sacrifices."[100]

Now as for his statement, *Whoever has ears to hear, let him hear what the Spirit is saying to the churches*, its interpretation is as follows. Whoever has two healthy sensory organs of hearing and is engaged in listening, let him hear what the Holy Spirit is saying to the churches. As for his statement, *Whoever achieves victory, to him I will give permission to eat from the tree of life, which is in the midst of a divine paradise*, by the word *victory* he means

97. I.e., the conditions of love.

98. Lit., "contexts."

99. James 3:14–15. I translate the Arabic term, *nafsānī* (lit., "of the soul"), as "psychic," an adjective derived from the Greek word for "soul" (*psychē*). Here, James (and by extension, the commentary) operates according to a tripartite anthropology, in which the body, soul, and spirit exist in an ascending hierarchy. Here, to be "psychic" or "soulish" is to fall short of the "spiritual" (*rūḥānī*) ideal.

100. 1 Samuel 15:22.

a spiritual *victory*, which may be summed up in three imperatives. The first is obedience to God by doing his commandments. The second is victory over Satan and turning away from his temptation. The third is the support of truth and the repudiation of falsehood.[101] Finally, his statements, *the tree of life* and *a divine paradise*, [refer to] the heavenly Jerusalem, and [my] discourse on it will come in its proper place, by God's will.[102]

12. (2:8) "To the angel of the church of Smyrna, write: 'This is what the first and the last, the one who died and lived again, says. (2:9) "I know your strain and your poverty, but [in fact] you are rich. [Among you,] I have not found anyone[103] from that so-called race of Jews (who are not a race, but rather a synagogue of Satan). (2:10) Do not fear the sufferings that you receive. Look, the devil will throw some of you in prison to sadden you and to persecute you for ten days. Be faithful unto death and I will give you the crown of life. (2:11) Whoever has ears to hear, let him hear what the Spirit says to the churches, for whoever conquers will not be defeated by the second death."'"[104]

The angel of the church of Smyrna is its bishop, Polycarp [*Fīlfāriyūs*] the disciple of the apostle. As for [the phrase] *the first and the last, the one who died and lived again*, its interpretation has been presented already.[105] As for

101. Būlus al-Būshī (Vat. Ar. 459, f. 5r; Sbath 1014, f. 9r; Edelby, "Commentaire," 15) also notes that this *victory* is not related to a tangible war, but rather "he achieves victory over depravity (*al-radhīlah*) through the raising up of virtue (*al-faḍīlah*)."

102. Būlus al-Būshī (Vat. Ar. 459, f. 5r; Sbath 1014, f. 9r–v; Edelby, "Commentaire," 15–16) interprets the adjective *divine* here in specifically Christological terms: "He says, *divine*, because he became fully incarnate with a rational soul completely like us in every way except sin. And he called humankind his brothers, just as it is written, 'I will proclaim your name to my brothers' (Psalms 22:22). And the apostle also says, 'Just as all the children have flesh and blood in common, so he in like manner has shared in these things' (Hebrews 2:14). Therefore, just as he manifested his divine work through the power of miracles, so too he has manifested the manner of his incarnation by these things. He is God incarnate. The one to whom divinity properly belongs is also the one to whom incarnation properly belongs."

103. The Bohairic biblical text on which this Arabic translation is based mistakes the phrase ⲙ̄ⲡⲓϫⲉⲙ ⲟⲩⲁⲓ ("I have not found anyone") for the phrase ⲙ̄ⲡⲓϫⲉⲟⲩⲁ ("the blasphemy"): see Horner, *CoptNT-North*, 4.454 (and 4.455, note a).

104. Lit., "for the second death will not defeat whoever conquers."

105. Būlus al-Būshī uses the statement, *the one who died and lived again*, repeated from 1:18, as an opportunity to return to the subject of Christ's divinity, a divinity maintained even in "the human economy" of the incarnation: "He accepted suffering and death corporeally and not as a phantasm. 'He is the life, the living one who gives life by the power of his divinity, who does not suffer and does not die,' as Cyril the Great, the patriarch of Alexandria, has said. The Lord is neither seen nor perceived in the substance of his divinity. He has united with a

his statement, *I know your labor and your poverty, but [in fact] you are rich*, his *labor* was his struggle for the faith, for he was martyred in the end. It refers to his *poverty* because he was poor and did not own anything from the fleeting things of this world. And his *riches* were his wealth in virtues and his perseverance in the midst of hardships.

As for his statement, *I have not found anyone from among that so-called tribe of Jews*, the term *Jew*ish has application in five senses concurrently.[106] The first is the person who is Jewish in terms of lineage—one of the sons of Judah, a son of Jacob, if his ancestry traces to Judah. The second is the person who is Jewish by affiliation—whoever is from one of the remaining tribes—for the general word, Jewish, applies to him even if he is not a son of Judah. The third is by way of figurative expression—the person who converts to the sons of Israel, for to him is also applied the designation, Jewish. The fourth is the person who is Jewish in terms of legal custom—the one who believes in God and the prophet Moses, and who practices the commandments of the Torah. The fifth is the person who is Jewish in name [only]—the one who traces his lineage to the religion of Judaism but does not practice it, whether he is from the sons of Israel or not. In view of this, the implicit sense of his statement, *I have not found anyone* who is Jewish may be taken according to the fourth meaning related to [legal] custom; or *from among those so-called Jews* may be taken according to the fifth meaning related to [one's] name. To these two meanings, the apostle Paul points in his statement, "For the one who is Jewish in appearance is really not the [true] Jew; but rather, the one who is Jewish on the inside is really the [true] Jew"[107]—that is, [when he speaks of one who is Jewish in appearance, he is speaking of one who is] a Jew by legal custom. Now as for his statement, *they are not a race*, indeed, whoever among that people becomes sunken in the use of lustful power, [that power] takes hold of him

human body in order to accept suffering and death on our behalf. He did not, however, unite with a body devoid of a rational soul. Rather, he became united with a rational, reasoning soul having the capacity to accept suffering and to taste death. So, he suffered corporeally. The body is his by virtue of the union. Therefore, the suffering is reckoned to him by virtue of the union and not by virtue of any change." (Vat. Ar. 459, f. 5v–6r; Sbath 1014, ff. 10v–11r; Edelby, "Commentaire," 18).

106. Būlus al-Būshī interprets this reference to the Jews in relation to the Jewish practice of circumcision, which he says has been superseded by baptism, just as the sacrifice of the lamb has been superseded by the eucharistic body and blood of Christ (Vat. Ar. 459, f. 6r–v; Sbath 1014, f. 11v; Edelby, "Commentaire," 19).

107. Romans 2:28.

and he comes to resemble donkeys and pigs. And whoever among the people tends toward the use of angry power, [that power] takes hold of him and he comes to resemble beasts of prey and small birds. But whoever has a reason-endowed soul that takes mastery over his lustful and angry powers and whoever uses those two [powers] in whatever way is necessary—[only] just as necessary and where necessary—that one is truly an excellent person. But whoever belongs to those first two types will tend toward that which is bestial in human nature. Such a one is signaled by the statement, *they are not a race*. In other words, no humanity is credited to them. As is customary, if an excellent person is praised, it is said, "This one is truly a human being." But if an evil person is criticized, it is said, "This one is not a human being at all." It is in this respect that he says, *they are not a race*.

His statement, *but rather a synagogue of Satan*, means that they are tools that Satan manipulates for corruption and evil deeds, and on this account they are placed in the genitive case in relation to him as a genitive of possession. As for the statement, *Do not fear the sufferings that you receive*, this is a prophecy concerning the martyrdom of this aforementioned bishop and an encouragement for him to accept [those sufferings]. As for his statement, *Look, the devil will throw some of you in prison to sadden you and to persecute you for ten days*, this is a second prophecy concerning him [i.e., that bishop]. He has informed [us] that the trial and testing of the righteous are attributed to Satan so that the [martyr's] pure essence might be distinguished from that which is counterfeit and that the one who endures might be distinguished from the one who does not endure, just as in the story of Job, the righteous one, and just like the Gospel parable of the seed that fell on the pure [soil], where it says, "In the narrow spaces, they sprang up quickly, for they had no root or soil."[108] And [it is also] just like it says, "Look, Satan sifts you like wheat."[109] It says, "He leads many of the chosen ones astray,"[110] and "Whoever endures to the end will be saved."[111]

This bishop, Polycarp, was arrested at the instigation of Satan, and his community was with him: They were finally set free and the bishop was burned. It was for this reason that the [divine] inspiration told him, *Be faithful unto death and I will give you the crown of life*. The word *crown* [*iklīl*]

108. Matthew 13:5. The form of the verb in the quoted Matthean text is *yashukūna* (= *yawshukūna*; "to be quick, to hurry").

109. See Luke 22:31.

110. See Matthew 24:24.

111. Matthew 24:13.

gives notice of his martyrdom and signals his status [*manzilah*], for the Lord said, "The dwelling places [*manāzil*] in my Father's house are many."[112] On that account, the crown signaled the honor of the martyr's status in the kingdom of heaven. The genitive construction in which the word *crown* is paired with the word *life* is a genitive of specification. *Life* is the happiness and eternal delight of the righteous in the hereafter, and [this is] also because the two terms, miter [*tāj*] and crown [*iklīl*] have one [and the same] meaning. The latter [word] functions as a sign, and it symbolizes seven things. The first of them is sovereignty. The second is judgment. The third is martyrdom. The fourth is prophecy. The fifth is the [apostolic] message. The sixth is the priesthood, just as the Torah says in its second book, "They fastened the holy crown over the turban."[113] The seventh is acclamation, just as Jeremiah says, "The crown of your acclamation has been removed from your heads."[114] Each one of these [meanings] will come [to our attention] in its proper place. The interpretation of *Whoever has ears to hear, let him hear, etc.* has already taken place. So too in the case of his statement, *whoever conquers*. But as for *the second death*, it is the punishment of evil people in the hereafter, because it is both severe and eternal. He calls it *death* by way of indicating what he elucidates in section 120 of this revelatory vision,[115] in his statement that in the second death the fate of all the sinners will be in the lake of fire and sulfur.

13. (2:12) "To the angel of the church in Pergamum, write: 'This is what the one who has the sword that strikes with two edges [lit., "mouths"] says. (2:13) "I know where you used to be: where the throne of Satan is.

112. John 14:2. Here, the interpreter engages in a play on words involving two terms with the same root: *manzilah* (status, rank) and *manzil* (pl. *manāzil*; dwelling place[s]).

113. Exodus 39:30.

114. Jeremiah 13:18.

115. Ibn Kātib Qayṣar is alluding to Revelation 20:10–15 here, but the section number indicated in Birmāwī's edition (p. 59) does not correspond to section numbering for those verses. Section 120 in Birmāwī corresponds to the commentary on Revelation 21:8, while the commentary on Revelation 20:10–15 is actually found in sections 108 through 113. At this point in the text, Par. Ar. 67 (f. 21r) has a different reading: "in this revelatory vision (chapter 31 according to the system of small chapter numbering)." The small chapter number indicated at this point in Par. Ar. 67 does not find any correspondence in the manuscript either. This lack of internal correspondence may partly be explained by the fact that in the manuscript tradition Ibn Kātib Qayṣar's commentary breaks off after Revelation 20:6, with the ending of Būlus al-Būshī's commentary substituted for Revelation 20:7–22:21 (= Birmāwī, 403–24 [sections 108–41]).

You have believed in my name and you have not denied my faith in the days that offered opposition to the faithful witness,[116] the one who was killed among you, [which is] where Satan is. (2:14) But then I have a few other names among you, people who hold fast to the teachings of Balaam [*Bal'ām*], who taught Balak [*Bālāq*] to place doubt before the children of Israel, so that they would eat sacrifices to idols and commit adultery. (2:15) So too, you hold fast to the teaching of the troublemakers.[117] (2:16) Repent then, lest I come to you quickly and make war with them with the sword of my mouth. (2:17) Whoever has ears to hear, let him hear what the Spirit says to the churches, and whoever conquers, I will give him the hidden manna. I will give him a white ring stone, and on the stone a new name is written, which no one knows except the one who has received it."'"

We learn from this that the angel of the church at Pergamum is its leader [*ra'īs*], and that the sword that strikes with two edges [lit., "two mouths"] symbolizes the divine power of vengeance.

As for his statement, *I know where* [*ayna*] *you used to be: where* [*ḥaythu*] *the throne of Satan is*, the two words, "where" [*ayna*] and "where" [*ḥaythu*], indicate the house of the Holy One—that is, the earthly Jerusalem, as evidenced by his statement after that: *the faithful witness, the one who was killed among you, [which is] where Satan is.* This *witness* is the Lord Jesus Christ (to him be the glory), and the place he was killed was in Jerusalem. Now as for his mention that it [i.e., Jerusalem] is Satan's place, it is clear that he appeared to the Lord at the time of [his] temptation there.[118] [Satan] stayed there and established his *throne* there, which is a symbol for his occupation

116. The Greek names the "faithful witness" as Antipas, an early Christian martyr about whom little is known, although the name is mentioned in an inscription at Pergamum (G. A. Deissmann, *Bible Studies*, ed. A. Grieve [New York: Harper, 1901], 187). According to later legends, the martyr was roasted to death inside a bull's carcass under the emperor Domitian (Robert H. Mounce, *The Book of Revelation* [Grand Rapids, Mich.: Eerdmans, 1977], 97). Antipas's name is not transmitted in either the Sahidic or Bohairic versions. The Sahidic has ⲡⲁⲙⲛ̄ⲧⲣⲉ ⲙ̄ⲡⲓⲥⲧⲟⲥ ("my faithful witness"; Horner, *CoptNT-South* 7.276); the Bohairic has ⲡⲓⲙⲁⲣⲧⲩⲣⲟⲥ ⲡⲓⲡⲓⲥⲧⲟⲥ ("the martyr/witness, the faithful one"; Horner, *CoptNT-North*, 4.456). The syntax of the Arabic follows the Bohairic, although it may be translated in either way.

117. The Greek, Sahidic, and Bohairic texts all identify the source of this teaching as the Nicolaitans. For the Sahidic version, see Horner, *CoptNT-South* 7.278; for the Bohairic version, see Horner, *CoptNT-North* 4.456.

118. Matthew 4:1–11; Mark 1:12–13; Luke 4:1–13.

[of the place], since the most important matter for him at that time was the location where the Jews put on the trial that was so unusual in the world—namely, the crucifixion of the Lord of all—and the conspiracy of the [Jewish] leaders [*ru'asā'*] against the apostles and the believers. It is as if [the text] points to the fact that [only] this one leader [*ra'īs*] came to believe among all the Jews of Jerusalem, and that, prior to believing, he had participated in defaming Christ the Lord. [Satan's] *opposition*, along with his proxies among the Jews who were there, is evidenced by the statement, *in the days that offered opposition to the faithful witness*. Divine inspiration discloses his [i.e., Satan's] original wicked behavior.

His statement, *You have believed in my name and you have not denied my faith*, indicates his patience after he came to believe, as well as his devotion, his confession of Christ the Lord, and his pious struggle [*jihad*] on account of his faith in [Christ]. As for his statement, *in the days that offered opposition to the faithful witness*, along with what follows, he mentioned the time in what he said about certain *days*, after he had mentioned the place earlier. For it is customary in confirming matters to mention their place and time. This is for the sake of [providing] full information and notification about what preceded and was hidden to the rest of the listeners. The one mentioning it provides notification about the future, so that the two things[119] might be part [of the disclosure] of what was hidden.

When he elucidated his situation, both before faith and after faith, he supplemented [this] by saying: *But then I have a few other names among you, people who hold fast to the teachings of Balaam,*[120] *who taught Balak to cast doubt before the children of Israel, so that they would eat sacrifices to idols and commit adultery.* His statement, *other names*, means people other than those opponents who were in Jerusalem when you were of their number. He had already interpreted what the teaching of Balaam was—namely, that it was the cause of idol worship and adultery. For Balak the king, when he feared the army of the Israelites, went to Balaam the fortuneteller and brought him to curse them. But it was revealed to [Balaam] by God that he should bless them. In the wickedness of his opinion, [Balak] believed that God had completely withdrawn his help, so he brought forward offerings and raised

119. The meaning here is unclear: the commentator's reference to "two things" (expressed by the dual pronomial suffice, *humā*) may refer to "place and time," but it also may refer to the leader's past and future (before faith and after faith).

120. Numbers 22–25; 31:1–16.

up sacrifices. But with great force [Balaam] pronounced a blessing on them and [proclaimed] that he would not curse them at all. And on account of his greed for silver, which is the root of all evils, Balak the king, when he learned [of this], had the idea to adorn women, and he set [them] loose in the midst of the army of the Israelites. When the sons of Israel presented themselves to them, they settled down with them, such that they ate sacrifices to idols with them and had intercourse with them. This was a reason for God's anger against the Israelites. [The word] *names* means those who are called by name—that is, the archheretics who were in every place dogging the apostles' footsteps and corrupting the hearts and conditions of believers and defiling the chastity of women. As for the statement, *So too, you hold fast to the teaching of the troublemakers*, the corruption of those heretics had penetrated deeply into [their] opinions, sayings, and deeds to the extent that it reached the leaders who were engaged in teaching. You ought to understand that people of this ilk have two meanings, and both are secretive and deceptive. The first is their so-called opinion, which they strengthen with argumentation. The other is their argumentation itself and their methodology, just as we have clarified all of this previously. This leader lied, his heart was swayed, and he capitulated when they made their allegations against him.[121] It is for this reason that it says, "I hold fast to their teaching, not to their method of teaching."

As for his statement, *Repent then, lest I come to you quickly and make war with them with the sword of my mouth*, its portent is simply the coming of God. For the divine foreordainment of this threat is sufficient for [prompting] one to renounce, repent, and relinquish his sick opinion, and it remains vigilant with regard to the cause of his specious argument. But as for their being rebuked, [God's] coming was not sufficient to overcome them with vengeance or to censure them in actuality without this [additional] reproach. With that in mind, he said, *I make war with them with the sword of my mouth.* The interpretation of the *sword of his mouth* was presented earlier.

As for his statement, *whoever conquers, I will give him the hidden manna*, by *hidden manna* he means the body of our Lord Jesus Christ united with his divinity, in which believers partake. The proof that this is the intended meaning is the statement by the same apostle John in the sixteenth section

121. Par. Ar. 67 (f. 23v) reads *lammā iddaʿawūhu*. In Birmāwī (p. 63), the word *lammā* (when) is omitted.

of his gospel: "I am the bread that comes down from heaven, not like the manna the your fathers ate in the desert and then died."[122] His statement, "not like the manna" gives notice that he called it "manna," but it was not like the manna eaten in the desert. The two things have the aspect of a simile with regard to the term, "manna," and the intended difference between them is that the latter is perceptible manna in its literal expression and meaning. As for the phrase(s), *died* [and] *ate it*, this is the hidden manna obtained by whoever is worthy to eat it. And *ate it* refers to the Incarnation [*ḥulūl*] of the Son[123] in the world, along with his infinite duration in eternal life, as evidenced by his statement, "Whoever eats this bread will live forever."[124] Thus, he has revealed that he identified it [i.e., the bread] as a synonym for the *hidden manna*, "the bread that comes down from heaven,"[125] and "the bread of life,"[126] all of this according to a spiritual language.

I know that it is not necessary for us to interpret some of the more cryptic texts for two reasons. The first is that the interpretation becomes protracted and one thing leads to another. The second is that for every [textual] locus there is something to be said. But it is our obligation [simply] to clarify the meaning cited, if it proves to be cryptic for explaining what follows.

Now, as for his statement, *I will give him a white ring stone, and on the stone is written a new name that no one knows except the one who receives it*, I think by *ring stone* [*faṣṣ*] he means the kingdom [of heaven]. If the term is [understood] in terms of its perceptible sense, then its meaning is a symbolic one; but if the term is [understood] in terms of its imperceptible sense, then it is an expression [to be read] in its spiritual sense.[127] This interpretation is derived from what God prepared for his chosen ones in the kingdom, and for this reason we have favored it over the alternative. But as for the *new name* written upon it, he indicates by it the totality of [spiritual] gifts prepared in the kingdom. Just as the apostle Paul said, "What no eye has seen, nor ear has heard, nor human heart conceived,"[128] the matter is one that no one can comprehend except for the one who has

122. John 6:48–49.

123. Arabic, *ḥulūl al-ibn fīhi* (lit., "descent of the Son in him"). The term *ḥulūl* was commonly used as a *terminus technicus* for the incarnation of the Word in the person of Jesus.

124. John 6:51.

125. John 6:32, 41, 49, 58.

126. John 6:35, 48.

127. Lit., "spiritual language."

128. 1 Corinthians 2:9.

attained [knowledge of] it. For this reason, he said, *no one knows except the one who receives it.* Regardless of whether the pronoun in the phrase *received it* refers to the *ring stone* or to the *name,* they both are related to each other and the intended meaning is one and the same. The [true] understanding here connotes the revelatory vision [*al-ru'yā*], just as we said earlier. In any case, the *ring stone* in this text is among the cryptic things [found] in this book. May God be the guide to what is right.

14. (2:18) "To the angel of the church of Thyatira, write: 'This is what the Son of God says, whose eyes are like the flame of fire and whose feet are like the copper[129] of Lebanon. (2:19) "Indeed, I know about your deeds, love, faith, service, and your perseverance. Your last deeds are better than your first ones. (2:20) But I hold against you the fact that you have given place to the woman Jezebel [*Izbāl*], who says: 'I am a prophet and teacher.' She is a woman who leads astray my servants to commit adultery and to eat sacrifices to idols. (2:21) I have granted her time to repent and she has not turned back to repent from her adultery. (2:22) Behold, I am throwing her on a bed, and the ones who have committed adultery with her into great misfortune. If she does not repent from her deeds, (2:23) I will strike her sons dead. All the churches know that I am the one who examines hearts and minds,[130] and I will give recompense to each person according to his deeds. (2:24) To you, the rest of those at Thyatira who do not have this teaching and have not learned, as they say, 'the depth of Satan,' I say: I will not place another burden on you, (2:25) but rather let those who are with you hold fast to it until I come. (2:26) Whoever prevails and preserves my deeds until the end, I shall give him authority over the nations, (2:27) and he shall control them with an iron rod and he shall crush them like a clay vessel. (2:28) Just as I received [this authority] from my Father, I shall give him the eastern star in the early morning. (2:29) Whoever has ears to hear, let him hear what the Spirit says to the churches."'"

The angel of Thyatira is its leader, just as was the case before. Thyatira is the fourth city to which the apostle wrote.

As for his statement, *This is what the Son of God says, whose eyes are like the flame of fire and whose feet are like the copper of Lebanon,* we have already spoken about it. So too with his statement, *Indeed, I know about your*

129. Or "brass" (*nuḥās*).

130. Lit., "hearts and kidneys" (*al-qulūb wa-l-kulā*). See chapter 4, note 65.

deeds, love, faith, service, and your perseverance: It was interpreted with regard to the point [*faṣṣ*][131] of what was written to the church of Ephesus.[132] On [that point], nothing has changed apart from the fact that he has put [the church leader's] *service* here in the place of his *labor* there, and he has added to this *your love and your faith*, both of which are self-evident. Then he said, *Your last deeds are better than your first ones*. This is contrary to what was said to the leader of the church of Ephesus: *You have left your first love behind*.[133] [By contrast,] here he says, *Your last deeds are better than your first ones*. What he thanks him for now is five things: worship, faith, love, service in teaching, and perseverance in the face of the difficulties caused by the archheretics. But regarding the totality of his perseverance in the face of the opposition caused by the followers of heresy, he followed up by saying: *But I hold against you the fact that you have given place to the woman Jezebel* [*Izbāl*], *who says: "I am a prophet and teacher."* How strange is this heretical woman's height of audacity for precedence and teaching! This indicates that she pretends at Christianity; otherwise, why does this leader put her in a position to teach? [It also indicates that] she is at core a fortuneteller; otherwise, why was she invited to prophesy? [It also indicates that] she has experience with the pagan mysteries; otherwise, why was she invited to teach? Nonetheless, she attracted a host of people to her viewpoint! I know that some of these mysteries involve adultery and other depravities like presenting sacrifices and offerings to idols and consuming them. As for why the revelatory vision names her Jezebel, this is with respect to the fact that Jezebel's deeds resembled those of the wife of Ahab, the king of old.[134] She was someone who had five traits. [She was] unbelieving, murderous, adulterous, defiant, and deceitful. Now as for her unbelief, it was because she was the daughter of the king Sidon from among the Gentiles.[135] Ahab, king of Israel, married her, and she opened

131. This may have functioned as a pun in the original Arabic. In Revelation 2:17, the term *faṣṣ* refers to a "ring stone"; however, when placed in a genitive (*iḍāfa*) construction with a generic noun such as *amr* (or, in this case, *mā*) it can mean "the point upon which a thing, or an affair, turns, or hinges; or the point in which it is distinguished, or discriminated, from other things" (Lane, *Arabic-English Lexicon*, vol. 6, 2495).

132. See Revelation 2:2.

133. Revelation 2:4.

134. 1 Kings 16:31–34; 18:1–19:3; 21; see also 2 Kings 9.

135. 1 Kings 16:31 introduces Jezebel as "daughter of King Ethbāʿal of the Sidonians [i.e., the Phoenicians]." Instead of understanding her father as the "king of Sidon," the author of this commentary mistakes "Sidon" as her father's name.

the houses of the idols and invited people to worship them. As for the fact that she was a murderess, this was because she murdered many of the prophets of God and searched for the prophet Elijah in order to kill him, but she did not capture him. As for her adultery, in her worship of idols were things that included adultery, as we said. As for her defiance, when her husband Ahab disregarded the matter pertaining to Naboth [*Nābūt*], the owner of the vineyard, she said to him, "Are you fit to be king of Israel? Get up and eat your bread and I will give you the vineyard."[136] As for her deceit, she acted deceitfully with the people of the village regarding the aforementioned Naboth with the result that they raised up false witnesses against him, saying that he cursed the gods and the king, and they stoned him until he died unjustly.[137]

This Jezebel resembles the earlier one. She has the [same] five traits as well. As for her unbelief, she invited [others] to the worship of idols through her secret teaching. As for the fact that she was a murderess, [it is evidenced] in her destruction of the souls belonging to whomever she led astray. As for her adultery, it was elucidated earlier. As for her defiance, [it was] on account of her audacity in [trying to do] what outstanding men were incapable of doing. And as for her deception, it was because she feigned Christianity and kept her paganism hidden. That was the worst wickedness, and the greatest form of duplicity and deception.

As for his statement, *I have granted her time to repent and she has not turned back to repent from her adultery*, it is well known that the power of desire grows strong in youth, weakens with maturity and the progression of years, and goes away in old age. It is out of divine mercy that [God] has cleared a way during the period of desire's lifespan that the desire for adultery might diminish from it, and that repentance from it might be made easier. But this woman continued her will[fullness] in her wicked thoughts along with her impurity, even though she had advanced in years. For she did not renounce her will and determination to realize her desire, and since [her] nature was unstable and followed [the behavior] to which it was accustomed, and [since it was] stuck [in its ways], avoiding that to which it was not accustomed, for this reason, *she has not turned back to repent from her adultery*, and her punishment was: *Behold, I am throwing her on a bed.* By this act of throwing, he means an affliction with some serious illnesses,

136. 1 Kings 21:1–7, quote from vs. 7.
137. 1 Kings 21:8–16, esp. vss. 8–14.

because sick people must stay in their beds. Thus, the Psalm says, "May he have mercy on you in your sickbed."[138] This again comes from divine acts of kindness toward her that she might become vigilant in her self-discipline. If she should persist and not repent, she would be disciplined with a harsher discipline—namely, the death of her natural children before her [eyes]. Thus, his statement: *If she does not repent from her deeds, I will strike her sons dead.*

As for his statement, *the ones who have committed adultery with her into great misfortune,* this is a nod toward his [other] statement, *I am throwing her on a bed.* It is as if he said, "I am throwing her on a bed, and I am throwing the ones who have committed adultery with her into great misfortune"—that is, an affliction that their endurance is unable [to match]. Perhaps it should be understood that the *adultery* in her and in them is the worship of idols. This is found many times in the books of the prophets, but we have given more weight to what we have discovered in the [immediate semantic and syntactical] contexts that are the main point at issue in such a case.

As for his statement, *All the churches know that I am the one who examines hearts and minds, and I will give recompense to each person according to his deeds,* it means: "With respect to the woman and those who followed her, I brought about whatever was imposed upon her and upon them as a warning and stern reprimand to the rest of the people in the churches. In this way, they will learn that I, to the contrary, am their recompense in and through their deeds, which they conceal and hide." It is also clear that he [i.e., God] (may he be exalted) is the one who examines hearts and minds. As for *hearts,* their goodness and wickedness hinges on [their] beliefs. As for *minds,* indeed their grounding principle is the movement of desire, and from it chastity and adultery come to be discerned.

As for his statement, *To you, the rest of those at Thyatira who do not have this teaching and have not learned, as they say, "the depth of Satan,"* by *teaching* he means the teaching of the woman who conceals it. The *depth of Satan* is the revealing of what is not concealed and the concealing of what is not revealed, just as this woman did along with those who followed her. Now as for his statement, *as they say,* its meaning is: "Just as you keep [certain things] secret, so too you should speak without wickedness, dissemblance, hypocrisy, or falsehood." His statement, *I will not place an-*

138. Psalm 41:3. Lit., "in the bed of your pain."

other burden on you, but rather let those who are with you hold fast to it until I come, means "I will not add to you another commandment, but rather, [you should] keep [the commandments] you received." Regarding his *coming*, he has come in the sense of what was promised and he has come in the sense of what was threatened, for at his coming he will recompense everyone according to his deed: if good, then in a good way, and if bad, then in a bad way. For this reason, we apportion [his] coming by the apportionment of the reward [or punishment].

As for the statement, *Whoever prevails and preserves my deeds until the end, I shall give him authority over the nations, and he shall control them with an iron rod and he shall crush them like a clay vessel*, what the act of prevailing is has already been interpreted. The intended referent of *whoever prevails* is the person who has authority over the nations in the dynasty of the thousand years that belong to the righteous. The report of what is spoken about it will come in its [proper] place. As for the prophecy in the second Psalm of David—namely, his statement, "I give you authority over the nations and you will oversee them with an iron rod"[139]—by it he meant Christ our Lord himself (to him be the glory). Whoever is worthy of this banquet has a share in its dominion. For it is as if he made this prophecy a general example: It is clear to whoever meditates upon it, regardless of whether he spoke by way of a special sign or did not speak [in this way].

The proof of the soundness of this interpretation is that this promise is not of this world, on account of his statement:[140] *Whoever prevails and preserves my deeds until the end, I shall give him authority.* The giving of authority to him is in accordance with the wording of the statement after *the end.* It is not possible that it is to occur in the hereafter, for he would not then have dominion over the nations. Indeed, [the hereafter] is the realm [lit., "house"] of punishment for everyone according to his own work. It was appointed to be what was promised[141] at the thousand-year banquet. The *control with an iron rod* is [his] retaliation against the Antichrist's dominion. The text explains this [in section 104] with its statement, "O all you flying birds in heaven, come and gather at the great banquet of the Lord God to eat the flesh of kings, the flesh of the commanders of the

139. Psalms 2:8–9.

140. Reading *li-qawlihi* (on account of his statement; Par. Ar. 67, 29r) in place of *fa-qawluhu* (and its statement; Birwāwī, 70).

141. Reading *al-wa'd* (the promise/what was promised; Par. Ar. 67, f. 29r), in place of *li-wa'd* (for a promise; Birmāwī, 70).

thousands, the flesh of the giants [*jabābirah*, "mighty ones"], the flesh of the horses and their riders, the flesh of free people, slaves, children, and adults."[142] [The text] likens their being broken or *crushed* to a clay vessel, [even though the vessel's] being broken is not explicitly mentioned, and nor is anything useful included regarding its [state of] being crushed.

As for the statement, *Just as I received [this authority] from my Father, I shall give him the eastern star in the early morning*, by this *star* he intends two meanings. One [meaning] is Christ the Lord (to him be the glory), as evidenced by his statement [in section 137], "I am the root and descendant of David, the bright star of the morning."[143] The other [meaning] is leadership and participation in dominion and conquest, as well as joy and happiness, in accordance with a number of proofs, among them his statement, *Just as I received from my Father, I shall give [to] him*. That which he received from his father is what Daniel the prophet mentioned: "While I was looking at the clouds of heaven, someone like the Son of Man emerged and approached the Ancient of Days. To him I give authority, dominion, and honor."[144] The statement of Isaiah the prophet conveyed the news, "They were all in agreement over the prisoner of the pit and he was rescued after some days. The sun is content and the moon is disgraced."[145] He means by these two the great king and the small king, and many other things besides. The second meaning is intended here. His final intention is the evidence of his statement, *Just as I received from my Father, I shall give him*. As for the rest of the section, its interpretation has already taken place.

Chapter Three (3:1–22)

15. (3:1) "To the angel who is at the church of Sardis, write: 'This is what the one who has the seven spirits of God and the seven stars says, "I know your deeds: You have the name of salvation, and you are alive even though

142. Revelation 19:17–18. The section number 104 indicated in Birmāwī (p. 70) is not original to the text: it corresponds to the section numbering at pages 376 to 378 in his edition. In Par. Ar. 67 (f. 29r), the section number given is 101.

143. Revelation 22:16. The section number 137 indicated in Birmāwī (pp. 70–71) is not original to the text: it corresponds to the section numbering at pages 421 to 422 in his edition. In Par. Ar. 67 (f. 29v), no section number is given; instead at this point the text reads "at the very end of the revelatory vision" (*fī awākhir al-ru'yā*).

144. Daniel 7:13.

145. Isaiah 24:22–23.

you are dead. (3:2) Watch out and strengthen the remnant, lest you die because I have not found your faith and your deeds perfect before my God. (3:3) Therefore, remember how you received and [how you] went astray. Take heed and repent. If you do not repent and if you do not watch out I will come like a thief and you will not know the hour in which I come to you. (3:4) But, furthermore, I have a few other names [of persons] in Sardis, those who have not soiled their clothes with a woman and who walk with me in white garments because they are worthy. (3:5) Whoever conquers in this way, I will clothe him with a white garment. I will not erase their names from the book of life and I will certainly manifest their names before my Father and before his angels (3:6) Whoever has ears to hear, let him hear what the Spirit says to the churches."''

As for his statement, *write to the angel who is at the church of Sardis*, the angel of the church of Sardis is its leader, and Sardis is an island in the districts of Asia,[146] and this is said to its patrician,[147] or to the delegate of the kingdom there. "The [island] that owns the sea," is how it is mentioned in the "Book of Travels and Kingdoms"[148] and it is called also "Sardinia."[149] His statement, *this is what the one who has the seven spirits of God and the seven stars says*, has contemplated these unearthly things through the superabundance of this spirit. Indeed, he first interpreted for us the stars as being seven spirits, so how did he here differentiate one from the other and distinguish stars from spirits when one thing cannot be differentiated from itself? How is this the case unless for the purpose of making clear to us that the seven spirits are different from the seven spirits of God, making this clear in a hidden way, while also hiding it in the open. This is because the seven spirits, which are also the seven stars, are the leaders of the seven churches, just as we have [already] interpreted them. The seven spirits of

146. The Birmāwī edition based on Cairo Arabic 666 reads *aʿmāl* (districts), Par. Ar. 67 (f. 30v, line 3) has the singular *ʿamal*. See also Birmāwī, 34, for the author's use of the same term. The same word form can also mean "deeds" (see Revelation 3:1 above).

147. Par. Ar. 67 and the Birmāwī edition both read *biṭrīq* (patrician). While it is possible that this originally read *baṭrak* (patriarch), the use of the word *biṭrīq* would indicate a delegate of the kingdom or a government official who may also have had an ecclesiastical role.

148. *Kitāb al-masālik wa-l-mamālik*, written in the ninth CE century by Ibn Khordādbeh, who was a Persian administrator in charge of directing postal routes. See C. Edmund Bosworth, "Ebn Kordādbeh, Abu'l-Qāsem ʿbn Ko-Allāh," *Encyclopædia Iranica* 8.1, 37–38 (http://www.iranicaonline.org/articles/ebn-kordadbeh, consulted March 29, 2018).

149. Ibn Kātib Qayṣar apparently confuses the word "Sardis" with the word "Sardinia" and hence thinks of the city of Sardis as an island in the Mediterranean Sea.

God are the angels that he previously said were before the throne, the ones who execute the divine commands, just as was made clear above.

As for his statement, *I know your deeds: You have the name of salvation, and you live even though you are dead*, by the phrase *his deeds* he means his diligence in worship, and by *the name of salvation* he means his belief in the name of Christ. This indicates that this leader, even though he was diligent in completing that which was assigned to him, nevertheless was neglectful in two aspects. The first is that he quickly was bent to the temptation of the one tempting him without exerting self-control. Thus it was said to him, *remember how you received and [how you] went astray.* The other aspect is his neglect for the strengthening and establishing of his people. Thus it was said to him, *strengthen the remnant.* With respect to his diligence in perfecting himself, it was said to him *you are alive.* And with respect to his neglect regarding his self-control,[150] it is said to him *you are dead.* As for [the author's] intention in saying *alive*, he means the one who possesses life. Here, life is the knowledge of truth and the doing of good, as evidenced by the statement of this apostle in his Gospel concerning our Lord, "The word by which I have spoken to you is [both] spirit and life."[151] That is, it is true and right(eous). His statement, "because God did not send his Son to the world in order to judge the world but to give life to the world,"[152] means in order to acquaint them with the knowledge of the truth and the doing of good. His intention in his [use of the word] *dead* is that [the leader of the church] is deficient in perfection. Deficiency is incompatible with perfection, just as existence is incompatible with nonexistence. Paul the apostle mentioned this meaning with regard to the property [or legal claim] of widows;[153] "And as for she who delights in pleasure, she has died even though she is alive."[154] This way of life is not a way [of life] at all.[155] Thus, it is necessary to juxtapose two contradictory things.

As for his statement, *watch out and strengthen the remnant, lest you die*, the *watchfulness* concerns falling short of attaining perfection. And the

150. Reading *ḍibṭ* for *ḍābiṭ*, though *ḍābiṭ* is in both the Birmāwī edition (p. 73) and Par. Ar. 67 (f. 31r, line 5).

151. John 6:36.

152. John 3:16.

153. Par. Ar. 67 (f. 31r, line 15, to f. 31v, line 1) reads: "and Paul the apostle mentions this meaning in section five from the first letter to Timothy regarding believing widows."

154. 1 Timothy 5:6.

155. Par. Ar. 67 (f. 31v, lines 2–3) reads: "It is not the way of life; it is the way of death."

strengthening of the remnant means [his] establishment of them [i.e., his flock] in their faith and their deeds. So indeed their perfection is collectively [derived] from his perfection, and his perfection from their perfection. By *the remnant* he means his people, the flock of [his] parish, those under his leadership. As for his statement *lest you die*, he was warning [the leader] in case he failed to strengthen the remnant through the ultimate death,[156] and if not, by necessity he would die the natural death, whether he has strengthened them or not.

As for his statement, *because I have not found your faith and your deeds perfect before my God*, indeed, according to this intention, *perfection* has two degrees. The first is the perfection of the person in himself by his faith and righteous deeds. With respect to this degree [of perfection], the gospel has indicated that rich man who kept the commandments in its statement, "If you want to be perfect, go and sell all that you have and give it to the poor and follow me."[157] This is the first [degree of] perfection. The other degree is the degree of leaders and teachers who do not benefit from their perfection in themselves; rather, their perfection abounds to someone else and it perfects [that person] through faith and deeds.[158] Our Lord indicated this degree in his statement, "Whoever does and teaches this will be called great in the kingdom of heaven."[159] No doubt, this leader did not possess the first perfection nor the second, as we explained, either because he went astray and was tempted, or because he did not strengthen his people. As for the statement *before my God*, his understanding concerning the Lord of all only proves true insofar as he is human.[160]

He says, *remember how you received and [how you] went astray*. As for his [act of] receiving, it is clear that he received from someone else, and

156. Lit., "destroying death" (*al-mawt al-ikhtirāmī*). Ibn Kātib Qayṣar is likely referring here to the "second death" of Revelation 21:8, which stands in contrast to the natural death that everyone will experience.

157. Matthew 19:21.

158. Here, I follow the reading in Par. Ar. 67 (f. 32r, line 3), which ends with *fa-yukammiluhu bi-l-imān wa-l-aʿmāl* (and it perfects [that person] through faith and deeds), instead of the reading in Birmāwī (p. 74), which mistakes the phrase as *bi-kalimat al-imān wa-l-aʿmāl* (through the word of faith and deeds).

159. Matthew 5:19.

160. Ibn Kātib Qayṣar here is concerned that Jesus has called God "my God," which implies his differentiation from God. The commentator's explanation is that this statement only applies to the humanity of Jesus. Par. Ar. 67 (f. 32r, lines 8–9) reads "except regarding his receiving the body of our nature."

that other person is either an evil spirit or a deceitful, heretical person. This is evidenced by his lack of precision and [lack of] reliability. As for *going astray*, [the meaning] is plain [i.e., to be taken literally]: It is deviation from the way of truth and goodness. He says, *Take heed and repent.* As for *taking heed*, it is with respect to what he attained and what he received praise for. As for *repentance*, it pertains to his [experience of] temptation and his lack of care in teaching his parish. The faithful wise person is the one who gives to his flock their spiritual nourishment in its proper time. As for the divine ordinance of repentance it is a warning that he should not do in the future like [he did in] the past, for which he repented. [The meaning of] *taking heed* is obvious. It is holding fast to the requirements of repentance and being on guard from falling into whatever contradicts its wisdom [i.e., the wisdom of repentance]. Indeed, people in their behavior are of five categories.

The first is the category of the righteous person. This is the one who walks and does not stumble, and thus must rise up from his error. This category is very precious: No one from among humankind reaches it except one who is in accordance with the life of the Lord of all in the body. The one who said, "Who from among you reproaches me for sin?"[161] The one who said "I am the good Shepherd."[162] Likewise, he said, "There is no one good except God alone."[163] This category resembles the sun.

The second is [the category of] the heedful person.[164] This is the one who rarely stumbles and who stands so he does not keep stumbling, like Moses and Isaiah and Jonah and Zechariah and Peter the apostle and whoever follows the path of these luminaries. This category resembles the moon.

The third is [the category of] the pure person. This is the one who walks and stumbles, then stands and in the end remains standing. This is the category of the pure people belonging to the old and new [scriptures], like David the prophet,[165] Josiah the King, and others besides these two. This category resembles the stars.

The fourth is [the category of] the fallen person. This is the one who walks and stumbles but does not stand up [again]. [This category] has two

161. John 8:46.

162. John 10:11.

163. Luke 18:19.

164. Birmāwī (p. 75) omits the word *ṭabaqah* (category), but Par. Ar. 67 (f. 32v, line 11) includes it.

165. It is curious Ibn Kātib Qayṣar names David as a prophet instead of as a king.

divisions. The first is to repent and not receive [forgiveness] like Cain, Esau, Saul the King, Eli the priest, and Judas Iscariot. The other is not to repent at all but to continue in one's errors, like Jeroboam son of Nebat and whoever follows his path. This category resembles a lamp that shines a little and then is extinguished.

The fifth is the category of the wicked, like those who from their upbringing concern themselves with evil or the worship of idols, or whoever resembles them. This category resembles the outer darkness. This is the opposite of the first category. The person cited here is the second category.[166]

As for his statement, *and if you do not repent and if you do not watch out I will come like a thief and you will not know the hour in which I come to you*, he means by his *coming* here the coming of his command and judgment, designating what is necessarily implied by what necessarily implies it.[167] He is warning him about what brings about the ultimate death.[168] This is conditioned upon his failure to repent. As for *coming like a thief*, one aspect of the analogy is that the thief does not stop watching for the carelessness, absentmindedness, or indifference of the owner of the house with respect to [the need for] vigilance,[169] or his disregard for prudence, until [the thief] perceives the opportune time and breaks in quickly. Thus, the coming of death is sudden. [It comes] at an unknown hour, at an imperceptible moment, and at an unknown time, like a trap shut upon a bird when it is careless.

As for his statement *but furthermore I have a few other names [of persons] in Sardis who have not soiled their clothes with a woman*, this concurs with his statement *and strengthen the remnant*. It is as if he says, "but furthermore I have other names different from this remnant, and they are [only] a few in number in relation to the former group." You have come to know that by the [word] *names* he means their designations. As for their *garments*, he means the power of desire [lit., "desirous power"] as evidenced by the

166. Ibn Kātib Qayṣar is indicating that the bishop being discussed in the letter belongs to the second behavioral category. Par. Ar. 67 (f. 33r, lines 11–12) confirms the reading of the printed edition.

167. Arabic, *iṭlāqan lism al-malzūm 'alā al-lāzim*. Here, the commentator uses a standard phrase referring to the relation between the plain sense of the phrase (in this case, the reference to "his coming") and its figurative sense (i.e., "the coming of his command and judgment"). See also Ibn Kātib Qayṣar's commentary on Revelation 3:15 (Birmāwī, 88), where he uses the same phrase for a similar purpose.

168. Lit., "destroying death" (*al-mawt al-ikhtirāmī*).

169. Par. Ar. 67 (f. 33v, line 2) reads: "indifference regarding [the owner's] vigilance."

statement of the apostle Jude in the ninth section of his epistle, "Be haters of garments, the dress of the soiled flesh,"[170] which means the use of his desirous power in depravities. Insofar as desire is [categorically] broader than depravity and depravity is broader than fornication in a certain respect, he distinguishes depravity with his statement *the defiled [flesh]*[171] and he distinguishes fornication by his statement *with a woman*, which means they did not [even] approach a woman. These *names* are the purest people who fully held fast to the sum of their virtues through abstinence from touching a woman at all, whether licitly or illicitly.[172] For his disavowal of women[173] is generally applicable. The evidence that the command is like this is his statement in the fourteenth section of Revelation,[174] when he saw the lamb standing on Mount Zion, and with [the lamb] were one hundred forty-four thousand. Indeed, a voice like thunder said to him, "These are the ones who have not soiled their clothes with a woman because they are virgins and these are those who walk with the Lamb wherever he goes."[175]

Indeed, if they were Israelites—I am speaking about the names in Sardis—they would be from the cohort of the one hundred forty-four thousand. If they were not Israelites, they would not be from the cohort of that number, but from the faithful virgins from among the nations [i.e., Gentiles]. Would that I knew—even while the bed of the wife is pure in this text and generally—how this aforementioned defilement prevails over it. The answer is that virginity is more honorable than marriage because in [the former] one associated with the pure angels and in [the latter] one associated with beasts and the rest of the animals. And for this reason

170. Jude 1:23. The Birmāwī edition (p. 76) has the phrase "the soiled flesh" (*al-jasad al-najas*), which links the vocabulary of Jude 1:23 (*al-najas*) with the verb form used in Revelation 3:4 (*najisa*). By contrast, Par. Ar. 67 (f. 33v, line 12) has "the defiled flesh"(*al-jasad al-danis*), which seems an attempt to reconcile the text with the subsequent commentary by the author.

171. Both the Birmāwī edition (p. 76) and Par. Ar. 67 (f. 33v, line 15) cite the adjective *al-danis*. In the case of the former, this is different from the verbal and adjectival forms cited above in Revelation 3:4 and Jude 1:23. In the case of the latter, the adjective used here by the scribe is consistent with the adjectival form in his citation of Jude.

172. Here Ibn Kātib Qayṣar makes use of the Islamic legal terms for purity: *ḥalāl* and *ḥarām*.

173. Lit., "the woman."

174. Revelation 14:1. The section referred to here does not correspond to the section numbering in Birmāwī's edition, where Ibn Kātib Qayṣar comments on this passage in section 65. For its part, Par. Ar. 67 (f. 34r, line 4) appears to read: "the tenth section."

175. Revelation 14:4. Par. Ar. 67 (f. 34r, line 7) reads "walk with the lamb."

abstinence is more honorable than marriage, and in this respect he has labeled [marriage] as *soiled* in distinction to abstinence.[176]

As for his statement, *and they walk with me in white garments because they are worthy*, this [act of] *walking* is a report on their friendship with the lamb and their journeying with him wherever he walks. And that, moreover, will take place in the first resurrection; otherwise their bodies would not have risen till now.[177] [The phrase] *white garments* here symbolizes abstinence[178] and its honor, with respect to the fact that white is a pure color resembling light and [even] the most insignificant impurity has an effect upon it. It is noteworthy because the white garments came in the vision [*al-jalayān*]. [It is] a symbol with two meanings. The first is the preeminence[179] of abstinence as evidenced by his statement *the ones who have not soiled their clothing with a woman and walk with me in white garments.* As for the second [meaning], it symbolizes praise, thankfulness, grace, and divine joy. In this class, there are categories according to aptitude, for Scripture says, "The lodgings in the house of my father are many."[180]

The vision refers to four categories.[181] The first is the category of the preeminence of abstinence as evidenced by his statement,[182] *Whoever conquers in this way, I will clothe him with a white garment.* The second is the category of prophecy,[183] as evidenced by his statement in the fifth section concerning the twenty-four elders that "they are wearing white garments."[184] It is not said that they had that [dress] on account of their abstinence, because there were married people among them like Moses, David, and others besides these two. The third is the category of the martyrs,[185] as evidenced by his statement "I will give to each one of them a white robe."[186]

176. Par. Ar. 67 (f. 34v, line 1) supports the reading of the printed edition here.

177. Revelation 20:5–6. See the introduction for further discussion on the meaning of the phrase "the first resurrection."

178. Par. Ar. 67 (f. 34v, line 5) reads *manzilat al-ʿiffah* (the status/dignity of chastity).

179. Literally, "primogeniture" (*bikriyyah*).

180. John 14:2.

181. Par. Ar. 67 (f. 34v, line 13) enumerates three categories (see notes 185 and 188 below).

182. Par. Ar. 67 (f. 34v, line 14) adds "in section 15."

183. Par. Ar. 67 (f. 34v, line 15) reads "the martyrs" instead of "prophecy," and then provides "section 28" as a cross-reference for the verse that follows.

184. Revelation 4:4.

185. Par. Ar. 67 (f. 35r, lines 2–3) combines the third and fourth categories and labels it "the category of the people [who experience] oppression and martyrdom."

186. Revelation 6:1.

The fourth is the category of the people of oppression and tribulation, as evidenced by his statement, "These are they who have come from oppressive tribulations, so their robes have been made white and washed in the blood of the lamb."[187] The Lord of all (glory be to him), if he is [in fact] the foundation of every virtue, possesses these three ranks—I mean, abstinence (both mental and sensory), kingship, and the suffering of tribulations.[188] When he appeared on Mount Tabor, he was seen in a white garment, "pure and bright-shining like lightning and snow, [and it was] impossible for any whitened thing on earth to be like it."[189] This virgin apostle is among those who saw and testified to this vision.[190]

As for his statement, *they are worthy*, it means that they are worthy of this status regarding this virtue due to their readiness to honor it [i.e., abstinence], because they struggled against the enticements of nature, and they were in their bodies upon the earth like angels in heaven. And it is right that triumph and victory is theirs. He raised his standard, which is *white*ness, and accordingly he says, *whoever conquers in this way I will clothe him with a white garment*, although whiteness is also the emblem of those who endure tribulations, like the martyrs, confessors, and those similar to them, just as will be discussed in its [proper] place.

As for his statement, *I will not erase their names from the book of life*, it appears that what this *book* indicates is more specific than what the book that will be mentioned later indicates.[191] For this reason, it is specified by its genitival relationship to the word *life*, for this [book] symbolizes the one who has become established in divine knowledge[192] from among the righteous especially. Luke the evangelist signaled this in his gospel when the seventy returned two by two from our Lord's mission, rejoicing over the [evil] spirits' obedience to them. So [the Lord] said to them, "Rejoice that

187. Revelation 7:14.

188. It appears that Par. Ar. 67, with its three (rather than four) categories, provides the earlier reading, and that the manuscript on which the Birmāwī edition is based has added the fourth category, without fully reconciling that addition to what follows, insofar as it concludes with a summary of only three categories. The category of "kingship" seems to map onto that of martyrdom, insofar as the martyrs were understood to earn crowns in heaven.

189. Mark 9:3.

190. Ibn Kātib Qayṣar ascribes authorship of Revelation to the apostle John the son of Zebedee.

191. See Revelation 20:13–15.

192. Par. Ar. 67 (f. 36r, lines 3–4) reads *al-ʿilm al-ilāhī* (divine knowledge), while the Birmāwī edition (p. 78) has *al-ʿālim al-ilāhī* (the divine knower).

your names are written in the heavens,"[193] which is to say: [that they are] among the cohort of the victorious. As for the fact that he does not erase their names, divine knowledge is disclosed when the end of each person comes upon him, whether good or evil. Whatever has been established in divine knowledge is not able to contradict what is commanded concerning [that person]. So it is not possible for the end of these people to be good unless it is good and they prove victorious. Blessed be the one whose name is established in this place.

As for his statement, *I will certainly manifest their names before my father and before his angels*, he wanted [to use] the verbal noun along with its verb for emphasis.[194] It is also known that their names are manifest to God and his angels. But what is the benefit in manifesting something [that is already] manifest? What he means is that they are not shown to be the forsaken ones, but their names are made public and they are mentioned to signal [God's] concern for them and [his] pleasure with them. Indeed that [concern/pleasure] belongs to the cohort of the blessed ones. As for his statement, *Whoever has ears to hear, let them hear*, and the rest of the section, its interpretation has already taken place.

I know that what he writes here to the leader of Sardis and what he wrote to the leader of Ephesus [have] similarities and analogies between them, for there he said, *This is what the one who holds the seven stars in his right hand says*, and here he says, *This is what the one who has the seven spirits of God and the seven stars says*. Moreover, there he said, *I know your deeds*, and here he says, *I know your deeds*. There he said, *[But I have] against you the fact that you have left your first love behind*, and here he says, *I have not found your faith and your deeds perfect before my God*. There he said, *Remember then how you have fallen and repent, lest I come*, and here he says, *So remember how you received and [how you] went astray. Take heed and repent. If you do not repent and if you do not watch out I will come.*[195]

16. (3:7) "To the angel of the church of Philadelphia, write:[196] 'This is what the Most Holy, the Truth,[197] says, the one who has in his hand the

193. Luke 10:20.

194. The commentator is referring to the text's use of the "cognate accusative." The phrase in the text of Revelation reads literally "I will manifestly manifest their names before my father."

195. Par. Ar. 67 (f. 36r, lines 13–14) summarizes this verse instead of quoting it verbatim.

196. Par. Ar. 67 (f. 36r, lines 15–16) reads "Write to the angel of the church that is for the love of the brethren (*maḥabbat al-ikhwa*), and in Coptic it is Philadelphia."

197. This is one of the Islamic names for God.

keys of the house of David, who opens and no one shuts, and when he shuts then no one is able to open: (3:8) "I know your deeds and your faith. Behold, I have set before you an opened door that no one is able to shut, for you have [only] a little strength and [yet] have kept my word and have not denied my name. (3:9) Behold, I will rescue you from the synagogue of Satan, [from] the ones who say that they are Jews, though they are not a people and they tell lies. Behold, I will make them come and bow down to you and be cast down before your feet. All of them will know that I myself have loved you. (3:10) As for you, you have kept my word and [preserved] my patience, and on account of this I also will preserve you from the trial that is coming upon all creation in order to test all who are upon the earth. (3:11) I myself am coming quickly, so hold fast to what you have so that no one takes your crown. (3:12) Whoever overcomes I will place him as a pillar in the house of my God. He shall no longer go out, and I will write the name of my God upon him and the name of the new city that belongs to my father, Jerusalem, which descends out of heaven from [the presence of] my God and [I will write upon him] my new name. (3:13) Whoever has ears to hear let him hear what the Spirit says to the churches."'"

His statement, *Write to the angel of the church of Philadelphia,* [refers to] a city called by the name of the one who founded it, whose name is Attalus Philadelphus,[198] which means "the one who loves the sister." It is a Greek term whose translation is as follows: *filō*, "the one who loves," and *dalfiyā*, "the sister," because at the end [of the word] there is a marker of the feminine.[199]

As for his statement, *This is what the Most Holy, the Truth, says, the one who has in his hand the keys of the house of David*, the *Most Holy* and the *Truth* are among the divine attributes, and he has modified the formulation of the active participle into a verbal noun for the purposes of emphasis, just as one says [that] in the Just One there is Justice, so that in this way, it might be distinguished from human attributes.[200] By the *keys* he

198. Attalus II Philadelphus (220–138 BCE). Par. Ar. 67 (f. 37r, line 6) reads *Baṭlīmūs Qushāsh*.

199. Ibn Kātib Qayṣar misunderstands the Greek derivation here. The second part of the Greek word *philadelphia* is not the term for "sister," which has a different feminine ending (Gr. *adelphē*). Rather, the feminine ending of *philadelphia* is simply a grammatical feature of the compound noun form connoting the abstract concept of "brotherly love."

200. Ibn Kātib Qayṣar here appears to situate his discussion of divine names within an Islamic context, because the terms "Most Holy," "Truth," and "Justice" are also the divine names

means legal force, because the obedience of the one who is commanded to [his] commander is like the obedience of the lock to its key. This is by way of [presenting] a simile and a comparison designed to produce understanding in the hearer.[201] By the *house of David* he means his familiarity with Judah and Israel. The beauty of this comparison is that when he recalls keys, he [also] recalls a house. This meaning moreover confirms that it is understood with respect to his excellent humanity. As for him, even though he is King of heaven and earth, indeed God promised to the sons of Israel to wait expectantly on the tongues of his prophets [for the Messiah], and indeed it happened this way: Accordingly, Gabriel the angel[202] said to the Virgin Mary, the mistress of the women inhabiting the world, "He will sit upon the throne of David his father."[203] Even though he did not have a father from humankind,[204] his human kinship in relation to his mother[205] came via David, then Judah.

As for his statement, *who opens and no one shuts, and when he shuts then no one is able to open*, by *opening* and *shutting* he means the execution of his judgments concerning life and death, happiness and unhappiness, condemnation and forgiveness, giving and depriving, including examples of this from the sources of the exalted power [of God],[206] just as it is mentioned in the gospel of this apostle:[207] "But He has given all judgment to the Son."[208] He [i.e., Christ] said concerning himself: "I have been given all authority in heaven and on earth."[209] He does not deprive once he has given, nor does he give once he has deprived. As for his statement,

of God in Islamic theology: see L. Gardet, "al-Asmā' al-Ḥusnā," *EI*^{2}, ed. P. Bearman, *et al.*, BrillOnline *Reference Works*, http://referenceworks.brillonline.com/entries/encyclopaedia-of-islam-2/al-asma-al-husna-COM_0070, consulted March 24, 2018.

201. Par. Ar. 67 (f. 37r, line 14) reads *sāmiʿ* (hearer), while the Birmāwī edition (p. 81) has *samʿ* (hearing).

202. Par. Ar. 67 (f. 37v, line 4) omits "angel" and instead reads "peace be upon him."

203. Luke 1:32.

204. Following the text of Par. Ar. 67 (f. 37v, line 6), which reads *ab min al-bashar* (a father from humankind), instead of *ab al-bashar* (the father of humankind; Birmāwī, 81).

205. Following the text of Par. Ar. 67 (f. 37v, line 7), which reads *al-umm* (mother), instead of *al-umam* (nations; Birmāwī, 81).

206. Par. Ar. 67 (f. 37v, line 11) omits *quwwah* (power) and instead reads *qudrah* (capacity).

207. Ibn Kātib Qayṣar identifies the author of the gospel of John with the author of Revelation.

208. John 5:22.

209. Matthew 28:18.

I know your deeds and your faith, an interpretation of something similar took place earlier.

As for his statement, *Behold, I have set before you an opened door and no one is able to shut it*, by this *door* he means preparedness and acquiescence toward him, as evidenced by the statement of the apostle Paul, "A great door has opened to me in the gospel,"[210] meaning the preparedness of a people who enter the faith. Thus, this leader brought it about that he called the archheretics who were in the city to obey and submit to him. As for the fact that *no one is able to shut* it, no one is able able to move them toward obedience. Thus his statement concerning the synagogue of Satan: *Behold I will make them come and bow down to you and be cast down before your feet.*

He says, *for you have [only] a little strength and [yet] have kept my word and have not denied my name.* The *strength* that he has is the safeguarding of the faith, as well as the fact that he does not deny [his name]. His statement *a little* means that [the leader's] punishment was not prolonged nor did his suffering increase, such that his endurance would disappear and his perseverance would become difficult. But [the leader] took on martyrdom as an easy battle, as evidenced by his statement, *so hold fast to what you have so that no one takes your crown.* As for his statement, *you have kept my word*, by this he means his keeping of the commandments by his diligence in worship and his perseverance in it.

As for his statement, *Behold, I will rescue you from the synagogue of Satan, [from] the ones who say that they are Jews, though they are not a people and they tell lies*, the *synagogue of Satan* is everyone who has departed from the truth. Belonging to their group are *the ones who say that they are Jews, though they are not a people and they tell lies*, but we have already interpreted this very same text with regard to what he wrote to the church of Smyrna.

As for his statement, *Behold, I will make them come and bow down to you and be cast down before your feet*, their *coming* to him is their obedience to him. This is the first gift. Their *bowing* to him and their *being cast before his feet* constitute their submission to him. This is the second gift. As for his statement, *All of them will know that I myself have loved you. As for you, you have kept my word and [preserved] my patience*, he taught them that our Lord (to him be glory) *loved* this leader. This is the third gift. *The keeping of his word* has [already] been explained. Now, as for the genitive construction

210. 1 Corinthians 16:9.

of *patience* in relation to the Lord of all, indeed a word is joined sometimes to its subject as in how you might say, "This sword is my workmanship," and sometimes to its object as in how you might say to the wounded, "This is your wound."[211] Here, the meaning of his statement, *and my patience*, is that of a genitive of a word with its object. So, the implication of the statement is that he teaches all of them, "I have loved you and you have kept my word and confirmed my name."

As for his statement, *on account of this I also will keep you from the trial coming upon all creation in order to test all who are upon the earth*, it means that on account of *keeping* my commandments, *I will keep you from the coming trial.* The trial that descends upon creation concurs with the outbreak of the unbelieving kings in those days at the instigation of Satan against all of the believers. Their punishments were innumerable in kind: being consumed by fire, being flayed,[212] boiling in oil and tar, having limbs dismembered piece by piece, having the body basted on iron grills,[213] being crushed with the breaking wheel,[214] having vinegar and lime poured on wounds, being sawed with a saw, being crucified with nails, being cast to lions, snakes, and other beasts, and finally being killed by the sword. For this reason, the end of the canons of the apostles was composed from the chronicles, [and] what was transcribed was [as follows]: "When the disciples had finished laying down the new traditions [*sunnah*, pl. *sunan*], and believers had multiplied upon the earth, the emperors—under the deceptions of Satan—were unbelievers, and they hastened to kill the believers and to torture them so that they would worship idols. In distress, [facing] adversity, and under compulsion, they were occupied with the establishment of other traditions [*sunan*], about 356 years [after the birth of Christ], around the time of Emperor Constantine the Great. If someone was about to obtain the crown of martyrdom hastily [and] without

211. Ibn Kātib Qayṣar is referring to Revelation 3:10 and discussing the difference between an objective genitive and a subjective genitive. In the two examples he gives, he is demonstrating how in the first case the person is the agent in creating the sword but in the second case the person is the subject of receiving the wound.

212. Par. Ar. 67 (f. 39r, line 7) reads "and ice" (*wa thalj*) instead of "flaying."

213. Lit., "combs, rakes" (*amshāṭ*).

214. Arabic, *al-hanbāzīn*: See http://st-takla.org/Coptic-Faith-Creed-Dogma/Coptic-Rite-n-Ritual-Taks-Al-Kanisa/Dictionary-of-Coptic-Ritual-Terms/9-Coptic-Terminology_Heh-Waw-Yeh/henbazeen.html (consulted March 29, 2018).

punishment, his situation would be prolonged and his patience would disappear, so there is no doubt that this involved protection and care."[215]

As for his statement, *I myself am coming quickly*,[216] this *coming* is a sign regarding the death of this leader by martyrdom,[217] and on account of this he followed it with his statement, *so hold fast to what you have so that no one takes your crown.*

As for his statement, *Whoever overcomes I will place him as a pillar in the house of my God. He shall no longer go out*, we have [already] interpreted what his *overcoming* is. The *pillar* means the permanent foundation [of the house] as evidenced by his statement, *he shall no longer go out*, and by the saying of the apostle Paul,[218] "That we might know how there must be in the house of God—which is the church of the living God—a pillar and permanent foundation for the truth."[219] By the *house of his God* he means the heavenly Jerusalem, and by his statement *he shall no longer go out* he means that this perpetual condition in blessedness shall not end, nor will it have a termination, but rather it shall be eternal and everlasting. As for his statement, *I will write the name of my God upon him and the name of the new city that belongs to my father, Jerusalem, which descends out of heaven from [the presence of] my God and [I will write upon him] my new name*, you know that *the name* sometimes means nothing more than the name, just as he said, "a stone, and upon it a name is written."[220] But sometimes it means a named individual, as with his statement, "but I have among you a few names"[221]—that is, a few persons. Just as [the book of] Acts says, "in those days Peter rose in the midst of the brethren and there were many gathered there, totaling one hundred twenty names."[222] Its meaning here is "persons." There are three names whose writing is mentioned here. The first is his statement, *the name of my God*. I think that this name is the one mentioned in section 20 concerning the one who is faithful and true: "Upon his

215. Reference unknown.

216. Par. Ar. 67 (f. 39v, line 5) begins this phrase with "Behold."

217. Ibn Kātib Qayṣar evidently views the coming of Jesus as symbolic for the personal judgment awaiting every Christian at his or her death.

218. Par. Ar. 67 (f. 39v, line 10–11) adds "in the fourth section of his letter to Timothy his disciple."

219. 1 Timothy 3:15.

220. Revelation 2:17.

221. Revelation 3:4.

222. Acts 1:15.

head are many crowns."[223] A name is written there that no one is capable of knowing except for that one alone, so any attempt to know this name after this statement is foolishness because it is among the mysteriously hidden secrets guarded from humanity and other [creatures] besides them. Perhaps in the knowledge of this greatest name or its pronunciation there is [special] influence, and for this reason it has been hidden and concealed because among the names of God (may he be exalted) that are mentioned in the old and new scriptures there are names never mentioned, nor [is it said] how they are in harmony. But rather, [they are only mentioned] at great festivals and special times, like the Hebrew name that has four letters and the name that has six letters,[224] as well as other names along the same vein. Now this written name is the greatest of them, and this is what his statement conceals with respect to it. In the book containing the stories of the apostles, there is mentioned something that corresponds to this meaning: "Indeed, they were working wonders in [his] name,"[225] and also, according to the statement of Peter the apostle to the paralytic who asked him for help, "What I have, I give it to you. In the name of Jesus of Nazareth, get up."[226]

The second [use of the word "name"] is his statement, *[I will write] the name of my God upon him and the name of the new city which belongs to my father,*[227] *Jerusalem, which descends out of heaven from [the presence of] my God.* If he indicates by this *name* the term Jerusalem, then it is revealed, but if he indicates this city by other names, then it is secret. Perhaps it [i.e., the name] is that which he said about it at first: that it was written on the stone. May God grant [us] knowledge with certainty about that. [My] discourse regarding the city *which descends out of heaven* will come [later] in its place, according to the will of God (may he be exalted).

The third [use of the word "name"] is his statement, *my new name.* This name is mentioned in section 20,[228] in which [the following] was said about

223. Revelation 19:12. The passage referred to here actually corresponds to section 103 in Birmāwī's edition.

224. Ibn Kātib Qayṣar is here probably speaking of the two divine names in Hebrew: *YHWH* and *Elohim*.

225. See Acts 4:30.

226. Acts 4:6.

227. Par. Ar. 67 (f. 40v, line 8) omits "my father."

228. Par. Ar. 67 (f. 40v, line 15) reads "twenty-eight." The passage referred to here in fact corresponds to section 103 in Birmāwī's edition.

the Lord of all: "A name is written upon his robe and his thigh, King of Kings and Lord of Lords."[229] So this is his new name. As for the [act of] writing contained in his statement, *I will write the name of my God upon him*, indeed the method of its *writing* is an improbable difficulty if the expression is taken literally, for it belongs to the domain of sign and symbol. The closest thing to what he means by *writing* is identification. An example of this is when you know from a person that he is a son of so-and-so and a brother of so-and-so and a relative of so-and-so. Therefore, these three identifications refer to three associated meanings, and they [all] pertain to him.[230] You are made aware of [the different names] by him, and you know them just as you know from something written down what it refers to. *Writing* is the knowledge of this. Thus, the report of this section in this respect is in accordance with the following picture. "Whoever overcomes, I will take him into the kingdom [of heaven], and he knows that he has a relationship of favor to my God and to me, and he belongs to the people of the kingdom." As for the order in the mentioning of these three names, he began with the name of God to honor him, and he concluded with the name of our Lord because he is the last to be named and he remains in mind. And it is ordained that the name of the city comes in the middle. As for the remainder of this section, a similar interpretation has already taken place.

17. **(3:14) "To the angel of the church of Laodicea, write: 'This is what the Truth says, the faithful and true witness, the head of God's creation: (3:15) "I know your deeds, that you are neither coarse [*kathīf*] nor refined [*laṭīf*]. If you were cold water that at first was hot [*ḥār*], (3:16) then [you should] be water that is lukewarm [*fātir*]. You are not [to be] hot water [*sukhn*], nor are you [to be] cold [*bārid*] water, lest I cut you off at your extremity.[231] (3:17) For you say, 'I am rich, and I do not need to acquire anything,' yet, do you not know that you are weak and miserable, that you are beggarly and poor, blind and naked? (3:18) I advise you to buy gold from me refined in fire, in order that you may become rich. I**

229. Revelation 19:16.

230. Lit., "him."

231. The Greek text of Revelation 3:15–16 reads: "I know your works; you are neither cold nor hot. I wish that you were either cold or hot. So, because you are lukewarm, and neither cold nor hot, I am about to spit you out of my mouth." Both the Sahidic and Bohairic follow the Greek of this passage quite closely (Horner, *CopticNT-South* 7.298–99; Horner, *CopticNT-North* 4.467–68).

will clothe you with bright garments lest the disgrace of your nakedness be made manifest, and I will put ointment[232] in your eyes that you may see clearly, (3:19) for the ones whom I love, I myself discipline and instruct. So be zealous for good and repent; (3:20) for, behold, I stand at the door and I knock, so whoever hears and opens the door for me, I will enter with him and I will eat with him, and he [will remain] with me. (3:21) To whoever conquers I will grant that he sits with me upon my throne just as I did when I conquered [and] sat with my Father upon his throne. (3:22) Whoever has ears to hear, let him hear what the Spirit says to the churches."'"

As for his statement, *Write to the angel of the church of Laodicea*, it is known that its angel is its leader and that the city is famous. As for his statement, *This is what the Truth says, the faithful and true witness*, *Truth* is an attribute of our Lord insofar as he is divine, and we have [already] mentioned the reason for [its] description by [its] verbal noun form and not in [its] subject form. *Faithful witness* is his description [i.e., his attribute] insofar as he is human. As for *witness*, it is because he was crucified in the body for the sake of calling creation to the knowledge of the truth. As for *faithful*, it is because he did not go astray and did not deviate from correctness in his speech, nor from grace in his action; nor did he wander from completeness in his instruction. In this he fulfilled faithfulness in a worthy manner.[233] For this reason he says after that, *and true*, for his relationship to the truth functions to confirm these indicated meanings.

As for his statement, *the head of God's creation*, by *head* [*ra's*] he means the ruling leader [*ra'īs*]. This is language known extensively in the law:[234] I mean the designation of our Lord as *head*. The basis of that comparison and analogy is that the head has leadership [*ri'āsah*] and control over the remainder of the body. On account of this, the location [of headship] was placed above [the body] as a form of honor for [the head]. On that subject, Paul the apostle says,[235] "He made himself head of the church, which is his body."[236] In section 9 of the epistle to the Colossians, [he writes,] "Just as Christ is the head of the church and in him—insofar as he is head—are

232. Arabic, *dharr* (powder).
233. Lit., "according to its worthiness."
234. Arabic, *sharī'ah* (law).
235. Par. Ar. 67 (f. 42v, line 6) adds "in the first section of the epistle to the Ephesians."
236. Colossians 1:18.

all [temporal] leaders [*ru'asā'*] and rulers."[237] And in section 16 of [the same letter, he also writes]: "You boast in vain, and you do not cling to the head from which is [derived] the entire composition of the body."[238] By *the creation of God* he means the heavenly and earthly creations, both elemental and composite, because [God] (may he be exalted) subjected everything to [Christ] and made him the heir and bearer of everything.

As for his statement, *I know your deeds, that you are neither coarse nor refined*, by *deeds* he means worship, just as we have said. By *coarse* he means the sinner, for the definition of coarseness in its plain sense is that it is a natural power by which the body naturally moves to [its] intermediate state.[239] So too, the sinner sinks with the allurements of nature and becomes rooted with them at the lowest level, like the stone that seeks out its place while falling to the depths, and [the sinner] becomes corporeal. This is one aspect of the analogy between the two meanings.[240] By *refined* he means the good person, and the definition of refinedness in its plain sense is that it is a natural power by which the body naturally moves from [its] intermediate state. Thus, the good person is elevated over the filth of nature and the allurements of lusts, being disdainful of them, and he becomes spiritual. Thus, he is not engrossed in [self-]reform, nor has he, through foolishness, fallen into evil, but [he occupies] an intermediate state between these two extremes. I know that the words "coarse" and "heavy" are one and the same in Coptic—namely, ϩⲟⲣϣ.[241] Likewise the [Coptic] word ⲥϧⲏⲙ[242] indicates in its plain sense "heat," and [indicates] in its figurative sense "refined," designating what is necessarily implied by what necessarily implies it.[243]

237. This seems to be a conflation of Colossians 1:18 and 2:10.

238. See Colossians 2:18–19.

239. Par. Ar. 67 (f. 43r, line 1) inserts "his discourse about deeds and" prior to the clause beginning with "the definition of base coarseness."

240. Par. Ar. 67 (f. 43v, line 6) reads "between the two meanings" instead of "of the two meanings" as in Birmāwī's edition (p. 88).

241. Here, Ibn Kātib Qayṣar seems to have confused two Coptic verbs: (1) ϩⲣⲟϣ (*hrosh*), which means "be heavy, slow, difficult" (Crum, *Coptic Dictionary*, 706a), and (2) ⲱⲣϣ (*ōrsh*), which means "be cold" (Crum, 530a) but in Bohairic is written ϩⲟⲣϣ (*horsh*).

242. Par. Ar. 67 (f. 43r, line 12) reads ⲥϧⲉⲙ (*s-hem*). Ibn Kātib Qayṣar or one of his copyists has here incorrectly recorded the Coptic word ϩⲙⲟⲙ (*hmom*; "be hot"), which has the Bohairic form ϧⲏⲙ (*hēm*) (Crum, *Coptic Dictionary*, 677a).

243. Here again, Ibn Kātib Qayṣar's uses a standard phrase referring to the relation between the plain sense of the phrase (in this case, the reference to "heat") and its figurative

As for his statement, *If you were cold water that first was hot, then [you should] be water that is lukewarm. You are not [to be] hot water, nor are you [to be] cold water*, by [the phrase] *cold water* he means [having] little or no zeal in good deeds as evidenced by his statement after that, *be zealous for good and repent.*

By *hot water* he means intemperance and rash zeal beyond what is appropriate so that the natural [states] of hot and cold encounter [one another] in opposition. By *lukewarm water* he means the moderation between the extremities of excess and renunciation. For that reason, he says, *You are not [to be] hot water, nor are you [to be] cold water*, because the ideal condition belonging to the two extremes is their mean. It is as if he said, "Be zealous in a situation conducive to zeal, tranquil in a situation conducive to tranquility, just as in your deeds you [should] occupy a mean between goodness [*al-ṣalāḥ*] and wickedness [*al-ṭalāḥ*]." Wickedness is not at the extremity of goodness, so moderation in it is a virtue,[244] but [wickedness] is still in conflict with [righteousness]. [The leader] ought to have been contrary to that. Namely, "you should advance far in goodness, neglect wickedness entirely, and be moderate in zeal."[245]

As for his statement, *lest I cut you off at your extremity*, this threatened him if he persisted in two matters. The first is the tendency toward some evil things. The second is a lack of zeal for the good. By the *extremity* he means the neck or the head, because the word ϩⲑⲏⲕ in the Coptic language combines [the senses of] the *extremity* and the heart,[246] for it appears in the parable of the rich man and Lazarus with the meaning "extremity" when [the Gospel of Luke] says, "he might moisten the extremity of his

sense (i.e., "refined"). See also his commentary on Revelation 3:3 (Birmāwī, 76), where he uses the same phrase for a similar purpose.

244. Par. Ar. 67 (f. 43v, line 10) omits the phrase "so moderation in it is a virtue."

245. Ibn Kātib Qayṣar apparently is making a distinction between goodness and virtue by claiming that virtue consists of a moderate zeal. At the end of this sentence, Par. Ar. 67 (f. 43v, lines 12–13) adds the phrase "so moderation in it is a virtue, but [wickedness] is different from [goodness]." The placement of these clauses here juxtaposes this comment on moderation with the immediately preceding discussion of "moderation in zeal." The cases, however, do not match up: "Zeal" (*al-ghīrah*) is a feminine noun, while the subsequent pronoun—"moderation in *it* [*fīhi*]"—is masculine. This may suggest that, despite its difficulties, the Birmāwī edition (p. 89) presents an earlier reading here, and that the scribe of the Paris manuscript tried, with only partial success, to address what he saw as a problem in the text.

246. The Coptic word here should probably be ϩⲑⲏ (*ht-hē*), which in Bohairic means both "tip, edge" (Crum, 718a) and "heart" (Crum 714a).

finger,"[247] and it [also] appears in the parable of the two sons of the owner of the vineyard [when the Gospel of Matthew says], "it ate away at his heart,"[248] which means he felt remorse. Some of translators have translated it here as "the middle," used figuratively with respect to the heart, because the heart of everything is its middle. This [meaning] is permissible sometimes,[249] but its translation as the "extremity" is more suitable when we speak of it. On account of the fact that this statement is in the form of a threat, it is not conceivable that it is symbolic in its testimony.

His statement, *For you say, "I am rich, and I do not need to acquire anything,"*[250] means that this leader thus speaks within himself about himself. Wealth [means] accumulating a lot, generally speaking, whether with respect to money, knowledge, or intellectual virtue. The opposite of [wealth] is poverty, which is a lack of abundance[251] of these things or their scarcity.[252] By *rich* here he means privately owned, trivial things that make this leader believe that through them he is rich. [These things] suggest to him associations that are still to be mentioned and detailed, and these [associations] involve six most excellent characteristics. The first of them is zeal, and its opposite is negligence. The second of them is modesty, and its opposite is haughtiness. The third of them is endurance, and its opposite is fatigue. The fourth of them is intellectual alertness, and its opposite is forgetfulness. The fifth of them is knowledge, and its opposite is ignorance. The sixth of them is preparedness for eternal life through righteousness,[253] and its opposite is readiness for dissolution through evil.

As for his statement, *yet, do you not know that you are weak and miserable, that you are beggarly and poor, blind and naked?*, he applies common meanings by means of spiritual language to six particular meanings. These meanings indicate to us the six most excellent characteristics mentioned earlier. *Weak* is a term that pertains to the person who is weak in zeal and

247. Luke 16:24.

248. Matthew 21:29.

249. Lit., "at a distance" (*'alā bu'd*).

250. Par. Ar. 67 (f. 44r, line 10) adds "this is in the form of a story."

251. Par. Ar. 67 (f. 44r, line 13) omits "of abundance."

252. Ibn Kātib Qayṣar appears to be reflecting on the paradoxical meanings of "wealth." Literally, it refers to riches and is therefore deemed to be negative. Allegorically, however, it can refer to various virtuous characteristics and is therefore understood in positive terms.

253. Par. Ar. 67 (f. 44v, line 4) reads *bi-l-barr* (through righteousness), while the Birmāwī edition gives a nonsensical reading of *ri-l-barr*, which may be mistaken transcription of *dhī al-birr* (possessing of righteousness).

in other things. By this he means the person who is weak in zeal particularly, namely, the one who is negligent, as is evidenced by his statement after that, *be zealous for good.*[254] *Miserable* is a term that pertains to the misery of arrogance or pride,[255] as well as other things. By this he means arrogance especially, as is evidenced by his statement, *and repent*[256]—that is, [he should repent] of the kind of obnoxious characteristic that ruins every virtue. *Beggarly* is a term that pertains to [his] asking for alms in poverty, his taking refuge from degradation, [his] patience in the face of weakness, and the like. He means weakness particularly because the person possessing [weakness] takes refuge with whomever he sees, asking him for help as if begging from him [and] in need of him, though he does not benefit at all from it. The patient person is silently steadfast, as if content with whatever endurance is in him with regard to expecting support [from any source] other than from God. On account of this he says, *I advise you to buy gold from me refined in fire, in order that you may become rich.* We will resume the interpretation of this later.[257] *Poor* is a term that pertains to poverty in money, status, vigilance, and other things. Among these [options], its meaning [here] is poverty in[258] intellectual vigilance as if he was deprived or destitute of it. This is negligence on account of [his] lack of purity of heart and the abundance of his distress. Now, the one who is alert in his intellect is in contact with divine things, a witness to their fullness. Concerning this he says in the Gospel [of Matthew], "Blessed are those whose hearts are pure, for they will see God."[259] When he says in the revelatory vision, *Because, behold, I stand at the door and I knock, so whoever hears and opens the door to me, I will enter*, etc., the [act of] *entering* depends on two conditions: *hearing* and *opening. Hearing* is obedience, and *opening* is preparedness, just as was the case with his interpretation of what he wrote to the angel of the church of Philadelphia. We will elaborate upon

254. Revelation 3:19.

255. Par. Ar. 67 (f. 44v, line 13) omits "or pride."

256. Revelation 3:19.

257. Par. Ar. 67 (f. 45r, line 8) omits "further on."

258. The following section of text—"money, status, vigilance, and other things. Among these [options] its meaning is poverty in"—appears in Par. Ar. 67 (f. 45r, lines 9–10) but is missing from the Birmāwī edition (p. 92) due to the error of *homoteleuton* (when a scribe or editor skips from one line to another because of the repetition of a word or phrase, often at the end of a line). In this case, the repetition of the words "poverty in" probably caused the error.

259. Matthew 5:8.

that with clarity when [the time] comes. *Blind* describes the blindness of vision, and [this meaning] is well-known, but the blindness of mental perception is ignorance. [Here] he means the second [definition], as evidenced by his statement, *that I might put ointment in your eyes that you may see clearly.* We will relate the interpretation of this in its [proper] place.

As for [the word] *naked*, by *nakedness* he means the body of corruptibility. For human beings in the world are, on account of their deeds, of three classes: a class of good people, a class of evil people, and a class in which good and evil are mixed. In the hereafter, two [of these] classes will exist no more, because the third class will be singled out. Whoever has triumphed over his error[260] is from the first class. The one whose evil triumphs is from the second class. The holy Gospel indicates these two classes in its statement, "Indeed the judge will divide the sheep on his right and the goats on his left. He will send the former to comfort, and he will dismiss the latter to hell."[261] As for those on the right side, on account of their preparedness, their bodies shall become spiritual, imperishable, luminous, neither suffering pain nor being susceptible to corruptibility, which is the second death. This noble body Paul called "the body of immortality" with his statement,[262] "When we have put on the body of immortality, we will not be naked thereafter."[263] And he called it the spiritual body with his statement, "He will die in a corporeal body and he will rise in a spiritual body."[264] This revelatory vision calls the bodies, with respect to their existence, immortal and wearing *garments*, and with respect to their honor and their illumination, [it calls them] *bright*.[265] On account of this, he said, *bright garments*. As for those on the left, on account of their [lack of] preparedness, their bodies[266] are corporeal,[267] dark, and susceptible to the second death and to extreme pains. These bodies Paul called psychic,[268] and Revelation calls them *naked* with its statement, *lest the disgrace of your*

260. The Arabic word *khusr* may also mean "punishment for sin" (Lane, *Arabic-English Lexicon*, 2.740; see Qur'ān 103:2).

261. This quotation paraphrases Matthew 25:31–46.

262. Par. Ar. 67 (f. 46r, line 4) adds "in his second letter to the Corinthians."

263. See 2 Corinthians 5:2–3.

264. 1 Corinthians 15:44.

265. Par. Ar. 67 (f. 46r, line 8) reads "white" (*bīḍ*) instead of "bright" (*zāhiyah*).

266. Par. Ar. 67 (f. 46r, line 9 reads *ajsāduhum* and not *ajāduhum* as in the Birmāwī edition, p. 93).

267. Par. Ar. 67 (f. 46r, line 9) adds "psychic" (*nafsāniyyah*).

268. Arabic, *nafsāniyyah*.

nakedness be made manifest, because *nakedness* implies disgrace and sins imply humiliation.

He says: *I advise you to buy gold from me refined in fire in order that you may become rich.* As for his *advising* of him, [it is] evidence for [his] authorization of [free] choice and the absence of fate, with respect to the doing[269] of good or evil. But he, without compulsion, has certainly advised for the sake of benefit, if the one who hears[270] accepts [the call] and thus makes it his own. If he declines it, then it is on him. As for *buying,* [it is] business and a contract. If he acts righteously, there is a good reward; if he acts wickedly, there is an evil reward. By *gold* he means beautiful patience and endurance in the face of the onset of accidents and trials, for the characteristic of this metal is to endure the flames of a forge and various kinds of tests.[271] Regarding the thing he gives as his surety, as if it has a price or valuation, it is a trust placed in him, a commission [to be delivered] to him, and the determination that it will not be redeemed apart from him. There is [the phrase,] *refined in fire,* which means tried, tested, purified, inimitable. As for his *becoming rich,* it concerns whoever places his trust in him among the leaders or [whoever] seeks his help from among humankind. The Psalm says, "Do not place your trust in the principalities, nor in human beings."[272] The explanation of the text is as follows: "I advise you to turn to me, to place your trust in me, and I will give you pure patience by which you will be purified, and you can dispense[273] with needing or seeking help from anyone in this [matter]." That is [the reason for] his statement, *for the ones whom I love, I myself discipline.*[274]

As for his statement, *I will clothe you with bright garments lest the disgrace of your nakedness be made manifest,* you know that the *garments*[275] are

269. Following Par. Ar. 67(f. 46r, line 15), which correctly reads *'amal* (doing) instead of the mistaken repetition of the word *'adam* (absence) in Birmāwī (p. 93).

270. Par. Ar. 67 (f. 46v, line 2) reads *al-sāmi'*, and not *al-sāmah* as the Birmāwī edition (p. 93) mistakenly reads.

271. Par. Ar. 67 (f. 46v, line 7) adds "and it is that which he purchases."

272. Psalm 146:3.

273. The Arabic verb *tastaghanā* (to dispense with; to have no need for) is from the same root as "to be rich."

274. The final sentence—"That is [the reason for] his statement, *for I myself discipline the ones whom I love*"—appears in Par. Ar. 67 (f. 46v, line 15), but it is absent from the Birmāwī edition (p. 93).

275. Par. Ar. 67 (f. 47r, line 2) reads *thiyāb* (garments), while the Birmāwī edition (p. 94) has the nonsensical *ṣiyāb.*

the body of immortality and that their splendor is their illumination and their honor. The *clothing*, the *manifestation*, and the *disgrace* are plain [in their meaning]. *Nakedness* is the body of corruptibility. The explanation of the statement, *buy from me*, [refers to] an eternal body that entails the joy of eternity in a luminous way, such that your disgrace through the body of dark corruptibility, which entails misery in the place of judgment, is not made manifest.

As for his statement, *I will put ointment in your eyes that you may see clearly*, by *ointment* he means their preparedness for revelation because it is just like when ointment clarifies the vision for sight. Thus, preparedness clarifies the mental perception for revelation. By *his eyes* he means his mental perception, not his [physical] vision. But when he mentions ointment, it is good that he mentions vision in a figurative way. The evidence for the fact that he meant mental perception, not [physical] vision is his statement, *for the ones whom I love, I myself discipline and instruct.* The *knowledge* [of his instruction][276] means revelation, not sight through [physical] sense. By *seeing*, he means intellectual perception as is evidenced by the statement of that apostle,[277] "As for the one who does evil, he will not see God."[278] God is not seen by the [physical] sense [of sight]. By his [use of the] word, *clearly*, he means authentically, which involves no doubt and does not derive from the uncertainties[279] of fantasy and illusion. Concerning this, he was careful in his statement, *clearly*, when he said, *for the ones whom I love, I myself discipline and instruct. Love* is plain in its meaning, but as for their *discipline*, it is by trials so that the substance of the virtue of patience may become manifest in them. As for their *instruction*, it is by the superabundance of the revelation that came upon them. And as for his statement, *So be zealous for good and repent*, its interpretation has already taken place.

He says, *for, behold, I stand at the door and knock, so whoever hears and opens the door for me, I will enter with him and I will eat with him, and he [will remain] with me.* By *standing at the door*, he means [the fact that he is] extremely near and close, as evidenced by the statement of the apos-

276. The Arabic word for "knowledge" (*ʿilm*) comes from the same root as the verb "to instruct" (*ʿalima/yaʿlamu*).

277. Par. Ar. 67 (f. 47v, line 1) adds "in his third letter."

278. 3 John 1:11.

279. The commentator engages in a play on words here: *tashbīhāt* can mean both "uncertainties" and "allegories."

tle Mark,[280] "Then, when you see these events know that he is near, at the gates."[281] As *for knocking*, he means by it [his] warning[282] through his messengers [*rusul*] and his books [*kutub*]. As for *hearing*, he means obedience and many other things mentioned like that. As for *opening the door*, it is preparedness, welcoming, and acceptance.

As for his statement, *I will enter with him*, by that he means, "I will pour out upon him the Spirit and will illuminate his intellect." For this reason, this apostle said in his gospel, "We will come and take lodging with him."[283] As for his statement, *I will eat with him, and he [will remain] with me*, by *eating* he means the perception of divine things—attaining them and coming to knowledge of them. Indeed hunger and thirst have both come, meaning the longing for [divine things], in the word of the Lord on the tongue of Amos the prophet to the sons of Israel: "'Behold, days are coming' says the Lord [God], '[when] I will send hunger on the earth, not hunger for bread and not thirst for water, but for listening to the words of the Lord.'"[284] By longing, he means a yearning for the perception of divine things. If there is hunger and thirst, they are the longing for these [divine things], and it is clear that eating and drinking are the attainment of them. Drinking and eating have other meanings besides this, which we will not prolong [our discourse] by mentioning and [thus] depart from [our] intended purpose.

As for his statement, *To whoever conquers I will grant that he sits with me upon my throne*, it was mentioned earlier that *conquering* is being made manifest to the end of this life in the knowledge of the truth, the doing of good works,[285] and patience in the face of trials. *Granting* is plain [in its meaning]. By *sitting* he means dignity and solemnity, and by this *throne* upon which the victorious one sits, he means nobleness and the distinction granted to him by God (may he be exalted). Its genitive construction

280. Par. Ar. 67 (f. 47v, line 11) adds "in his Gospel."

281. Mark 13:29. The Arabic term used in Mark for "gates" is the same as that used in Revelation for "door" (*bāb*, pl. *abwāb*).

282. Ar. *indhār* (warning; announcement).

283. John 14:23.

284. Amos 8:11. Par. Ar. 67 (f. 48r, lines 5–7) does not cite Amos but instead cites Isaiah: "In the word of Isaiah the prophet to the sons of Israel, 'They will be hungry and thirsty, not for bread and not for water, but for every word which comes out of the mouth of God.'" In fact, this does not come from Isaiah, but seems to be an amalgam of Amos 8:11 and Deuteronomy 8:3 or Matthew 4:4.

285. Lit., "work of the good" (*ʿamal al-khayr*).

with our Lord is a genitive of possession. To this [may be added] a genitive of specification, in contradistinction to the *throne* that is the second noun of a genitive construction with the Father. By it [i.e., the throne], he means majesty, splendor, magnificence, kingship, and whatever is similar to [those things]. Its genitive construction is also one of possession. As for his statement, *just as I did when I conquered [and] sat with my Father upon his throne*, this is like the preceding statement, and by analogy [it has] three aspects. The first is [the act of] *conquering*, the second is [the act of] *sitting*, and the third is [the act of] sitting *upon the throne*. The explanation of the two statements together relates to knowledge, [good] work, and patience to the utmost extent among whomever I have warned, such that they have obeyed and prepared themselves: "I have poured out upon him the spirit of wisdom and knowledge. I have raised him up and distinguished him, just as I have *conquered*, and my Father has granted me majesty, splendor, and all authority in heaven and on earth." As for the rest of the section, an interpretation of something similar took place earlier. The interpretation of the first revelatory vision has [now] been completed in its entirety.

Works Cited

Abū Shākir Ibn al-Rāhib, *Kitāb al-tawārīkh*, al-juz' al-awwal, al-abwāb 1–47. Edited by S. Moawad. Silsilat Madrasat al-Iskandariyyah li-l-dirāsāt al-masīḥiyyah. Cairo: Madrasat al-Iskandariyyah, 2016.

Accad, Martin. "The Ultimate Proof-Text: The Interpretation of John 20:17 in Muslim-Christian Dialogue (Second/Eighth–Eighth/Fourteenth Centuries)." In *Christians at the Heart of Islamic Rule: Church Life and Scholarship in 'Abbasid Iraq*, edited by David Thomas, 199–214. Leiden: Brill, 2003.

Acts of Paul. Edited by Carl Schmidt, *Acta Pauli aus der Heidelberger koptischen Papyrushandschrift Nr. 1*, rev. ed. Leipzig: J. C. Hinrichs, 1905. Repr. 1965. Translated by W. Schneemelcher, in *New Testament Apocrypha*, rev. ed. Volume 2, 213–70. Cambridge: James Clarke & Co.; Louisville: Westminster/John Knox Press, 1992.

Adams, A. W. ed. *Commentarium libri quinque in Apocalypsim Joannis Evangelistae.* CSEL 92. Turnhout: Brepols, 1985.

Amphilochius of Iconium, *Seleuc.* (*Iambics to Seleucus*). Edited by E. Oberg, *Amphilochii Iconiensis iambi ad Seleucum.* Patristische Texte und Studien 9. Berlin: De Gruyter, 1969.

Andrew of Caesarea. *Commentary on the Apocalypse.* Published as *Studien zur Geschichte des griechischen Apokalypse-Textes.* Edited by J. Schmid. Volume 1, 1–268. Münchener theologische Studien 1. Munich: Karl Zink, 1955. Translated by Eugenia Scarvelis Constantinou. Washington, D.C.: The Catholic University of America Press, 2011.

Arethas of Caesarea, *Commentary on the Apocalypse.* Published as *Studien zur Geschichte des griechischen Apokalypse-Textes.* Edited by J. Schmid. Volume 1, 207–458. Münchener theologische Studien 1. Munich: Karl Zink, 1955. See also PG 106.

Artemidorus, *Onir.* (*Interpretation of Dreams*). Published as *Artemidori Daldiani onirocriticon libri V.* Edited by R. A. Pack. Leipzig: Teubner, 1963.

Assfalg, J. *Die Ordnung des Priestertums: ein altes liturgisches Handbuch der koptischen Kirche.* Cairo: Publications du Centre d'études orientales. Coptica 1. Cairo: Centre d'études orientales, 1955.

Athanasius of Alexandria. *C. Ar.* (*Orations against the Arians*). PG 26.12–468.

———. *gent.* (*Against the Nations*). Edited by R. W. Thomson. Oxford: Clarendon Press, 1971.

———. *v. Anton.* (*Life of Antony*). Edited by G. J. M. Bartelink, SC 400. Paris: Cerf, 1994.

———. *virg.* (*On Virginity*). Edited by R. Casey. "Der dem Athanasius zugeschriebene Traktat PERI PARTHENIAS," *Sitzungsberichte der preussischen Akademie der Wissenschaften* 33 (1935): 1026–45.

Atiya, Aziz S. "Būlus al-Būshī," *CE* 2.423–4.

ʿAwaḍ, Jirjis Fīlūthāʾus. Introduction to *Tafsīr Sifr al-Ruʾyā li-l-Qadīs Yūḥannā al-Lahūtī l-Ibn Kātib Qayṣar*, edited by al-Qummuṣ Armāniyūs Ḥabashī Shattā al-Birmāwī. Cairo, 1939. Repr. Cairo: Maktabat al-Maḥabbah, 1994.

Awad, Wadi. "al-Asʿad Ibn al-ʿAssāl." BrillOnline *Reference Works*, http://dx.doi.org/10.1163/1877-8054_cmri_COM_25903, consulted March 24, 2018.

———. "al-Muʾtaman Ibn al-ʿAssāl," in CMR, vol. 4, 530–37. BrillOnline *Reference Works*, http://dx.doi.org/10.1163/1877-8054_cmri_COM_24900, consulted March 24, 2018.

———. "Al-Rashīd Abū l-Khayr Ibn al-Ṭayyib," CMR, vol. 4, 431–37. BrillOnline *Reference Works*, http://dx.doi.org/10.1163/1877-8054_cmri_COM_24906, consulted March 24, 2018.

———. "al-Ṣafī Ibn al-ʿAssāl," in CMR, vol. 4, 538–51. BrillOnline *Reference Works*, http://dx.doi.org/10.1163/1877-8054_cmri_COM_24904, consulted March 24, 2018.

———, ed. *Studio su al-Muʾtaman Ibn al-ʿAssāl* (*Dirāsah ʿan al-Muʾtaman ibn al-ʿAssāl*). Studia Orientalia Christiana Monographiae 5. Cairo and Jerusalem: The Franciscan Centre of Christian Oriental Studies and Franciscan Printing Press, 1997.

ʿAwāḍallah, Manqariyūs. *Maqālāt al-Anbā Būlus al-Būshī.* Cairo: al-Maṭba'ah al-tujāriyyah al-ḥadīthah, 1972.

Babcock, W. S. *Tyconius: The Book of Rules.* Texts and Translations 39. Atlanta: Scholars Press, 1989.

Beaumont, Mark. *Christology in Dialogue with Muslims: A Critical Analysis of Christian Presentations of Christ for Muslims from the Ninth and Twentieth Centuries.* Bletchley: Paternoster, 2005.

al-Birmāwī, al-Qummuṣ Armāniyūs Ḥabashī Shattā, ed. *Tafsīr Sifr al-Ru'yā li-l-Qadīs Yūḥannā al-Lahūtī l-Ibn Kātib Qayṣar*. Cairo, 1939. Repr. Cairo: Maktabat al-Maḥabbah, 1994.

Blau, Joshua. *The Emergence and Linguistic Background of Judaeo-Arabic*. London: Oxford University Press, 1965.

———. *A Grammar of Christian Arabic*. 3 volumes. CSCO 267, 276, 279. Louvain: Secrétariat du CorpusSCO, 1966–67.

Bosworth, C. Edmund. 'Ebn Kordādbeh, Abu'l-Qāsem 'bn Ko-Allāh.' In *Encyclopædia Iranica* 8.1, 37–38, http://www.iranicaonline.org/articles/ebn-kordadbeh.

Boysson, A. de. "Avons-nous un commentaire d'Origène sur l'Apocalypse," *Revue Biblique* 10 (1913): 555–67.

Brakke, David. *Athanasius and the Politics of Asceticism*. Oxford: Clarendon Press, 1995.

Bright, Pamela. *The Book of Rules of Tyconius: Its Purpose and Inner Logic*. Notre Dame, Ind.: University of Notre Dame Press, 1988.

Brock, Sebastian. "A Neglected Witness to the East Syriac New Testament Commentary Tradition, Sinai Arabic ms 151." In *Studies on the Christian Arabic Heritage in Honour of Prof. Dr. Samir Khalil Samir S. I. on the Occasion of His Sixty-fifth Birthday*, edited by R. Ebied and H. Teule. Eastern Christian Studies 5, 205–15. Leuven: Peeters, 2004.

al-Bukhārī, Muḥammad ibn Isma'īl. *Ṣaḥīḥ al-Bukhārī*. Edited by M. Ludolf Krehl. 4 volumes. Leiden: Brill, 1862. Edited by Aḥmad Muḥammad Shākir, *al-Jāmi' al-Ṣaḥīḥ*. 9 volumes. Beirut: Dār al-Jīl, n.d.

Būlus al-Būshī. *Commentary on the Apocalypse*. Edited and translated by Shawqi Talia, "Bulus al-Buši's Arabic Commentary on the Apocalypse of St. John: An English Translation and Commentary." Ph.D. dissertation, The Catholic University of America, 1987. For an uncritical edition, published serially, see *Tafsīr Sifr al-Ru'yā (al-Abūghālimsīs) li-l-Anbā Būlus al-Būshī usquf Miṣr (ayy al-Qāhirah al-qadīmah)*. In *Majallat Marqus* 491–503 (February 2008–April 2009). For a recent critical edition and French translation, see Nagi Edelby, "Le Commentaire de l'Apocalypse de Būlus al-Bušī (évêque du Caire en 1240 A.D.): Étude, edition critique, traduction et Index exhaustif." Ph.D. dissertation, Université Saint-Joseph-Beyrouth, 2015. For a recent edition based on a manuscript at the Monastery of St. Macarius (MS 22 Tafsīr [Commentary]), see Bishop Epiphanius (al-Anbā Ibīfānīyūs), *Tafsīr Sifr al-Ru'yā (Abūghālumsīs) li-l-Anbā Būlus al-Būshī Usquf Miṣr*. Cairo: Dār Majallat Marqus, 2017.

Cheiko, Louis, ed. *Petrus ibn Rahib: Chronicon orientale*. Beirut: E Typographeo catholico, 1903. Repr. Louvain: L. Durbecq, 1955.

Christe, Yves. *L'Apocalypse de Jean: Sens et développements de ses visions synthétiques.* Paris: Picard, 1996.

Const. Ap. (*Apostolic Constitutions*). Published as *Didascalia et constitutiones apostolorum.* Edited by F. X. Funk. Volume 1. Paderborn: F. Schoeningh, 1905.

Constantinou, Eugenia Scarvelis. *Guiding to a Blessed End: Andrew of Caesarea and the Apocalypse.* Washington, D.C.: The Catholic University of America Press, 2013.

Courreau, J., ed. *L'Apocalypse expliquee par Cesaire d'Arles. Scholies attribuée à Origène.* Paris: Desclée de Brower, 1989.

Cowley, R. *The Traditional Interpretation of the Apocalypse of St. John in the Ethiopian Orthodox Church.* Cambridge: Cambridge University Press, 1983.

Crum, W. E. *A Coptic Dictionary.* Oxford: Clarendon, 1939.

Cyril of Alexandria. *schol. inc.* (*Scholia on the Incarnation*). PG 75.1369–1412. Translated by J. A. McGuckin, *St. Cyril*, 294–335.

Cyril of Jerusalem, *catech.* (*Catechetical Lectures*). PG 33.331–1180. NPNF 7.

Dagron. G. "Rēver de Dieu et parler de soi: le rēve et son interpretation d'après les sources byzantines." In *I sogni ne medioevo*, edited by T. Gregory, 37–55. Lessico Intellettuale Europeo 35; Rome: Edizioni dell' Ateneo, 1985.

Davis, Stephen J. "Biblical Interpretation and Alexandrian Episcopal Authority in the Early Christian Fayoum." In *Christianity and Monasticism in the Fayoum Oasis*, edited by G. Gabra, 45–61. Cairo: American University of Cairo Press, 2005.

———. "Cataloguing the Coptic and Arabic Manuscripts in the Monastery of the Syrians: A Preliminary Report," *Studia Patristica* 90 (2018): 179–85.

———. *Coptic Christology in Practice: Incarnation and Divine Participation in Late Antique and Medieval Egypt.* Oxford: Oxford University Press, 2008.

———. "The Copto-Arabic Tradition of *Theosis*: A Eucharistic Reading of John 3:51–57 in Būlus al-Būshī's Treatise *On the Incarnation.*" In *Partakers of the Divine Nature*, edited by M. J. Christensen and J. A. Wittung, 163–74. Madison, N.J.: Fairleigh Dickinson University Press, 2007.

Deissmann, G. A. *Bible Studies.* Edited by A. Grieve. New York: Harper, 1901.

Devress, R. "Châines exégetiques grecques." In *Dictionnaire de la Bible*, edited by F. G. Vigouroux. Supplement edited by L. Pirot, et al. Volume 1, 1084–1233. Paris: Letouzey et Ané, 1928.

Didymus the Blind. *comm. Zach.* (*Commentary on Zechariah*). Edited by Doutreleau, SC 84. Paris: Cerf, 1962. Translated by R. C. Hill, FC 111. Washington, D.C.: The Catholic University of America Press, 2006.

Dozy, R. *Supplément aux dictionnaires arabes.* 2 volumes. Leiden: Brill, 1881.

Drexl, Francis, ed. *Achmetis oneirocriticon.* Leipzig: Teubner, 1925.

Dulaey, M., ed. *Sur l'Apocalypse: suivi du fragment chronologique et de La construction du monde.* SC 423. Paris: Cerf, 1997.

Dvorjetski, E. "The History of Nephrology in the Talmudic Corpus," *American Journal of Nephrology*, 22, no. 2–3 (2002): 119–29.

Dyobouniotes, C. I., and A. von Harnack, eds. *Der Scholien-Kommentar des Origenes zur Apokalypse Johannis*. Texte und Untersuchungen 38.3. Leipzig: Hinrichs, 1911.

Ebied, R. Y., and M. J. L. Young, eds. *The Lamp of the Intellect of Severus ibn al-Muqaffaʿ, Bishop of al-Ashmūnain*. CSCO 365. Louvain: Secrétariat du CorpusSCO, 1975.

Edelby, Nagi. "Le Commentaire de l'Apocalypse de Būlus al-Bušī (évêque du Caire en 1240 A.D.): Étude, edition critique, traduction et Index exhaustif." Ph.D. dissertation, Université Saint-Joseph-Beyrouth, 2015.

———. "L'Homélie de l'Annonciation de Būlus al-Būšī." *Parole de l'Orient* 22 (1997): 503–65.

Eusebius of Caesarea, *h.e.* (*Ecclesiastical History*). Edited by G. Bardy. SC 31, 41, 55, 73. Paris: Cerf, 1955. Translated by NPNF, ser. 2, 1.

Ewald, Heinrich. Untitled article in *Abhandlungen zur orientalischen und biblischen Literatur*, 1–11. Göttingen: Dieterich, 1832.

Fahd, Toufic. *Artemidorus: Le livre des songes*. Damascus: Institut français de Damas, 1964.

Faltas, Joseph. *O megas Athanasios ōs pēgē tēs theologias tou Būlūs al-Būšī*. Ph.D. diss., University of Athens, 1994.

———. *al-Rūḥ al-qudus: Maymar ʿīd al-ʾanṣarah lil-usquf Būlus al-Būshī*. Cairo: Mu'assasat al-Qadīs Anṭūnīyūs, 2006.

al-Fārābī, Abū Naṣr Muḥammad. *Al-Fārābī on the Perfect State: Abū Naṣr al-Fārābī's* Mabādi' ārā' ahl al-madīna al-fāḍila. Edited by R. Walzer. Oxford: Clarendon, 1985.

Ford, J. Massyngberde. *Revelation*. The Anchor Bible 38. Garden City, N.Y.: Doubleday, 1975.

Fox, Robin Lane. *Pagans and Christians*. New York: Knopf, 1987.

Gardet, L. "al-Asmā' al-Ḥusnā," *EI²*. BrillOnline *Reference Works*, http://referenceworks.brillonline.com/entries/encyclopaedia-of-islam-2/al-asma-al-husna-COM_0070, consulted March 24, 2018.

———. "Ḳiyāma." *EI²*. BrillOnline *Reference Works*. http://referenceworks.brillonline.com/entries/encyclopaedia-of-islam-2/kiyama-COM_0526, consulted March 24, 2018.

Goldziher, I. *Muhammedanische Studien*. 2 volumes. Halle: Niemeyer, 1888–90.

Graf, Georg. "Arabische Übersetzungen der Apokalypse," *Biblica* 10 (1929): 170–94.

———. *Geschichte der christlichen arabischen Literatur*. Studi e Testi 118, 133, 146, 147, 172. Vatican City: Biblioteca Apostolica Vaticana, 1944–52.

———. "Die koptische Gelehrtenfamilie der Aulād al-'Assāl und ihr Schrifttum," *Orientalia*, n.s. 1 (1932): 34–56, 193–204.

———. "Das Schriftstellerverzeichnis des Abū Isḥāq ibn al-'Assāl," *Oriens Christianus* n.s. 2 (1912): 205–26.

———. *Der Sprachgebrauch der ältesten christlichen-arabischen Literatur: ein Beitrag zur Geschichte des Vulgar-Arabisch*. Leipzig: Harrossowitz, 1905.

———. *Verzeichnis arabischer kirchlicher Termini*. Leuven: Imprimerie Orientaliste L. Durbecq, 1954.

Green, Nile. "The Religious and Cultural Roles of Dreams and Visions in Islam," *Journal of the Royal Asiatic Society*, Series 3, 13, no. 3 (2003): 287–313.

Gregory of Nazianzus, *carm.* (*Poems*). PG 37.

Gregory of Nyssa, *De hominis opificio* (*On the Creation of Humankind*). PG 44.125–256.

Griffel, Frank. "The Muslim Philosophers' Rationalist Explanation of Muḥammad's Prophecy." In *The Cambridge Companion to Muḥammad*, edited by Jonathan E. Brockopp. 158–79. Cambridge: Cambridge University Press, 2010.

———. "Philosophy and Prophecy." In *The Routledge Companion to Islamic Philosophy*, edited by R. C. Taylor and L. X. López-Farjeat, 385–98. London: Routledge, 2016.

Griffith, Sidney H. "Answering the Call of the Minaret: Christian Apologetics in the World of Islam." In *Redefining Christian Identity: Cultural Interaction in the Middle East since the Rise of Islam*, edited by J. J. van Ginkel, H. L. Murre-van der Berg, and T. M. van Lint, 91–126. Leuven: Peeters, 2005.

———. *The Beginnings of Christian Theology in Arabic: Muslim-Christian Encounters in the Early Islamic Period*. Variorum Collected Studies Series. Aldershot: Ashgate, 2002.

———. *The Bible in Arabic: The Scriptures of the "People of the Book" in the Language of Islam*. Princeton: Princeton University Press, 2013.

———. *The Church in the Shadow of the Mosque: Christians and Muslims in the World of Islam*. Princeton: Princeton University Press, 2008.

Gryson, R., ed. *Bedae presbyteri expositio apocalypseos*. CCSL 121a. Turnhout: Brepols, 2001.

———, ed. *Commentaria minora in Apocalypsin Johannis: Variorum auctorum*, CCSL 107. Turnhout: Brepols, 2003.

Gumerlock, Francis X. "Patristic Commentaries on Revelation," *Kerux* 23, no. 2 (2008): 49–67.

———. "Patristic Commentaries on Revelation: An Update," *Kerux* 27, no. 3 (2012): 37–43.

———. *The Seven Seals of the Apocalypse: Medieval Texts in Translation*. TEAMS Commentary Series. Kalamazoo, Mich.: Medieval Institute Publications; Western Michigan University, 2009.

Haddad, Rachid. *La Trinité divine chez les théologiens arabes (750–1050).* Beauchesne religions 15. Paris: Beauchesne, 1985.
"*al-Hanbāzīn.*" Article in the *Dictionary of Ecclesiastical Terms* (*Qāmūs al-muṣṭalaḥāt al-kanīsiyyah*) on the St. Takla Haymanout Coptic Orthodox Website. http://st-takla.org/Coptic-Faith-Creed-Dogma/Coptic-Rite-n-Ritual-Taks-Al-Kanisa/Dictionary-of-Coptic-Ritual-Terms/9-Coptic-Terminology_Heh-Waw-Yeh/henbazeen.html.
Hanson, John S. "Dreams and Visions in the Graeco-Roman World and Early Christianity," *ANRW* II.23.2 (1980): 1395–1427.
Ḥarfūsh, Ibrāhīm. "Die Bibliothek der Maroniten in Ḥaleb," *Mashriq* 17 (1914): 96.
al-Ḥasan ibn al-Bahlūl. *Kitāb al-dalā'il li al-Ḥasan ibn al-Bahlūl.* Edited by Yūsuf Ḥabbī. Kuwait: Manshūrāt ma'had al-makhṭūṭāt al-'arabiyyah, 1987.
Heijer, Johannes den. "Coptic Historiography in the Fatimid, Ayyubid, and Early Mamluk Periods," *Medieval Encounters* 2 (1996): 67–98.
Heininger, B. *Paulus als Visionär: Eine religionsgeschichtliche Studie.* Herdersbiblische Studien 9. Freiburg: Herder, 1996.
History of the Patriarchs of the Coptic Church [*HPCC*]. Edited by B. T. Evetts. 4 volumes. PO 1.2; 1.4; 5.1; 10.5. Paris: Firmin-Didot, 1904–15.
History of the Patriarchs of the Egyptian Church [*HPEC*]. Edited by A. Khater and O. H. E. KHS-Burmester. 4 volumes. Cairo: Imprimerie de l'Institut français d'archéologie orientale, 1943–74.
Hofmann, Josef. *Die äthiopische Johannes-Apokalypse, kritisch untersucht.* CSCO 297, Subsidia 33. Louvain, Secrétariat du CorpusSCO, 1969.
———. *Die äthiopische Übersetzung der Johannes-Apokalypse*, 2 volumes. CSCO 281–82, Aethiopici 55–56. Louvain: Secrétariat du CorpusSCO, 1967.
Horner, G. *The Coptic Version of the New Testament in the Northern Dialect* [= *CoptNT-North*]. Oxford: Clarendon Press, 1898–1905. Repr. Osnabrück: Otto Zeller, 1969.
———. *The Coptic Version of the New Testament in the Southern Dialect* [= *CoptNT-South*]. Oxford: Clarendon Press, 1911–24. Repr. Osnabrück: Otto Zeller, 1969.
Hoskier, H. C., ed. *The Complete Commentary of Oecumenius on the Apocalypse.* Ann Arbor: University of Michigan Press, 1928.
Hoyland, Robert. *Seeing Islam As Others Saw It: A Survey and Evaluation of Christian, Jewish and Zoroastrian Writings on Early Islam.* Studies in Late Antiquity and Early Islam. Princeton: Darwin Press, 1998.
Ibn Sīnā (Avicenna). *Avicenna's* De Anima *(Arabic Text): Being the Psychological Part of* Kitāb al-Shifā'. Edited by F. Rahman. Oxford: Oxford University Press, 1959.
Ibn al-Ṭayyib. *Commentary on Genesis.* Edited by J. C. J. Sanders, *Ibn aṭ-Ṭaiyib, Commentaire sur la Genèse.* 2 volumes. CSCO 274–75. Louvain: Secrétariat du CorpusSCO, 1967.

Ibn Ḥajar al-ʿAsqalānī. *Fatḥ al-Bārī*. 13 volumes plus index. Cairo: Maktabat al-Salafiyyah, 1986.

Ibn Kātib Qayṣar. *Commentary on the Apocalypse*. Edited by al-Qummuṣ Armāniyūs Ḥabashī Shattā Birmāwī, *Tafsīr Sifr al-Ruʾyā li-l-Qadīs Yūḥannā al-Lahūtī l-Ibn Kātib Qayṣar*. Cairo, n.p., 1939. Repr. Cairo: Maktabat al-Maḥabbah, 1994. Also Par. Ar. 67.

Irenaeus *haer.* (*Against Heresies*). Edited by A. Rousseau and L. Doutreleau. 5 volumes. SC 100, 152–53, 210–11, 263–264. Translated by ANF 1.

Jeffrey, A. *The Foreign Vocabulary of the Qurʾān*. Baroda: Oriental Institute, 1938.

Jerome, *v. Pauli* (*Life of Paul the Hermit*). PL 23.17–28. Translated by H. Waddell, *The Desert Fathers*, 26–39. Ann Arbor: University of Michigan Press, 1957.

John of Nikiu, *Chronicle*. Translated by R. H. Charles. In *The Chronicle of John (c. 690 A. D.) Coptic Bishop of Nikiu*. Text and Translation Society 3. London: William & Norgate, 1916.

Junod, E. "À propos des soi-disant scolies sur l'Apocalypse d'Origène," *Rivista di storia e letteratura religiosa* 20 (1984): 112–21.

Juynboll, G. H. A., and D. W. Brown. "Sunna," *EI*². BrillOnline *Reference Works*, http://referenceworks.brillonline.com/entries/encyclopaedia-of-islam-2/sunna-COM_1123, consulted March 24, 2018.

Kashouh, Hikmat. *The Arabic Versions of the Gospels: The Manuscripts and Their Families*. Berlin: de Gruyter, 2012.

Kelhoffer, James A. *The Diet of John the Baptist: "Locusts and Wild Honey" in Synoptic and Patristic Interpretation*. Wissenschaftliche Untersuchungen zum Neuen Testament 176. Tübingen: Mohr Siebeck, 2005.

Kelly, Joseph F. T. "Early Medieval Evidence for Twelve Homilies by Origen on the Apocalypse," *Vigiliae Christianae* 39 (1985): 273–79.

Khoury, Paul. *Matériaux pour servir à l'étude de la controverse théologique islamo-chrétienne de langue arabe du VIIIe au XIIe siècle*. 6 volumes. Würburg: Oros, 2000.

Kretschmar, Georg. *Die Offenbarung des Johannes: Die Geschichte ihrer Auslegung im 1. Jahrtausend*. Stuttgart: Calwer, 1985.

Kruger, Steven F. *Dreaming in the Middle Ages*. Cambridge Studies in Medieval Literature 14. Cambridge: Cambridge University Press, 1992.

Kussaim, S. "Contribution à l'étude du moyen arabe des coptes," *Le Muséon* 80 (1967): 153–209; and 81 (1968): 5–77.

Lamoreaux, John C. *The Early Muslim Tradition of Dream Interpretation*. Albany: SUNY Press, 2002.

Landron, Bénédicte. *Chrétiens et musulmans en Irak: attitudes nestoriennes vis-à-vis de l'Islam*. Paris: Cariscript, 1994.

Lane, Edward W. *An Arabic-English Lexicon*. London: Williams and Norgate, 1863–93.

Larson, S. "The Earliest Syriac Commentary on the Apocalypse: Transcription, Translation and Importance of Brit. Lib. MS. ADD. 17,127." Ph.D. dissertation, University of Birmingham, 1984. See also https://search.proquest.com/docview/1928847856/59FDFF4AB84344A7PQ/3?accountid=15172, consulted March 29, 2018.
Lazarus-Yafeh, Hava. "Tawrāt," in *EI²*. BrillOnline *Reference Works*, http://referenceworks.brillonline.com/entries/encyclopaedia-of-islam-2/tawrat-COM_1203, consulted March 24, 2018.
Lentin, Jérôme. "Middle Arabic." In *Encyclopedia of Arabic Language and Linguistics*, Managing Editors Online Edition: Lutz Edzard, Rudolf de Jong, http://dx.doi.org/10.1163/1570-6699_eall_EALL_COM_vol3_0213, consulted March 24, 2018.
Leontius of Neapolis. *Life of Saint John the Almsgiver*. Published as *Leontios' von Neapolis Leben des heiligen Johannes des Barmherzigen, Erzbischofs von Alexandrien*. Edited by H. Gelzer. Freiburg i. B.: J. C. B. Mohr (P. Siebeck), 1893.
Life and Miracles of Saint Thecla. Published as *Vie et miracles de Sainte Thècle*. Edited by G. Dagron. Bruxelles: Société des Bollandistes, 1978.
Life of St. Onnophrius. In *Journeying into God: Seven Early Monastic Lives*, edited and translated by Tim Vivian, 172–87. Minneapolis: Fortress Press, 1996.
Livingstone, E. A. "Docetism." In *The Oxford Dictionary of the Christian Church*, 3rd edition, edited by F. L. Cross and E. A. Livingstone, 496. Oxford: Oxford University Press, 2005.
Lo Bue, Francesco. *Turin Fragments of Tyconius' Commentary on Revelation*. Cambridge: Cambridge University Press, 1963.
Lowry, Charles W. "Did Origen Style the Son a *KTISMA*?," *Journal of Theological Studies* 39 (1938): 39–42.
MacCoull, Leslie S.B. "MS. Morgan 591: The Apocalypse Commentary of Pseudo-Cyril of Alexandria," *Studia Patristica* 20 (1989): 33–39.
MacKay, Thomas W. "Early Christian Millenarianist Interpretation of the Two Witnesses in John's Apocalypse 11:3–13." http://publications.maxwellinstitute.byu.edu/fullscreen/?pub=1128&index=15, consulted March 29, 2018.
Macrobius. *Commentary on the Dream of Scipio*. Published as *Macrobe: Commentaire au Songe de Scipion*. Edited by M. Armisen-Marchetti. 2 volumes. Paris: Les Belles Lettres, 2001–3.
Maio, G. "The Metaphorical and Mythical Use of the Kidney in Antiquity," *American Journal of Nephrology* 19, no. 2 (1999): 101–6.
Mart. Poly. (*Martyrdom of Polycarp*). Edited and translated by H. Musurillo, 2–22. Oxford: Clarendon, 1972.
Mavroudi, Maria. *A Byzantine Book on Dream Interpretation: The Oneirocriticon of Achmet and Its Arabic Sources*. Leiden: Brill, 2002.

McGuckin, J. A. *St. Cyril of Alexandria. The Christological Controversy: Its History, Theology, and Texts*. Leiden: Brill, 1994.

Metzger, Bruce M. *The Canon of the New Testament: Its Origin, Development, and Significance*. Oxford: Clarendon Press, 1987.

Michot, Jean. "La pandémie avicennienne au VIe/XIIe siècle: Présentation, edition princeps et traduction de l'introduction du livre de l'advenue du monde (*kitāb ḥudūth al-ʿālam*) d'Ibn Ghaylān al-Balkhī," *Arabica* 40, no. 3 (1993): 287–344.

Miller, Patricia Cox. *Dreams in Late Antiquity: Studies in the Imagination of a Culture*. Princeton: Princeton University Press, 1994.

———. "'A Dubious Twilight': Reflections on Dreams in Patristic Literature," *Church History* 55 (1986): 153–64.

Moss, Candida. *The Other Christs: Imitating Jesus in Ancient Christian Ideologies of Martyrdom*. New York: Oxford University Press, 2010.

Mounce, Robert H. *The Book of Revelation*. Grand Rapids, Mich.: Eerdmans, 1977.

Mu'taman ibn al-ʿAssāl. *Majmūʿ uṣūl al-dīn*. Edited by A. Wadi, OFM, in *Summa dei principi della Religione*. 5 volumes. Studia Orientalia Christiana Monographiae 6a–7a [text], 6b–7b [critical apparatus], 8–9 [Italian translation]. Cairo and Jerusalem: The Franciscan Centre of Christian Oriental Studies and Franciscan Printing Press, 1998–99.

Nestle, Eberhard and Erwin, and Barbara and Kurt Aland, eds. *Novum Testamentum Graece*, 27th rev. ed. Stuttgart: Deutsche Bibelgesellschaft, 2001.

Oberhelman, Steven M. *Oneirocriticon of Achmet: A Medieval Greek and Arabic Treatise on the Interpretation of Dreams*. Lubbock: Texas Tech University, 1991.

Oecumenius. *Commentary on the Apocalypse*. Translated by John N. Suggit. Washington, D.C.: The Catholic University of America Press, 2006.

Oiconomou, Elias V. "Authorities and Citizens in John's Book of Revelation." http://www.myriobiblos.gr/bible/studies/economou_revelation.asp, consulted March 29, 2018.

Origen of Alexandria. *princ.* (*On First Principles*). Edited by P. Koetschau, GCS 22 (1913). Translated by G. W. Butterworth. Gloucester, Mass.: Peter Smith, 1973.

———. *comm. Matt.* (*Commentary on the Gospel of Matthew*). PG 13.829–1800.

Orlandi, Tito, "Cirillo Vescovo Di Alessandria." In *Omelie copte. Aegyptiorum Patrum homilias*, edited by T. Orlandi, 121–44. Corona Patrum 7. Torino: Società editrice internazionale, 1981.

———. "Un testo copto sulla dominazione araba in Egitto." In *Acts of the Second International Congress of Coptic Studies*, edited by T. Orlandi and F. Wisse, 225–34. Rome: C.I.M., 1985.

Owens, Jonathan. *A Linguistic History of Arabic.* Oxford: Oxford University Press, 2006.

Peel, M. *The Epistle to Rheginos: A Valentinian Letter on the Resurrection.* London: SCM Press, 1969.

Périer, J. ed. *La Perle précieuse traitant des sciences ecclésiastiques par Jean, fils d'abou-Zakariyā, surnommé ibn Sabāʿ.* PO 16. Paris: F. Didot, 1922.

Plato, *Tim.* (*Timaeus*). Edited and translated by R. G. Bury. LCL. Cambridge, Mass.: Harvard University Press; London: William Heinemann, 1981.

Prigent, P., and R. Stehly, eds., "Les fragments du *De Apocalypsi d'Hippolyte,*" *Theologische Zeitschrift* 29 (1973): 313–33.

Ps.-Athanasius. *Apocalypse.* Edited and translated by F. J. Martinez, "Eastern Christian Apocalyptic in the Early Muslim Period: Pseudo-Methodius and Pseudo-Athanasius." Ph.D. dissertation, Catholic University of America, Washington, D.C., 1985.

Ps.-Dionysius. *The Celestial Hierarchy.* Published as *Corpus Dionysiacum*, II, second edition. Edited by G. Heil and A. M. Ritter. Patristiche Texte und Studien 67; Berlin: De Gruyter, 2012. English translation by J. Parker, *The Celestial and Ecclesiastical Hierarchy of Dionysius the Areopagite.* London: Skeffington & Son, 1894.

———. *Pseudo-Dionysius: The Complete Works.* Translated by Colm Luibheid. New York: Paulist Press, 1987.

———. *The Works of Dionysius the Areopagite.* Translated by John Parker. London: James Parker and Co., 1897.

Qur'ān. Edited and translated by M. M. Pickthall, *The Meaning of the Glorious Qur'ān.* Beirut: Dar al-Kitāb al-Lubnānī, 1970.

Rahman, Fazlur. *Prophecy in Islam: Philosophy and Orthodoxy.* London: Allen & Unwin, 1958.

Reiling, J. *Hermas and Christian Prophecy: A Study of the Eleventh Mandate.* Leiden: Brill, 1973.

Riedel, W. "Der Katalog der christlichen Schriften in arabischer Sprache von Abū'l-Barakāt." In *Nachrichten von der königlichen Gesellschaft der Wissenschaften zu Göttingen*, Philologisch-historische Klasse. Göttingen: Horstmann, 1902.

Robinson, J. A. "Origen's Comments on the Apocalypse," *Journal of Theological Studies* 13 (1912): 295–97.

Ryan, Stephen Desmond, O.P. *Dionysius Bar Salibi's Factual and Spiritual Commentary on Psalms 73–82.* Cahiers de la Revue Biblique 57. Paris: J. Gabalda et Cie, 2004.

al-Ṣafī ibn al-ʿAssāl, *Kitāb al-qawānīn.* Edited by M. Jirjis. Cairo: Tabaʿat al-usquf Īsūdhūrus, 1927.

Saʿīd ibn al-Biṭrīq [Eutychius of Alexandria]. *Kitāb al-burhān.* Edited by P. Cachia and W. M. Watt, *Eutychius of Alexandria. The Book of the Demonstration*

(Kitāb al-burhān). CSCO 192–93 and 209–10. Louvain: Secrétariat du CorpusSCO, 1960–61.

Samir, Samir Khalil. *Traité de Paul de Būš sur l'Unité et la Trinité l'Incarnation, et la Vérité du Christianisme* (*Maqālah fī al-tathlīth w-al-tajassud wa-Ṣiḥḥat al-Masīḥiyyah*). Patrimoine Arabe Chrétien 4. Zouk Mikhail: al-Turath al 'Arabi al-Masihi, 1983.

———, and Jørgen S. Nielsen, eds., *Christian Arabic Apologetics during the Abbasid Period, 750–1258*. Leiden: Brill, 1994.

Schmid, J., ed. *Studien zur Geschichte des griechischen Apokalypse-Textes*. Volume 1. Münchener theologische Studien 1. Munich: Karl Zink, 1955.

Sedláček, J. ed. *Dionysius bar Salibi In Apocalypsim, Actus et Epistulas Catholicas*, CSCO 53, Syr. 18. Louvain: Secrétariat du CorpusCSO, 1909.

Shenoute. *When the Word Says*. Edited by L. Depuydt, *Catalogue of Coptic Manuscripts in the Pierpont Morgan Library*. Corpus of Illuminated Manuscripts, Volume 4. Oriental Series 1, no. 71, 144–49. Leuven: Peeters, 1993. Edited and translated by D. W. Young, *Coptic Manuscripts from the White Monastery: Works of Shenute*, no. 22, 137–39 (text), 142–3 (trans.); no. 27, 160–66 (text), 166–69 (trans.). Österreichische Nationalbibliothek. Vienna: Verlag Brüder Hollinek, 1993, 162.41–9 and 167.228.

Shepherd of Hermas. See *Vis*.

Sidarus, Adel. "Ibn al-Rāhib." CMR, vol. 4, 471–79.

———. *Ibn ar-Rāhibs Leben und Werk: Ein koptisch-arabischer Enzyklopädist des 7./13. Jahrhunderts*. Islamkundliche Untersuchungen 36. Freiburg: Klaus Schwarz Verlag, 1975.

———. "Kitāb al-tawārīkh." In *Christian Muslim Relations 600–1500*, edited by D. Thomas. BrillOnline *Reference Works*, http://referenceworks.brillonline.com/entries/christian-muslim-relations-i/kitab-al-tawarikh-COM_24891, consulted March 24, 2018.

———. "Le renaissance copte arabe du moyen âge." In *The Syriac Renaissance*, edited by Herman G. B. Teule et al., 311–40. Leuven: Peeters, 2010.

———, and Samuel Moawad. "Un traité melkite sur le comput pascal de Yaḥyā ibn Sa'īd al-Anṭākī d'après Abū Šākir ibn al-Rāhib (auteur copte du XIIIe siècle)," *Le Muséon* 123 (2010): 455–77.

Simaika, M. *Catalogue of the Coptic and Arabic Manuscripts in the Coptic Museum, the Patriarchate, the Principal Churches of Cairo and Alexandria and the Monasteries of Egypt*. 2 volumes. Cairo: Government Press, 1939–42.

Skard, E. "Zum Scholien-kommentar des Origenes zur Apokalypse Johannis," *Symbolae Osloenses: Norwegian Journal of Greek and Latin Studies* 15, no. 1 (1936): 204–8.

Slusser, M. "Docetism—A Historical Definition," *The Second Century* 1 (1981): 163–72.

Suermann, Harald. "Koptische arabische Apokalypsen." In *Studies on the Christian Arabic Heritage*, edited by R. Ebied and H. Teule. Eastern Christian Studies 5, 25–44. Peeters: Leuven, 2004.

Suggit, John N., ed. and trans. *Oecumenius, Commentary on the Apocalypse*. Fathers of the Church 112. Washington, D.C.: The Catholic University of America Press, 2006.

Sundberg Jr., A. C. "Canon Muratori: A Fourth-Century List," *Harvard Theological Review* 66, no. 1 (1973): 1–41.

Swanson, Mark N. "Būlus al-Būshī," *CMR*, vol. 4, 280–87. BrillOnline *Reference Works*, http://dx.doi.org/10.1163/1877-8054_cmri_COM_25673, consulted March 24, 2018.

———. *The Coptic Papacy in Islamic Egypt (641–1517)*. Cairo: American University in Cairo Press, 2010.

———. "Ibn Kātib Qayṣar," CMR, vol. 4, 453–56. BrillOnline *Reference Works*, http://dx.doi.org/10.1163/1877-8054_cmri_COM_25670, consulted March 24, 2018.

———. "Patriarch Cyril III ibn Laqlaq," CMR, vol. 4, 320–24. BrillOnline *Reference Works*, http://dx.doi.org/10.1163/1877-8054_cmri_COM_25270, consulted March 24, 2018.

Talia, Shawqi. "Bulus al-Buši's Arabic Commentary on the Apocalypse of St. John: An English Translation and Commentary." Ph.D. dissertation, The Catholic University of America, 1987.

Thomas, Stephen. "Anthropology." In *The Westminster Handbook to Origen*, edited by John McGuckin, 53–58. Louisville, Ky.: Westminster John Knox Press, 2004.

Turner, C. H. "Document. Origen Scholia in Apocalypsin," *Journal of Theological Studies* 25 (1923): 1–16.

———. "The Text of the Newly Discovered Scholia of Origen on the Apocalypse," *Journal of Theological Studies* 13 (1912): 386–97.

Tyconius. *Reg.* (*The Book of Rules*). Edited and translated by W. S. Babcock. Texts and Translations 39. Atlanta: Scholars Press, 1989.

Tzamalikos, Panagiōtēs, ed. *An Ancient Commentary on the Book of Revelation: A Critical Edition of the Scholia in Apocalypsin*. Cambridge: Cambridge University Press, 2013.

Victorinus. *Commentary on the Apocalypse*. Edited by M. Dulaey. SC 423. Paris: Cerf, 1997. See also Hausleiter, J. CSEL 49. Vienna: F. Tempsky, 1916. For Jerome's heavily redacted edition of Victorinus's commentary, see ANF 7.344–60.

Vollandt, Ronny. *Arabic Versions of the Pentateuch: A Comparative Study of Jewish, Christian, and Muslim Sources*. Leiden: Brill, 2015.

Vis. (*Shepherd of Hermas*). In *The Apostolic Fathers: Greek Texts and English Translations*. Third edition. Edited by M. W. Holmes, 454–685. Grand Rapids, Mich.: Baker, 2007.

Walzer, R. "Aflāṭūn." *EI²*. BrillOnline *Reference Works*, http://referenceworks.brillonline.com/entries/encyclopaedia-of-islam-2/aflatun-COM_0023, consulted March 24, 2018.

Watt, W. M. *Islamic Philosophy and Theology*. Edinburgh: Edinburgh University Press, 1962.

Weber, Gregor. *Kaiser, Träume und Visionen in Prinzipat und Spätantike*. Stuttgart: Franz Steiner, 2000.

Wehr, Hans. *A Dictionary of Modern Written Arabic*. Edited by J. M. Cowan. 3rd edition. Beirut: Librairie du Liban, 1961. Repr. 1980. 4th edition. Wiesbaden: Harrassowitz, 1979.

Weinrich, William C. *Revelation*. Ancient Christian Commentary on Scripture 12. Downers Grove, Il.: InterVarsity Press, 2005.

Werthmuller, Kurt. *Coptic Identity and Ayyubid Politics in Egypt, 1218–1250*. Cairo: American University in Cairo Press, 2010.

Whittingham, Marin. "Prophecy." In *Encyclopaedia of Islamic Civilisation and Religion*, edited by Ian Richard Netton, 514–15. London: Routledge, 2008.

Wickham, L. *Cyril of Alexandria: Select Letters*. Oxford: Clarendon, 1982.

Witte, Bernd. "Der koptische Text von M 602 f. 52–f. 77 der Pierpont Morgan Library—wirklich eine Schrift des Athanasius?," *Orientalia Christiana* 78 (1994): 123–30.

Wojciechowski, Michał. *Pseudo-Orygenes, Uwagi do Apokalipsy* (= *Pseudo-Origen, Scholia on the Apocalypse*). Mała Biblioteka Ojców Kościoła 4. Kraków: Wydawnictwo "M", 2005.

Zibelius-Chen, K. "Kategorien und Rolle des Traumes in Ägypten," *Studien zur altägyptischen Kultur* 15 (1988): 277–93.

Zotenberg, H. "La Chronique de Jean de Nikioū," *Notices et Extraits des manuscrits de la Bibliothèque Nationale* 24, no. 1 (1883): 125–605.

Subject Index

Biblical Index